W9-BLM-853

Rod and Staff Books

(Milestone Ministries)
800-761-0234 or 541-466-3231
www.RodandStaffBooks.com

SPELLING

By Sound and Structure

For Christian Schools

SPELLING

By Sound and Structure

Grade 6

Rod and Staff Publishers, Inc.
P.O. Box 3, Hwy. 172
Crockett, Kentucky 41413
Telephone: (606) 522-4348

Acknowledgements

We acknowledge the everlasting God, the Lord, beside whom there is none else. His blessing made the writing and publishing of this book possible.

We express gratitude to Brother Marvin Eicher for revising and editing this textbook, to numerous ones involved in reviewing it, and to Brothers Lester Miller and A. Daniel Zook for the artwork.

We are grateful for the teachers and students who tested this revision in their classrooms and for all those who helped to make this book possible.

Copyright 2009
by Rod and Staff Publishers, Inc.
Crockett, Kentucky 41413

Printed in U.S.A.

ISBN 978-07399-0705-4

Catalog no. 166912

Outline of Concepts

A Sounds and Letters
B Using Your Words
C Building Words

Teacher Introduction

THE IMPORTANCE OF SPELLING IN A LANGUAGE

God has given man the ability to send messages by writing. The written word can be sent to people far away from the author. A written message can also be preserved over long periods of time. The written word can help to preserve a language as writers adhere to the prescribed rules governing the system that characterizes a given language.

Spelling is a vital part of the system of a language. For a message to be conveyed accurately, the writer and the reader must both be familiar with the same set of rules that dictate the forming of discernible words or word parts. Should someone write *oshin*, the reader may have difficulty understanding that he is referring to one of the large bodies of water on the earth. Spelling rules will help students to represent the various sounds in a word with the correct letters.

Although the phonetic approach to reading is good, students sometimes have difficulty translating phonetic sounds into standard spellings. For that reason the revised *Spelling by Sound and Structure* emphasizes the interpretation of phonetic spellings. The student is also required to write the words from the spelling lists in the exercises, sometimes more than once. The exposure that a student receives simply by writing a word will help to rivet the proper spelling in his mind. The primary goal is finally to teach the student the standard spellings of the words in the word lists, both by the use of spelling rules and by rote, as well as to give him practice with using those words intelligently.

Proper pronunciation is vital to good spelling skills. If a person has a habit of mispronouncing certain words, he may spell those words the way he says them. For example, if one says *travlin* for *traveling*, he may fail to insert an *e* between the *v* and *l*. Saying *excape* for *escape* is another example of careless speech that may hinder proper spelling.

ORGANIZATION OF *SPELLING BY SOUND AND STRUCTURE*

This book has thirty-four lessons divided into units of six lessons each except for the last unit, which has only four lessons. Each unit (except the last) has five regular lessons, followed by a review lesson for that unit. The units are generally self-contained, so that a student can find the spelling rules and helps for each review lesson within the same unit.

Each regular lesson has sixteen NEW WORDS and four REVIEW WORDS. Each lesson is divided into three main parts.

Part A, Sounds and Letters, drills the phonetic composition of the words in the spelling list. Spelling rules for the speech sounds taught in the lesson are given just before the work relating to them. In many of the lessons, students will need to interpret a number of phonetic spellings.

Part B, Using Your Words, emphasizes the vocabulary aspect of the spelling words. These exercises should show that the student is able to use the words intelligently. Part B also teaches some dictionary-related skills such as parts of speech and syllable division. As with other lesson parts, the student is expected to use the *Speller Dictionary* as needed to do Part B.

Part C, Building Words, emphasizes the use of words or word parts in forming other words. Plural and compound nouns, present and past tenses, prefixes and suffixes, and contractions are some of the concepts taught.

An additional part at the end of most lessons is entitled *Bible Thoughts*. This part is designed to link use of the spelling words to Bible concepts. The student is to use his Bible as needed in completing this part.

LESSON PLANS FOR *SPELLING BY SOUND AND STRUCTURE*

If spelling class is scheduled only once in a week, the test for the prior week's words should be given first. The new lesson should then be assigned. The teacher should read the words from the word list to the students or have the students read the words with him. This is essential so that the students learn the correct pronunciation of the words.

The lesson exercises should be assigned as written work. The teacher could discuss with the students any concepts that he thinks may be difficult for them. However, the students should be able to do most of the work by themselves. A second spelling test may be given at the discretion of the teacher.

If spelling class is scheduled two times per week, one class period could be used to correct the regular work and give the first spelling test. The second class could be used to discuss the work more thoroughly, give the second spelling test, and assign the new lesson.

SPELLING TESTS

After pupils have completed the work in the spelling lesson and have studied the words in the word lists sufficiently, the spelling test should be administered. If pupils are having problems with mastering the words, a trial test given a day or two before the final test may be desirable.

Testing procedures other than the ones suggested below may be acceptable if the results accurately portray the degree of word mastery.

Administering the Spelling Test

Use the test sentences provided with each lesson. Pronounce the word once, say the sentence, and pronounce the word again. The pupils will write only the words for numbers 1–16.

To test the REVIEW WORDS, you may elect to have the pupils write the entire sentence that contains two of the REVIEW WORDS. If using this method, say the sentence carefully twice before the pupils begin to write it.

Every sixth lesson reviews the words from the preceding five lessons. To test these lessons, use the test sentences provided if time permits. Be sure that pupils understand that they are to write only abbreviations for the specified words.

Scoring the Test

For tests from the regular lessons, you could apply 100 points and deduct 5 points for each misspelled word to get a percent grade. If you have pupils write the entire sentences for the REVIEW WORDS, deduct 5 points for any misspelled REVIEW WORDS in those sentences and 1 point for any other misspelled words in the sentence. Never deduct more than 10 points per sentence.

Tests for Review Lessons may again be ascribed 100 points, with each word or abbreviation counting 2 points. Make sure that pupils understand that they need to write the abbreviations only for the specified words.

The basic goal of Rod and Staff spelling courses is to help pupils master the spelling of the words in the word lists. Therefore, scores from the spelling tests should be given more weight on the final grades than scores from the regular work in the lessons.

Word List

A

abroad 20
abundant 9
accept 28
accident 28
according 9, 27
account 22
accurate 29
acquaint 27
ad 9
additional 31
addressed 3
adjustment 23
admitted 21
advanced 31
adventure 16
advertised 26
advertisement 9
affair 19
afford 33
agent 1
alligators 14
amendment 31
announce 22
announcement 33
annual 11
anxious 17
apiece 13
apostle 8
appeared 19
appreciate 17
approach 16, 32
approved 5, 21
arrival 32
articles 10
assemble 25
assist 4
assure 17
assured 21
attack 7

attempt 21
attic 7
audience 25
auditorium 33
author 20
automatic 7, 20
aware 19

B

baggage 23
banking 3
baptism 26
baptized 26
basis 23, 31
battery 2, 15
beautifully 11, 32
beef 2
believed 13, 21
believing 32
beneath 4
beyond 29
blizzard 26
blossoms 1, 8
blvd. 29
borrowed 5
bough 22, 33
boulevard 29
bound 22
breathe 4, 13
brook 27
bruise 21
bu. 29
buffalo 23
bull 3
bulletin 21, 33
burden 14
bureau 11
bushel 29
business 26
butcher 16

C

cabbage 1
calendar 31
capable 11
cedar 13
ceiling 13
channel 16
charity 16
cheerful 16
chickenpox 8
children's 13
chocolate 9
choice 2, 16
choir 27
chorus 5
Christian 16
circulation 14
citizen 26
clerk 27
cliff 3
clipping 5
closet 1
column 31
combination 17
communicate 11
community 32
companion 29
compass 1, 8
completing 4
composition 26
congregation 17
congress 3
connected 27
connection 33
constantly 33
construction 7
cont. 31
continued 31
contrary 5, 19
copies 1

2 Cor. 10
2 Corinthians 10
corrected 5
correction 7
couch 1
court 27
courtesy 14
credit 3
currant 9, 33
current 14
customer 8, 15

D

dash 1
data 32
dawn 20
deacon 10
deal 3
debtor 15
Dec. 9
deceive 13
December 9
declare 19
defective 7
definition 17
degree 1
delay 2
delicious 17
deliveries 15, 32
depot 13
description 32
design 11
dessert 26
destination 32
develop 21
devout 22
disappear 16
disappointed 16, 33
disciples 25
discontinued 33

disease 26
dispatch 16
division 22
domestic 7
doubt 22
drag 3
driven 22
drown 22
duties 3
dying 11

E

earnest 14
echo 5
education 32
effect 31
electrical 7, 27
electricity 7
elsewhere 28
embarrass 8, 25
embroidery 15
employ 2
encounter 22
enforce 33
engineer 16
Eph. 31
Ephesians 31
equipment 27
error 5
especially 17
estimate 32
et cetera 9
etc. 9
eternal 14
eternity 33
everlasting 8
exactly 26
exam 9
examination 9
example 26

excess 28
excitement 28
exclaimed 28
exercise 28
expedition 28
expensive 25
experience 28
express 28
expression 33

F

factories 2, 15
failure 15, 29
fashion 17
faucet 20
Feb. 9
February 9
fierce 25, 31
figures 1
final 3
firmament 14
fitted 5
foreign 10
fortunate 16
forwarding 28
foul 22
fountain 10
fowl 22
funeral 11
furious 9, 25
furnace 14
further 25

G

Gal. 31
Galatians 31
garage 22
garbage 19
generation 17
generous 9, 23
gentlemen 23
Gethsemane 8

glorify 20
gnawing 33
godliness 33
Gospel 10
gossip 8
government 8
governor 15, 31
grammar 31
grateful 11
grease 25
greetings 1, 11
grief 3
grieve 13
groan 11
groceries 2
guard 19

H

happiest 25
happiness 33
headache 8
hedge 23
height 13
heir 19, 29
hem 3
heretofore 19
heroes 23
honestly 29
honesty 29
honorable 32
Hosea 10
how's 20
humanity 32
humble 29
hunger 3
hygiene 23

I

ignorant 15
immediately 32
including 21
increased 11, 4

independence 16
industrial 8, 31
infant 4
influence 21
inherit 8
iniquity 31
injury 23
insects 1
instruction 27
instructor 15
insurance 17
international 15
introduced 5, 21
invitation 17
invoice 2
irrigate 19

J

Jan. 9
January 9
jealous 31
Jehovah 11
Jerusalem 21
jewel 21
journey 23
jury 23

K

kerosene 27
kingdom 7
kneel 29
knives 2
knock 7
knowledge 29
labor 3
ladies 1
laundry 20
lawyer 20, 29
league 13
leather 4
length 4
lightning 3, 11

linger 3
loneliness 11
losing 4, 21
loyal 2

M

machinery 17
manufacturing 16
materials 19
mature 21
meanwhile 28
measure 22
medium 13
merchant 14
mercies 2, 25
Messiah 11
metal 10
method 4
mg 29
milligram 29
millimeter 29
million 3
miners 15
miracles 19
mirror 32
missionary 14
misspell 8
mm 29
moderate 33
moisture 16
mortal 20
moss 3, 20
museum 11, 32
musical 7

N

Nahum 10
native 2
natural 16
Nazareth 9
necessary 25
neither 13

nephew 5, 11
nickel 10
nowadays 22

O

observation 15
occur 27
offer 3
onion 29
opposite 26
orchard 4, 20
ordain 20
ore 20
overalls 20
overlook 27
oyster 2, 15

P

pajamas 23
parable 31
paragraph 5
pardon 10
passover 8
patience 17
pattern 1
pavement 2
peck 29
penmanship 17
pennies 1
percentage 23
permission 15
personality 14
Phil. 10
Philem. 10
Philemon 10
Philippians 10
phone 9
physical 5
pickles 27
pier 19
pigeon 10, 23
pk. 29

plains 1
poison 2, 26
post office 8
practice 25
practicing 31
preferred 21
preparing 19
prettiest 25
priced 4
principal 10
principle 10
procured 21
produced 21
pronounce 22
propeller 21
prophecy 25
prophesy 25
prove 2
Psalms 10
public 7
publication 7
publish 17
puzzle 26

Q

qualified 27
qualities 27
quality 8
quarrel 20, 27
quotation 32

R

radar 19
readily 7

recently 25
recipe 11
Redeemer 16
reducing 21
reference 15, 25
regarding 5
regularly 15, 29
reindeer 13
relief 13
religious 9
replying 5
represented 5, 26
required 4
research 14
reserve 14
respectable 27
Rev. 10
Revelation 10
reverence 15
reverse 14
rural 10

S

salesman 23
satisfactory 25
satisfied 4
scenery 32
scholarship 15
scissors 23
Scripture 16
search 1
secret 1, 13
securing 4, 27
Sept. 9

September 9
series 23
serious 25
servant 14
severe 9
shelter 17
shield 13
shone 22
sincere 19
sister's 14
situation 17
society 32
solve 2
Song of Sol. 31
Song of Solomon 31
sought 22
source 20
stationary 17
stationery 17
stock 7
stole 22
strength 31
stretch 16
stroke 7
studying 4
successful 7
suggest 9, 23
supreme 11
surface 14
swear 19
syllable 8
synagogue 8

T

tabernacle 10
tailor 15
taxes 1
telegraph 5
telephone 9
territory 9, 20
testament 9
theirs 26
therefore 4
there's 26
they're 26
tickled 4
tithe 4
tongue 3
towel 1
traffic 7
transfer 33
typewriter 5

U

unbeliever 13
universal 29
unpleasant 26
usually 22

V

valuable 32
vanity 2
vary 33
veil 13
vice-president 26
volume 29
voyage 2, 23

W

watchful 28
weapon 28
weigh 28
weight 13
weren't 19
whatever 28
what's 20
whence 33
where's 20
whether 28
whirl 28
who'd 19
who'll 19
width 28
windmills 8
wolves 2
worried 4
worship 14
worst 14
worthy 28
wrap 5
wreck 7
wrestle 5

Y

yourselves 27

The Weekly Lesson Plan

Part **A, Sounds and Letters,** helps you to hear the sounds in words and helps you to spell those sounds with letters of the alphabet. In this part you will learn to use some patterns that will help you to spell words.

Part **B, Using Your Words,** helps you to learn the meanings of words that we use when we speak and write.

Part **C, Building Words,** helps you to use words and parts of words to build many more words. In this part you will learn to use more patterns that will help you to spell words.

LESSON 1

NEW WORDS

1. closet
2. agent
3. insects
4. secret
5. couch
6. figures
7. search
8. greetings
9. blossoms
10. copies
11. pennies
12. compass
13. plains
14. degree
15. taxes
16. dash

REVIEW WORDS

17. towel
18. ladies
19. cabbage
20. pattern

/k/ouch
cookie/z/

A. Sounds and Letters

1. The word *couch* has three sounds: /k/, /ou/, and /ch/. The first sound is spelled with the single letter *c*, and the other sounds are spelled with two letters each.

   In the word *pennies*, which letter spells /p/? Which letters spell /n/? Which letter spells /z/?

2. Look at exercise 1 again. Observe that the letters which represent sounds are placed between slashes like this: /k/. The symbol /k/ does not mean the letter *k* but the sound of the letter *k*.

Write four NEW WORDS and one REVIEW WORD that begin with /k/.

3. Write the two spelling words (NEW WORDS or REVIEW WORDS) that end with /s/. Be careful not to write any that end with /z/.

4. Write eight spelling words ending with /z/.

5. Write the symbol that represents the first sound in each of these words. Remember to place it between slashes.
   a. cedar   c. phone
   b. kneel   d. choose

6. For each sound, write NEW WORDS in which that is the first vowel sound. The numbers in parentheses tell you how many words to write. Check your Speller Dictionary.
   a. /ē/ (2)   b. /ā/ (2)

7. Write spelling words that have these short vowels as their first vowel sounds.
   a. /i/ spelled *i* (2)
   b. /a/ spelled *a* (4)
   c. /e/ spelled *e* (1)

8. Write spelling words in which these consonant sounds occur in the order given.
   a. /s/, /k/, /t/   d. /p/, /t/, /n/
   b. /t/, /l/   e. /d/, /sh/
   c. /s/, /r/, /ch/   f. /j/, /n/, /t/

6

A. 37 points
1. p; nn; s
2. closet, couch, copies, compass, cabbage
3. insects, compass
4. figures, greetings, blossoms, copies, pennies, plains, taxes, ladies
5. a. /s/
   b. /n/
   c. /f/
   d. /ch/
6. a. secret, greetings
   b. agent, plains
7. a. insects, figures
   b. taxes, dash, cabbage, pattern
   c. pennies
8. a. secret
   b. towel
   c. search
   d. pattern
   e. dash
   f. agent

Test Sentences

(Teacher: To give spelling tests, pronounce each spelling word, read the sentence, and pronounce the word again.)

1. *closet*   You should keep your *closet* neat.
2. *agent*   The real estate *agent* is here.
3. *insects*   Some *insects* are helpful to us.
4. *secret*   Many Christians must have *secret* meetings.
5. *blossoms*   The cherry *blossoms* are beautiful.
6. *couch*   You may sleep on the *couch* tonight.
7. *figures*   Be sure your *figures* are copied correctly.
8. *greetings*   Give my *greetings* to your parents.
9. *pennies*   Wasted *pennies* become wasted dollars.
10. *copies*   Please make two *copies* of this letter.

B. Using Your Words

1. Write the spelling word that belongs with each group.
  a. birds, mammals, reptiles
  b. nickels, quarters, dimes
  c. lettuce, broccoli, spinach
  d. cupboard, wardrobe, cabinet
  e. ruler, protractor, graph paper
  f. tariffs, levies, duties

2. A synonym is a word with nearly the same meaning as another word. For each sentence, write a spelling word that is a synonym of the underlined word.
  a. The <u>flowers</u> on our apple tree were damaged by a late frost.
  b. A <u>representative</u> from the real estate office was showing the house.
  c. Gerald was asleep on the <u>sofa</u>.

  d. Man's <u>quest</u> for knowledge never ends.

3. Do not confuse *plains* with *planes* or *decree* with *degree*. Write the correct words.
  a. The ninth grade is studying (plains, planes) in geometry.
  b. The geography lesson was about the western (plains, planes) of America.
  c. Water boils at 212 (decrees, degrees).
  d. Whoever disobeyed the king's (decree, degree) was punished.
  e. Mr. Fry holds a college (decree, degree).

Dictionary Practice
Use the Speller Dictionary for this part.
4. True or False: *Compass* should be pronounced (kəm pas′) when it is a verb.

C. Building Words

- The plural forms of most nouns are made by adding *-s* or *-es* to the singular form. **plain—plains tax—taxes**
- If a word ends with e preceded by a consonant, drop the e before adding *-es*. **cabbage—cabbages** If a word ends with y preceded by a consonant, change the y to i and add *-es.* **penny—pennies**

1. Write the plural form of each word.
  a. agent   c. towel
  b. degree   d. closet

2. Write the singular form of each word.
  a. insects   c. figures
  b. greetings   d. blossoms

3. Add *-es* to form the plurals of these.
  a. search   c. dash
  b. compass   d. couch

4. Change these to their singular forms.
  a. taxes   d. pennies
  b. cabbages   e. ladies
  c. harnesses   f. copies

Bible Thoughts
Use a spelling word to complete this Bible verse.

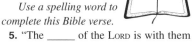

5. "The _____ of the Lᴏʀᴅ is with them that fear him" (Psalm 25:14).

7

B. 16 points
1. a. insects
   b. pennies
   c. cabbage
   d. closet
   e. compass
   f. taxes
2. a. blossoms
   b. agent
   c. couch
   d. search
3. a. planes
   b. plains
   c. degrees
   d. decree
   e. degree
4. False

C. 19 points
1. a. agents
   b. degrees
   c. towels
   d. closets
2. a. insect
   b. greeting
   c. figure
   d. blossom
3. a. searches
   b. compasses
   c. dashes
   d. couches
4. a. tax
   b. cabbage
   c. harness
   d. penny
   e. lady
   f. copy
5. secret

11. *plains*	The open *plains* were excellent pasture lands.
12. *degree*	The temperature was one *degree* above freezing.
13. *search*	The shepherd made a *search* for the sheep.
14. *taxes*	Our *taxes* are used to build roads.
15. *compass*	A good *compass* always points north.
16. *dash*	Put a *dash* of salt in the soup.

For the Rᴇᴠɪᴇᴡ Wᴏʀᴅs, you will write the entire sentences. Listen carefully as I say each sentence twice. Remember to begin each sentence with a capital letter and to use the correct end punctuation.

That *towel* has a pretty *pattern*.

Now listen as I say the second sentence twice.

Three *ladies* cut up *cabbage* for the soup.

LESSON 2

NEW WORDS

1. *oyster*
2. *mercies*
3. *wolves*
4. *beef*
5. *invoice*
6. *vanity*
7. *poison*
8. *employ*
9. *factories*
10. *native*
11. *pavement*
12. *voyage*
13. *prove*
14. *battery*
15. *delay*
16. *choice*

REVIEW WORDS

17. *loyal*
18. *groceries*
19. *solve*
20. *knives*

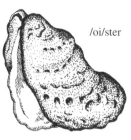

/oi/ster

A. Sounds and Letters

- At the beginning of a word or within a word, /v/ is usually spelled *v*. **vanity invoice** At the end of a word, /v/ is usually spelled *ve*. **native prove** The /v/ sound may also be spelled *ve* at the end of a syllable with a long vowel sound. **pavement**

1. Write these spelling words. Spell /v/ correctly in each one.
   a. wol/v/es
   b. pro/v/
   c. /v/oyage
   d. sol/v/
   e. pa/v/ment
   f. kni/v/es

8

2. Also write these words correctly.
   a. re/v/iew
   b. arri/v/
   c. en/v/y
   d. deser/v/
   e. /v/alue
   f. car/v/

- The /oi / sound is spelled *oi* or *oy*. **poison oyster** At the end of a word or before a vowel, /oi/ is usually spelled *oy*. **employ voyage**

3. Write these words, spelling /oi/ correctly.
   a. ch/oi/ce
   b. /oi/ster
   c. empl/oi/
   d. p/oi/son
   e. l/oi/al
   f. inv/oi/ce

4. Also spell these words correctly.
   a. n/oi/se
   b. destr/oi/
   c. p/oi/nt
   d. av/oi/d
   e. j/oi/ous
   f. ann/oi/ed

5. Write three NEW WORDS that have /a/ in the first syllable.

6. Write the spelling words that begin with these sounds.
   a. /d/
   b. /s/
   c. /g/
   d. /n/ (2 words)

A. 32 points
1. a. wolves
   b. prove
   c. voyage
   d. solve
   e. pavement
   f. knives
2. a. review
   b. arrive
   c. envy
   d. deserve
   e. value
   f. carve
3. a. choice
   b. oyster
   c. employ
   d. poison
   e. loyal
   f. invoice
4. a. noise
   b. destroy
   c. point
   d. avoid
   e. joyous
   f. annoyed
5. vanity, factories, battery
6. a. delay
   b. solve
   c. groceries
   d. native, knives

Test Sentences

1.	*oyster*	Do you like *oyster* stew?
2.	*wolves*	We saw five *wolves* in the zoo.
3.	*beef*	That rancher raises *beef* cattle.
4.	*factories*	Many *factories* make clothing.
5.	*mercies*	The Lord's *mercies* are sure.
6.	*vanity*	The Lord hates *vanity* and pride.
7.	*poison*	Some books will *poison* our minds.
8.	*invoice*	The package had an *invoice* inside.
9.	*pavement*	The road past our house is *pavement*.
10.	*native*	He was a *native* of Germany.
11.	*prove*	Can you *prove* your answer?
12.	*voyage*	Paul made a *voyage* to Rome.

B. Using Your Words

1. Write the spelling word that completes each comparison.
   a. *Hog* is to *pork* as *cow* is to ____.
   b. *Old* is to *young* as *foreign* is to ____.
   c. *Steep* is to *hills* as *sharp* is to ____.
   d. *Heal* is to *medicine* as *kill* is to ____.
   e. *Plane* is to *flight* as *ship* is to ____.
   f. *Lend* is to *loan* as *hire* is to ____.

2. Write spelling words with these meanings.
   a. A hard surface for walking or driving.
   b. Undeserved kindnesses.
   c. Establishments where things are manufactured.

   d. Find the solution to.
   e. Food and household supplies sold by certain stores.
   f. A mollusk with two shells.

3. Write the spelling words that are synonyms of these words.
   a. faithful   d. selection
   b. conceit   e. verify
   c. natural   f. postpone

Dictionary Practice

4. Write the part of speech that matches each use of *native*.
   a. Many people have a native tendency to speak too quickly.
   b. Pedro is a native of Guatemala.

C. Building Words

- When a noun ends with *y* preceded by a vowel, its plural is formed by adding *-s*. **boy—boys**
- The plurals of many nouns that end with *f* or *fe* are formed by changing *f* to *v* and adding *-es* or *-s*. Others are formed by simply adding *-s*. **wolf—wolves life—lives cliff—cliffs belief—beliefs**
- The plural of a proper noun is formed by adding *-s* or *-es*, even when the last letter is *y*. **Taylor— Taylors James—Jameses West Liberty—West Libertys**

1. Write the plurals of the following NEW WORDS.

   a. native   c. poison
   b. voyage   d. vanity

2. Also write the plurals of these.
   a. factory   c. knife
   b. journey   d. loaf

3. Write the plurals of these proper nouns.
   a. Smith   e. Judas
   b. Lewis   f. Wolfe
   c. Kanagy   g. Middlebury
   d. Jones   h. Quaker City

Bible Thoughts

Use a spelling word to complete this Bible verse.
4. "Great are thy tender ____, O LORD" (Psalm 119:156).

9

B. 20 points
1. a. beef
   b. native
   c. knives
   d. poison
   e. voyage
   f. employ
2. a. pavement
   b. mercies
   c. factories
   d. solve
   e. groceries
   f. oyster
3. a. loyal
   b. vanity
   c. native
   d. choice
   e. prove
   f. delay
4. a. adj.
   b. n.

C. 17 points
1. a. natives
   b. voyages
   c. poisons
   d. vanities
2. a. factories
   b. journeys
   c. knives
   d. loaves
3. a. Smiths
   b. Lewises
   c. Kanagys
   d. Joneses
   e. Judases
   f. Wolfes
   g. Middleburys
   h. Quaker Citys
4. mercies

---

13. *delay*   The snow will *delay* our trip.
14. *employ*   The company will *employ* more workers.
15. *battery*   There is a *battery* in the flashlight.
16. *choice*   Make a *choice* to do right.

The man's *loyal* friend brought *groceries*.

Will sharp *knives* help to *solve* the problem?

LESSON 3

NEW WORDS

1. *bull*
2. *deal*
3. *moss*
4. *cliff*
5. *hem*
6. *grief*
7. *congress*
8. *drag*
9. *banking*
10. *tongue*
11. *hunger*
12. *addressed*
13. *lightning*
14. *credit*
15. *labor*
16. *offer*

REVIEW WORDS

17. *million*
18. *linger*
19. *duties*
20. *final*

lightni/ng/

- Most consonant sounds are spelled with single letters at the beginning or the end of a word. **drag hem** After a long vowel sound also, most consonant sounds are spelled with single letters. **la<u>b</u>or grie<u>f</u>** Double consonants occur after many vowel sounds that are short. **mi<u>ll</u>ion o<u>ff</u>er**

- The consonants *f, l, s,* and *z* are doubled at the end of many one-syllable words when the vowel sound is short. **cli<u>ff</u> bu<u>ll</u> mo<u>ss</u> fu<u>zz</u>**

A. Sounds and Letters

- The /ng/ sound is usually spelled *ng*. **lightning** But when it comes before /g/ or /k/, /ng/ is usually spelled *n*. **hu<u>n</u>ger ba<u>n</u>k** In a few words, /ng/ is spelled /ngue/. **to<u>ngue</u>**

1. Add the correct spelling of /ng/ as you write these words.
   a. hu__ger
   b. li__ger
   c. ba__ki__
   d. lightni__
   e. co__gress
   f. thi__ki__

2. Which NEW WORD ends with /ng/ spelled in an unusual way?

3. Spell these words correctly, using single or double letters as needed.
   a. dea/l/   f. grie/f/
   b. cli/f/   g. mi/l/ion
   c. he/m/   h. la/b/or
   d. mo/s/   i. o/f/er
   e. bu/l/   j. du/t/ies

4. In which NEW WORD is there an exception to the usual pattern—a single *d* occurs between two short vowels?

5. *Final* ends with a (single, double) *l* because it has (one syllable, two syllables) and the last syllable (is, is not) accented.

10

A. 21 points
   1. a. hunger
      b. linger
      c. banking
      d. lightning
      e. congress
      f. thinking
   2. tongue
   3. a. deal
      b. cliff
      c. hem
      d. moss
      e. bull
      f. grief
      g. million
      h. labor
      i. offer
      j. duties
   4. credit
   5. single, two syllables, is not

Test Sentences

1.	*bull*	There is a *bull* in that field.
2.	*deal*	Laban made a *deal* with Jacob.
3.	*moss*	The pioneers used *moss* for chinking.
4.	*cliff*	The *cliff* overlooks the whole valley.
5.	*grief*	Jacob suffered much *grief* over Joseph.
6.	*drag*	Do not *drag* your feet.
7.	*hem*	The woman touched the *hem* of Christ's garment.
8.	*banking*	I do my *banking* in town.
9.	*tongue*	The *tongue* cannot be tamed by man.
10.	*hunger*	They had a *hunger* for the Word.
11.	*lightning*	The *lightning* struck a tree.
12.	*congress*	In the United States, *Congress* enacts laws.

B. Using Your Words

1. An *antonym* is a word whose meaning is opposite to the meaning of another word. Write spelling words that are antonyms of these.

   a. joy   d. first
   b. hasten   e. push
   c. rest   f. satisfaction

2. Write the same spelling word for both blanks in each sentence, changing the forms as needed to make them fit.

   a. The many duties were a _____ on the king; they even _____ down his health.
   b. Father enjoys _____ at that hardware store because Mr. White always tries to give him a fair _____.
   c. So many people were _____ at the main office on Grant Street that another _____ was opened on Maple Avenue.

3. Write spelling words that are synonyms.

   a. meeting   d. responsibilities
   b. precipice   e. border
   c. appetite   f. language

Dictionary Practice

4. The first syllable of *address* may be accented when that word is a (noun, verb).

5. Some words have more than one entry. Look up *bull²*. This official document is marked with the _____ (seal) of a pope.

C. Building Words

- Certain verb forms are made by adding *-ed*, *-ing*, *-s*, or *-es* to the root word. **offer—offered bank—banking deal—deals address—addresses**

- When a one-syllable word has one vowel and ends with a single consonant, the consonant is doubled to add *-ed* or *-ing*. **drag— dragged hem—hemming**

1. Add *-ed* to each word.

   a. labor   c. address
   b. bank   d. credit

2. Add *-ing* to each of these, doubling consonants as needed.

   a. bat   c. drag
   b. hem   d. offer

3. In *dread*, two vowels precede the final *d*. So the *d* (should, should not) be doubled when *-ing* is added.

4. Write the plurals of these NEW WORDS.

   a. bull   d. congress
   b. cliff   e. grief
   c. moss   f. tongue

5. Also write the plurals of these.

   a. valley   c. Davis
   b. match   d. Albany

Bible Thoughts

Use a spelling word to complete this Bible verse.

6. "If thine enemy _____, feed him; if he thirst, give him drink" (Romans 12:20).

11

13. *addressed*   This letter is *addressed* to you.
14. *credit*   Give a person *credit* for his effort.
15. *offer*   I made an *offer* to help her.
16. *labor*   It is hard *labor* to move rocks.

Do not *linger* over your *duties*.

The *final* cost was over a *million* dollars.

B. 20 points

  1. a. grief
    b. linger (*or* drag)
    c. labor
    d. final
    e. drag
    f. hunger
  2. a. drag, dragged
    b. dealing, deal
    c. banking, bank
  3. a. congress
    b. cliff
    c. hunger
    d. duties
    e. hem
    f. tongue
  4. noun
  5. bulla

C. 20 points

  1. a. labored
    b. banked
    c. addressed
    d. credited
  2. a. batting
    b. hemming
    c. dragging
    d. offering
  3. should not
  4. a. bulls
    b. cliffs
    c. mosses
    d. congresses
    e. griefs
    f. tongues
  5. a. valleys
    b. matches
    c. Davises
    d. Albanys
  6. hunger

LESSON 4

NEW WORDS

1. orchard
2. assist
3. infant
4. beneath
5. leather
6. length
7. priced
8. securing
9. breathe
10. tickled
11. required
12. losing
13. increased
14. method
15. tithe
16. completing

REVIEW WORDS

17. satisfied
18. studying
19. worried
20. therefore

A. Sounds and Letters

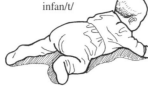

infan/t/

- Both /th/ and /th/ are usually spelled with the digraph *th*. **me<u>th</u>od lea<u>th</u>er** At the end of one-syllable words containing long vowel sounds, /th/ is often spelled *the*. **ti<u>th</u>e brea<u>th</u>e**

1. In the rule above, the word *digraph* refers to ___ letter(s) that spell ___ sound(s). (Write the missing numbers.)

2. The /th/ sound, as in *thin*, is unvoiced. Spell /th/ correctly as you write the following words.

   a. benea/th/   c. me/th/od
   b. leng/th/   d. /th/eft

3. The /th/ sound, as in *this*, is voiced. Spell /th/ correctly as you write these spelling words.

   a. ti/<u>th</u>/   c. /<u>th</u>/erefore
   b. lea/<u>th</u>/er   d. brea/<u>th</u>/

- Knowing whether a word has a suffix helps to determine the spelling of its final sound. If a word ends with /d/ or /t/ because it is a past form, the final sound is usually spelled *ed*. **required priced** If the word is not a past form, final /d/ or /t/ is spelled *d* or *t*. **method infant**

4. a. Write four spelling words in which final /d/ is spelled *ed*.
   b. Write two NEW WORDS in which final /t/ is spelled *ed*.

5. All the words you wrote for exercise 4 are the _____ forms of verbs.

6. Write the NEW WORDS that end with these consonant blends.
   a. nt   b. rd   c. st

7. Write the five spelling words that contain *-ng*.

8. Which NEW WORD has /k/ spelled *ck*?

A. 26 points

1. 2, 1
2. a. beneath
   b. length
   c. method
   d. theft
3. a. tithe
   b. leather
   c. therefore
   d. breathe
4. a. tickled, required, satisfied, worried
   b. priced, increased
5. past
6. a. infant
   b. orchard
   c. assist
7. length, securing, losing, completing, studying
8. tickled

Test Sentences

1. *assist*	Will you please *assist* me?
2. *infant*	The *infant* lay in a manger.
3. *orchard*	Mr. White's *orchard* is for sale.
4. *leather*	The man wore a *leather* apron.
5. *length*	They walked the *length* of the street.
6. *method*	Which *method* is best for studying?
7. *beneath*	The shoes stood *beneath* the chair.
8. *priced*	The eggs were *priced* at eighty cents.
9. *increased*	Jesus *increased* in wisdom.
10. *required*	Mother *required* sugar for the cake.
11. *breathe*	Fish *breathe* through their gills.
12. *tithe*	Abram paid a *tithe* to Melchisedec.

B. Using Your Words

1. *Breathe* and *breath* are easily confused, and so are *bathe* and *bath*. Write the correct word for each sentence.
   a. The air was so dusty that I could hardly (breath, breathe).
   b. Harold was out of (breath, breathe) from running so hard.
   c. We usually take more (baths, bathes) in warm weather than in cold weather.
   d. Pharaoh's daughter came down to (bath, bathe) in the river.

2. *Lose* and *loose* are also confused easily. Think of this phrase: *loose tooth.* (Both words have two *o*'s). Write the correct words for the following sentences.
   a. It is better to (lose, loose) a game than to win by playing unfairly.
   b. The horse got (lose, loose) because the rope was not tied tightly.
   c. Put the money in your purse, or you may (lose, loose) it.

3. Write spelling words that are antonyms.
   a. shortness   d. diminished
   b. discontented   e. carefree
   c. hinder   f. above

Dictionary Practice

4. What parts of speech may these words be?
   a. tithe   b. beneath

C. Building Words

- To add a suffix beginning with a vowel to a root word ending with *e*, the final *e* is dropped. **tithe—tithed** To add a suffix beginning with a vowel to a root word ending with a consonant and then *y*, the *y* is changed to *i*. No change is made if the *y* is preceded by a vowel or if the suffix begins with *i*. **study—studied enjoy—enjoyed satisfy—satisfying**

1. Add *-ed* to each word.
   a. breathe   c. tickle
   b. complete   d. increase

2. Write the NEW WORD that was formed by adding *-ing* to a one-syllable word. Also write its past form, which ends with *-t*.

3. Add *-ing* to each word.
   a. worry   d. reply
   b. study   e. satisfy
   c. obey   f. destroy

4. Write the plural of each word.
   a. length   e. orchard
   b. tithe   f. increase
   c. infant   g. method
   d. price   h. address

Bible Thoughts

Use a spelling word to complete this Bible verse.

5. "Moreover it is _____ in stewards, that a man be found faithful" (1 Corinthians 4:2).

13

B. 17 points
1. a. breathe
   b. breath
   c. baths
   d. bathe
2. a. lose
   b. loose
   c. lose
3. a. length
   b. satisfied (*or* tickled)
   c. assist
   d. increased
   e. worried
   f. beneath
4. a. noun, verb
   b. adverb, preposition

C. 21 points
1. a. breathed
   b. completed
   c. tickled
   d. increased
2. losing, lost
3. a. worrying
   b. studying
   c. obeying
   d. replying
   e. satisfying
   f. destroying
4. a. lengths
   b. tithes
   c. infants
   d. prices
   e. orchards
   f. increases
   g. methods
   h. addresses
5. required

---

13. *completing*   Are you *completing* your assignment?
14. *losing*   John is *losing* his grip on the heavy log.
15. *tickled*   The dust *tickled* his nose.
16. *securing*   The priests thought they were *securing* the tomb.

Therefore his desire could not be *satisfied*.

Mark looked *worried* as he was *studying*.

LESSON 5

NEW WORDS

1. chorus
2. physical
3. corrected
4. paragraph
5. introduced
6. telegraph
7. represented
8. nephew
9. typewriter
10. wrestle
11. contrary
12. error
13. approved
14. regarding
15. borrowed
16. replying

REVIEW WORDS

17. wrap
18. clipping
19. fitted
20. echo

A. Sounds and Letters

- The original spelling of a word affects its modern spelling. For example, *physical* is spelled as it is because it comes from the Latin word *physica*.

1. Write the spelling words that are derived from these words.
   a. Middle English *wrappen* (to cover)
   b. Latin *errare* (to wander)
   c. Latin *contra* (opposite)
   d. Latin *nepot* (brother's son)
   e. Greek *ēkhō* (sound)
   f. Greek *tēle* (distant) + *graphein* (to write)

/k/lipping

- The /k/ sound is usually spelled *c* or *k*. **clipping kind** Sometimes /k/ is spelled *ch*. **chorus**

2. Write spelling words with these sounds.
   a. two /k/ sounds spelled *c*
   b. beginning /kl/ spelled *cl*
   c. /k/ spelled *ch* (2 words)

- The /f/ sound is sometimes spelled *ph*. **nephew**

3. Write these words, spelling /f/ correctly.
   a. /f/ysical   d. sti/f/
   b. /f/itted   e. paragra/f/
   c. ne/f/ew   f. telegra/f/

- The /r/ sound is usually spelled *r* or *rr*. **contrary error** At the beginning of some words, /r/ is spelled *wr*. **wrestle**

4. Write spelling words by replacing the underlined letters with letters that spell /r/.
   a. chap   b. nestle   c. connected
5. Write the spelling words described here.
   a. A compound word whose second part begins with /r/ spelled *wr*.
   b. Words that begin with /r/ because they have the prefix *re-* (3 words).
   c. A word with /s/ is spelled *c*.
   d. A word with /ō/ spelled *ow*.
   e. A word with /ōōv/ spelled *ov*.

14

A. 26 points
1. a. wrap
   b. error
   c. contrary
   d. nephew
   e. echo
   f. telegraph
2. a. corrected
   b. clipping
   c. chorus, echo
3. a. physical
   b. fitted
   c. nephew
   d. stiff
   e. paragraph
   f. telegraph
4. a. wrap
   b. wrestle
   c. corrected
5. a. typewriter
   b. represented, regarding, replying
   c. introduced
   d. borrowed
   e. approved

Test Sentences

1.	*chorus*	The class sang the *chorus* loudly.
2.	*physical*	Jesus had a *physical* body like ours.
3.	*paragraph*	Write a *paragraph* to explain your thought.
4.	*telegraph*	The pony express was slower than the *telegraph*.
5.	*nephew*	My *nephew* is five years old.
6.	*typewriter*	Put this *typewriter* on the shelf.
7.	*wrestle*	We do not *wrestle* against flesh and blood.
8.	*introduced*	The teacher *introduced* the visitors.
9.	*contrary*	Such an idea was *contrary* to the truth.
10.	*represented*	Jesus *represented* the Father to us.
11.	*approved*	"Study to shew thyself *approved* unto God."
12.	*error*	A mistake is called an *error*.

B. Using Your Words

1. Words like *hear* and *here* are homophones. Which spelling word is a homophone for *rap*?
2. Write the correct homophone for each phonetic spelling.
   a. Mother (rapt) softly on the door.
   b. Hang your (raps) on these hooks.
   c. The gift was (rapt) in colorful paper.
   d. The officer (rapt) out swift orders.
3. Write the spelling word that belongs with each group.
   a. cousin, niece, uncle
   b. purchased, rented, leased
   c. cutting, shearing, trimming
   d. opposite, reverse, against
   e. sentence, essay, passage

f. accepted, favored, consented
g. repaired, mended, cured
4. Write spelling words that are synonyms of these words.
   a. mistake   d. reflection
   b. answering   e. suited
   c. cutting   f. struggle

Dictionary Practice

5. *Clip* may mean "to strike with a sharp blow." This meaning is (archaic, informal, obsolete).
6. A dictionary entry may include a boldface *idiom,* a phrase with a special meaning of its own. Look up *fit*[2], and copy an idiom that means "irregularly; not steadily."

C. Building Words

- An inflected form is divided into syllables between the root word and the suffix. If the final consonant is doubled to add the suffix, the division is made between the double consonants. **in/tro/duc/ing clip/ping**
- An inflected form is divided between the root word and the suffix only if the suffix forms a new syllable. **ap/proved ap/prov/ing**

1. Write each word, and use a slash (/) to divide it between the root word and the suffix. Divide it only if the suffix forms a new syllable.
   a. corrected   c. representing
   b. fitted   d. clipped

2. Write these words, and divide them into syllables. Do not divide between the double letters, because they belong to the root words.
   a. added   c. blessing
   b. calling   d. sniffing
3. Use the Speller Dictionary for help to divide these words into syllables.
   a. chorus   c. paragraph
   b. wrestle   d. typewriter

Bible Thoughts
Use a spelling word to complete this Bible verse.
4. "But the ship was . . . tossed with waves: for the wind was ____" (Matthew 14:24).

15

B. 20 points
   Homophone is preferred over *homonym* in current usage.
1. wrap
2. a. rapped
   b. wraps
   c. wrapped
   d. rapped
3. a. nephew
   b. borrowed
   c. clipping
   d. contrary
   e. paragraph
   f. approved
   g. corrected
4. a. error
   b. replying
   c. clipping
   d. echo
   e. fitted
   f. wrestle
5. informal
6. by fits and starts
C. 13 points
1. a. correct/ed
   b. fit/ted
   c. represent/ing
   d. clipped
2. a. add/ed
   b. call/ing
   c. bless/ing
   d. sniff/ing
3. a. cho/rus
   b. wres/tle
   c. par/a/graph
   d. type/writ/er
4. contrary

13. *regarding*   Father was *regarding* the man seriously.
14. *replying*   I am *replying* to your letter.
15. *borrowed*   The widow *borrowed* jars from her neighbors.
16. *corrected*   Have you *corrected* your mistakes?

The *echo* seemed to *wrap* itself around me.

Mother *fitted* the *clipping* into her book.

LESSON 6

1	2	3	4	5
closet	oyster	bull	orchard	chorus
agent	mercies	deal	assist	physical
insects	wolves	moss	infant	corrected
secret	beef	cliff	beneath	paragraph
couch	invoice	hem	leather	introduced
figures	vanity	grief	length	telegraph
search	poison	congress	priced	represented
greetings	employ	drag	securing	nephew
blossoms	factories	banking	breathe	typewriter
copies	native	tongue	tickled	wrestle
pennies	pavement	hunger	required	contrary
compass	voyage	addressed	losing	error
plains	prove	lightning	increased	approved
degree	battery	credit	method	regarding
taxes	delay	labor	tithe	borrowed
dash	choice	offer	completing	replying

A. Sounds and Letters Review

1. Write these Lesson 2 words, spelling the /v/ and /oi/ sounds correctly.

   a. __oyage   d. __ster
   b. nati__   e. inv__ce
   c. __anity   f. empl__

2. Write these Lesson 3 words, correctly spelling /ng/ and the final /f/, /l/, and /s/ sounds.

   a. banki/ng/   d. cli/f/
   b. co/ng/gress   e. dea/l/
   c. mo/s/   f. grie/f/

3. Which Lesson 3 word has /ng/ spelled *ngue*?

4. Write these Lesson 4 words, spelling the /th/ and /th/ sounds correctly.

   a. me__od   c. ti__
   b. leng__   d. lea__er

5. Add /d/ or /t/ to the end of each word.

   a. tickle   c. worry
   b. price   d. increase

6. Add the correct spelling of /k/, /f/, or /r/ as you write these Lesson 5 words.

   a. __orus   d. bo__owed
   b. __ontrary   e. __eplying
   c. __ysical   f. __estle

16

See page 82 for test sentences.

A. 27 points

1. a. voyage
   b. native
   c. vanity
   d. oyster
   e. invoice
   f. employ
2. a. banking
   b. congress
   c. moss
   d. cliff
   e. deal
   f. grief
3. tongue
4. a. method
   b. length
   c. tithe
   d. leather
5. a. tickled
   b. priced
   c. worried
   d. increased
6. a. chorus
   b. contrary
   c. physical
   d. borrowed
   e. replying
   f. wrestle

B. Using Your Words Review

1. Write whether the words in each pair are *synonyms, antonyms,* or *homophones.*
   a. physical, spiritual
   b. mercies, kindnesses
   c. plains, planes
   d. native, foreign

2. Write the correct word for each sentence.
   a. Caesar made a (decree, degree) that all the world should be taxed.
   b. Not many (plains, planes) were leaving the airport on that day.
   c. An adult (breaths, breathes) about twelve times per minute.
   d. After driving the combine all day, Lamar was glad to take a (bath, bathe).
   e. This (lose, loose) belt is slipping.

3. Write spelling words with these meanings. Lesson numbers are in parentheses.
   a. Hidden; not known to many people. (1)
   b. A very young child; baby. (4)
   c. Symbolized; stood for. (5)
   d. A grove of fruit trees. (4)
   e. A writing machine that produces printed characters. (5)

4. Write the spelling words that have these double meanings.
   a. (1) An adult male of cattle.
      (2) An edict issued by a pope.
   b. (1) A finished edge on cloth.
      (2) The sound of clearing the throat.

C. Building Words Review

1. Add the suffix /iz/ to each word.
   a. price   c. couch
   b. search   d. invoice

2. Write the plural of each word.
   a. penny   d. wolf
   b. valley   e. belief
   c. delay   f. cliff

3. Add *-ed* to each word.
   a. bank   c. hem
   b. prove   d. copy

4. Add *-ing* to each word.
   a. complete   c. employ
   b. wrap   d. reply

5. Write the plural of each proper noun.
   a. Lincoln   d. Christmas
   b. Jersey   e. Saturday
   c. Hilty   f. Goodrich

6. Add *-ed* to each word. If the suffix forms a new syllable, use a slash to show syllable division between the root word and suffix.
   a. assist   c. regard
   b. labor   d. represent

7. Add *-ing* to each word. Show syllable divisions between root words and suffixes.
   a. approve   c. introduce
   b. clip   d. drag

17

B. 16 points
   1. a. antonyms
      b. synonyms
      c. homophones
      d. antonyms
   2. a. decree
      b. planes
      c. breathes
      d. bath
      e. loose
   3. a. secret
      b. infant
      c. represented
      d. orchard
      e. typewriter
   4. a. bull
      b. hem

C. 32 points
   1. a. prices
      b. searches
      c. couches
      d. invoices
   2. a. pennies
      b. valleys
      c. delays
      d. wolves
      e. beliefs
      f. cliffs
   3. a. banked
      b. proved
      c. hemmed
      d. copied
   4. a. completing
      b. wrapping
      c. employing
      d. replying
   5. a. Lincolns
      b. Jerseys
      c. Hiltys
      d. Christmases
      e. Saturdays
      f. Goodriches
   6. a. assist/ed
      b. labored
      c. regard/ed
      d. represent/ed
   7. a. approv/ing
      b. clip/ping
      c. introduc/ing
      d. drag/ging

LESSON 7

NEW WORDS

1. attack
2. musical
3. automatic
4. domestic
5. traffic
6. correction
7. stock
8. defective
9. electrical
10. electricity
11. attic
12. public
13. publication
14. successful
15. readily
16. construction

REVIEW WORDS

17. knock
18. wreck
19. stroke
20. kingdom

A. Sounds and Letters

> • The /k/ sound at the end of a word is usually spelled *ck* after a short vowel when the last syllable is accented or when the word has only one syllable. **atta̱c̲k̲ sto̱c̲k̲** After a short vowel, final /k/ is usually spelled *c* in unaccented syllables. **atti̱c̲ publi̱c̲** The /k/ sound is spelled *c* or *k* when it occurs elsewhere in a word. **c̲onstru̱c̲tion k̲ingdom**

1. Write the spelling words that end with the following sounds.

18

atti/k/

   a. /ak/   b. /ek/   c. /ok/ (2 words)

2. Each answer in exercise 1 ends with /k/ spelled ___ after a (long, short) vowel.

3. Write the five NEW WORDS that end with /ik/. Is the last syllable in each word accented or unaccented?

4. Write these words, spelling /k/ correctly.
   a. musi__al   e. ele__tri__al
   b. defe__tive   f. lo__ation
   c. __orre__tion g. publi__ation
   d. ba__on   h. __onstru__tion

5. Also spell /k/ correctly in these words.
   a. stro__   d. mista__
   b. brea__   e. __ingdom
   c. __een   f. strea__

6. *Circle* and *accent* each have two *c*'s, one spelling /k/ and one spelling /s/. Write two NEW WORDS that also have two such *c*'s.

7. *Stroke* is a one-syllable word whose final sound is /k/. This /k/ is not spelled *ck,* because the vowel is (long, short).

8. Write two words for each of these, one with a long vowel and one with a short vowel. Spell final /k/ correctly each time.
   a. la/k/   d. li/k/
   b. pi/k/   e. sta/k/
   c. sto/k/   f. du/k/

A. 41 points
1. a. attack
   b. wreck
   c. stock, knock
2. *ck,* short
3. automatic, domestic, traffic, attic, public; unaccented
4. a. musical
   b. defective
   c. correction
   d. bacon
   e. electrical
   f. location
   g. publication
   h. construction
5. a. stroke
   b. break
   c. keen
   d. mistake
   e. kingdom
   f. streak
6. electricity, successful
7. long
8. a. lake, lack
   b. pike, pick
   c. stoke, stock
   d. like, lick
   e. stake, stack
   f. duke, duck

Test Sentences

1. *defective*   The fire was caused by *defective* wiring.
2. *musical*   He seems to have *musical* talent.
3. *electrical*   There was an *electrical* fuse missing.
4. *electricity*   The discovery of *electricity* changed the world.
5. *domestic*   A cow is a *domestic* animal.
6. *correction*   Make a *correction* on your paper.
7. *publication*   This newspaper *publication* is free.
8. *construction*   The *construction* of a sentence is important.
9. *readily*   The children *readily* accepted the changes.
10. *stock*   We must *stock* up on food.
11. *attic*   Please shut the *attic* door.
12. *traffic*   The *traffic* was moving slowly.

B. Using Your Words

1. Write spelling words that are antonyms.
   - a. demolition
   - b. wild
   - c. fruitless
   - d. reluctantly
   - e. defend
   - f. private

2. Write the spelling words that complete these comparisons.
   - a. *Act* is to *action* as *correct* is to ____.
   - b. *Barn* is to *loft* as *house* is to ____.
   - c. *Pipe* is to *water* as *wire* is to ____.
   - d. *Foot* is to *kick* as *knuckles* is to ____.

3. Write spelling words with these meanings.
   - a. Faulty; imperfect.
   - b. Pleasing to hear.
   - c. Pass the hand over; caress.
   - d. Ruin completely.

   - e. Something that is published.
   - f. Operating by itself.

Dictionary Practice

- The *connotation* of a word is the feeling that it gives besides its actual meaning. **discuss** (favorable connotation) **dispute** (unfavorable connotation)

4. a. Write the *-ed* and *-ing* forms of *traffic*.
   b. The words you wrote have a (favorable, unfavorable) connotation.

5. Compare *kingdom* and *dictatorship*. Which word has a more favorable connotation?

C. Building Words

- An *inflectional suffix* changes the form of a word but does not change its part of speech. **stock (verb)—stocks, stocked, stocking**

- Many words have a *derivational suffix*, which usually changes the root word to a different part of speech. **warm (adjective)— warmly (adverb)**

- The last letter of the root word is sometimes dropped or changed when a derivational suffix is added. **Make—making true— truly ready—readily**

1. Three common inflectional suffixes are *-es*, *-ed*, and *-ing*. Add *-ed* and *-ing* to each word.
   - a. knock   b. wreck   c. attack

2. The derivational suffixes *-ion*, *-ation*, *-ity*, and *-dom* are used to form nouns. Use them to make spelling words from these.
   - a. king   c. public
   - b. electric   d. construct

3. Form adverbs by adding *-ly* to these.
   - a. public   c. electrical
   - b. ready   d. successful

4. For most words ending with *-ic*, the ending *-ally* must be used to change them to adverbs. Add *-ally* to these words.
   - a. music   c. domestic
   - b. frantic   d. automatic

Bible Thoughts
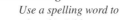
Use a spelling word to complete this Bible verse.

5. "Blessed are the poor in spirit: for theirs is the ____ of heaven" (Matthew 5:3).

19

B. 20 points
1. a. construction
   b. domestic
   c. successful
   d. readily
   e. attack
   f. public
2. a. correction
   b. attic
   c. electricity
   d. knock
3. a. defective
   b. musical
   c. stroke
   d. wreck
   e. publication
   f. automatic
4. a. trafficked, trafficking
   b. unfavorable
5. kingdom

C. 19 points
1. a. knocked, knocking
   b. wrecked, wrecking
   c. attacked, attacking
2. a. kingdom
   b. electricity
   c. publication
   d. construction
3. a. publicly
   b. readily
   c. electrically
   d. successfully
4. a. musically
   b. frantically
   c. domestically
   d. automatically
5. kingdom

---

13. *attack*   The Pharisees were ready to *attack* Jesus.
14. *automatic*   We have an *automatic* washer.
15. *public*   This was Jesus' last *public* discourse.
16. *successful*   We had a *successful* trip.

In one *stroke,* Saul lost the *kingdom.*

If you *knock* that down, you may *wreck* it.

(Teacher: You need not require the commas.)

LESSON 8

NEW WORDS

1. *industrial*
2. *misspell*
3. *embarrass*
4. *government*
5. *syllable*
6. *synagogue*
7. *customer*
8. *gossip*
9. *Gethsemane*
10. *apostle*
11. *inherit*
12. *passover*
13. *chickenpox*
14. *windmills*
15. *everlasting*
16. *quality*

REVIEW WORDS

17. *compass*
18. *blossoms*
19. *headache*
20. *post office*

A. Sounds and Letters

- The /a/ sound is usually spelled *a*. **p͟assover**

1. Write these words, spelling /a/ correctly.
   a. emb__rrass   c. p__ssover
   b. everl__sting   d. __dv__nce

- The /e/ sound is usually spelled *e* and sometimes *ea*. **inh͟erit h͟eadache**

2. Write these words, spelling /e/ correctly.
   a. missp__ll   c. G__ths__mane
   b. h__dache   d. prot__ct

w/i/ndm/i/lls

- The /i/ sound is usually spelled *i* and sometimes *y*. **w͟indm͟ills s͟yllable**

3. Add /i/ as you write these words.
   a. w__ndm__lls   c. __ndustrial
   b. __nher__t   d. post off__ce

4. Two NEW WORDS begin with /si/ spelled *sy* because the original Greek words began with the prefix *syn*. Write these words.

- The /o/ sound is usually spelled *o*. **apostle** After /w/ it is often spelled *a*. **qu͟ality w͟ash**

5. Add /o/ as you write these words.
   a. g__ssip   d. st__ck
   b. ap__stle   e. bl__ssoms
   c. qu__lity   f. w__tch

- The /u/ sound is usually spelled *u* and sometimes *o*. **c͟ustomer g͟overnment**

6. Add /u/ as you write these words.
   a. c__stomer   c. g__vernment
   b. ind__strial   d. c__mpass

7. Write the NEW WORD that ends with /poks/.

8. In the word you wrote for number 7, /k/ is spelled *ck* because it comes after a (long, short) vowel in a syllable that is (accented, unaccented).

20

A. 27 points
1. a. embarrass
   b. everlasting
   c. passover
   d. advance
2. a. misspell
   b. headache
   c. Gethsemane
   d. protect
3. a. windmills
   b. inherit
   c. industrial
   d. post office
4. syllable, synagogue
5. a. gossip
   b. apostle
   c. quality
   d. stock
   e. blossoms
   f. watch
6. a. customer
   b. industrial
   c. government
   d. compass
7. chickenpox
8. short, accented

Test Sentences

1. *industrial*   The United States is an *industrial* nation.
2. *misspell*   Do not *misspell* this word.
3. *embarrass*   The praise seemed to *embarrass* him.
4. *government*   The *government* needs our respect.
5. *syllable*   A *syllable* is a part of a word.
6. *synagogue*   Jesus went to the *synagogue* to teach.
7. *gossip*   Idle *gossip* does great harm.
8. *quality*   He has the *quality* of honesty.
9. *Gethsemane*   Jesus visited the Garden of *Gethsemane*.
10. *apostle*   Paul was an *apostle* called of God.
11. *inherit*   The meek will *inherit* the earth.
12. *customer*   Give the *customer* what he wants.

B. Using Your Words

1. Write spelling words that are synonyms.
   a. shopper   d. humiliate
   b. eternal   e. manufacturing
   c. characteristic   f. disciple

2. For each sentence, write the same spelling word (or a form of it) to fit in both blanks.
   a. Because he did not use his _____ as a guide in the darkness, the sailor only _____ the lake.
   b. Someone who has a habit of _____ about others will be known as a _____.
   c. There are thousands of _____ in the orchard when the apple trees _____.

3. Write a spelling word which is a synonym of *talk,* but which has an unfavorable connotation.

4. From each pair, copy the word with the more favorable connotation.
   a. curious, nosy
   b. stubborn, firm
   c. breakable, flimsy
   d. argue, discuss
   e. shout, bellow

Dictionary Practice

5. True or False: *Apostle* should be pronounced without a /t/ sound.

C. Building Words

• Most compound words are spelled solid (without a space between the parts). A compound spelled solid is called a closed compound. Some compounds are spelled open (with a space). **passover post office**

1. Write the compound NEW WORDS that contain *ever, wind, over,* and *chicken.*

2. Combine *ever* or *wind* with these words to form other closed compounds.
   a. when   c. whirl
   b. storm   d. green

3. Write the spelling word that contains *ache*. Then combine *ache* with *tooth* and *stomach* to form closed compounds.

4. Join *any* with each of these words to form closed compounds.
   a. where   c. one
   b. body   d. thing

5. Which REVIEW WORD is an open compound?

6. Join *master, cutter, school,* and *picket* with these words to build open compounds.
   a. fence   c. builder
   b. board   d. paper

Bible Thoughts
Use a spelling word to complete this Bible verse.

7. "Then cometh Jesus with them unto a place called _____" (Matthew 26:36).

21

B. 19 points
1. a. customer
   b. everlasting
   c. quality
   d. embarrass
   e. industrial
   f. apostle
2. a. compass, compassed
   b. gossiping, gossip *or* gossiper
   c. blossoms, blossom
3. gossip
4. a. curious
   b. firm
   c. breakable
   d. discuss
   e. shout
5. True

C. 21 points
1. everlasting, windmills, passover, chickenpox
2. a. whenever
   b. windstorm
   c. whirlwind
   d. evergreen
3. headache, toothache, stomachache
4. a. anywhere
   b. anybody
   c. anyone
   d. anything
5. post office
6. a. picket fence
   b. school board
   c. master builder
   d. paper cutter
7. Gethsemane

13. *chickenpox*   The baby has *chickenpox* too.
14. *everlasting*   The wicked shall go into *everlasting* fire.
15. *windmills*   Long ago, *windmills* were common in Holland.
16. *passover*   The *passover* lamb was killed and eaten.

Roy found a *compass* at the *post office*.

Will these *blossoms* make your *headache* worse?

LESSON 9

NEW WORDS

1. *testament*   9. *according*
2. *furious*   10. *territory*
3. *generous*   11. *religious*
4. *Nazareth*   12. *chocolate*
5. *abundant*   13. *et cetera etc.*
6. *severe*   14. *advertisement ad*
7. *suggest*   15. *examination exam*
8. *currant*   16. *telephone phone*

REVIEW WORDS

17. *January Jan.* 19. *September Sept.*
18. *February Feb.* 20. *December Dec.*

test/ə/m/ə/nt

NEW WORDS containing /ə/ are forms of these?
  a. examine   b. testator
3. a. Write the three NEW WORDS that begin or end with /ə/.
  b. When it forms the first or last syllable of a word, /ə/ is often spelled ___.

> • The /əs/ sound at the end of a word is usually spelled *ous*.
> **generous religious**

4. Write words that have the suffix *-ous*, which are different forms of these.
  a. religion   d. caution
  b. danger   e. envy
  c. fury   f. vigor
5. Use *ose* or *us* to spell /əs/ in these words.
  a. purp/əs/   b. radi/əs/
6. a. Write the NEW WORD with two *g*'s, one pronounced /g/ and one pronounced /j/.
  b. Write two other spelling words that have /j/ spelled *g*.
7. Which REVIEW WORDS have these sounds?
  a. two /e/ sounds   c. /yo͞o/ spelled *u*
  b. /s/ spelled *c*   d. two /r/ sounds

A. Sounds and Letters

> • The /ə/ sound occurs only in unaccented syllables. It is spelled *a, e, i, o,* or *u*. **test*a*ment exam*i*nation s*u*ggest**

1. Add /ə/ as you write these NEW WORDS.
  a. Naz__r__th   e. tel__phone
  b. curr__nt   f. choc__late
  c. s__ggest   g. advertisem__nt
  d. __bund__nt
2. You can often remember which letter spells /ə/ by thinking of how a different form of the word is spelled. Which

A. 29 points
1. a. Nazareth
  b. currant
  c. suggest
  d. abundant
  e. telephone
  f. chocolate
  g. advertisement
  h. examination
2. a. examination
  b. testament
3. a. abundant, according, et cetera
  b. a
4. a. religious
  b. dangerous
  c. furious
  d. cautious
  e. envious
  f. vigorous
5. a. purpose
  b. radius
6. a. suggest
  b. generous, religious
7. a. September
  b. December
  c. January
  d. February

22

Test Sentences

1.	*furious*	Jezebel was *furious* with Elijah.
2.	*testament*	A will is a *testament*.
3.	*generous*	Joseph was *generous* with his brothers.
4.	*suggest*	Did you *suggest* that?
5.	*chocolate*	We had *chocolate* ice cream.
6.	*abundant*	God's love is *abundant* toward us.
7.	*religious*	Jesus was crucified by *religious* leaders.
8.	*Nazareth*	Joseph went from *Nazareth* to Bethlehem.
9.	*according*	It came to pass *according* to the word of Elisha.
10.	*territory*	This *territory* is unfamiliar to me.
11.	*currant*	That is a *currant* bush.
12.	*severe*	We had a *severe* thunderstorm.

B. Using Your Words

1. The words *currant* and *current* are easily confused. Write the correct words.
   a. Mother uses (currants, currents) to make jellies and pies.
   b. A high-tension wire carries a powerful (currant, current) of electricity.
   c. The boat could make little headway against the swift (currant, current).
   d. A fungus sheltered by (currant, current) bushes is harmful to white pines.
2. Write the spelling word that belongs with each group.
   a. region, area, zone
   b. Bethlehem, Capernaum, Bethany
   c. caramel, fudge, peppermint
   d. hint, imply, indicate
   e. certificate, deed, title
3. Write spelling words that are antonyms.
   a. mild   c. scarce
   b. stingy   d. atheistic

Dictionary Practice

4. In Latin, *et cetera* means "___ ___ ___."
5. The word *currant* comes from a French phrase that refers to the city of _____.

C. Building Words

- Abbreviations may be used when it is important to save space, as in recipes, addresses, and notes. A few standard abbreviations, such as *Mr.*, *P.M.*, and *A.D.*, may be used in stories, reports, and letters.
- Most abbreviations are followed by periods. **etc.**
- In general writing, it is better to avoid *etc.* and to use *and so on* or *and so forth*.

1. Write the abbreviations for month names that are in the spelling list.
2. In the following sentences, find each abbreviation that does not follow the rules above. Write the word or words that should be used instead.
   a. The Dr. prescribed an antibiotic for Mrs. Porter.
   b. The archaeologists found pottery, tools, clay tablets, etc., which they dated around 1000 B.C.
   c. By 3:00 P.M., the river had risen to 12 ft. above its flood stage.
   d. We traveled over 100 mi. to reach Dr. Watson's office.
3. Some words are shortened forms rather than actual abbreviations. Write the full words for these shortened forms.
   a. phone   e. exam
   b. gym   f. ad
   c. bike   g. auto
   d. dorm   h. math

Bible Thoughts

Use a spelling word to complete this Bible verse.

4. "This is my blood of the new _____, which is shed for many" (Mark 14:24).

23

B. 15 points
1. a. currants
   b. current
   c. current
   d. currant
2. a. territory
   b. Nazareth
   c. chocolate
   d. suggest
   e. testament
3. a. severe
   b. generous
   c. abundant
   d. religious
4. and other things
5. Corinth

C. 17 points
1. Jan., Feb., Sept., Dec.
2. a. doctor
   b. and so on (so forth)
   c. feet
   d. miles
3. a. telephone
   b. gymnasium
   c. bicycle
   d. dormitory
   e. examination
   f. advertisement
   g. automobile
   h. mathematics
4. testament

For numbers 13–16, write the words *and* their abbreviations or clipped forms.

13.	*et cetera*	*etc.*	The words *et cetera* come from Latin.
14.	*examination*	*exam*	This *examination* is not hard.
15.	*advertisement*	*ad*	Put an *advertisement* in the paper.
16.	*telephone*	*phone*	The *telephone* is very useful.

The first two months are *January* and *February*.

He stayed with us from *September* to *December*.

Now write the abbreviations of the four month names in your sentences. (*Jan. Feb. Sept. Dec.*)

LESSON 10

NEW WORDS

1. *pardon*   9. *principal*
2. *fountain*   10. *principle*
3. *pigeon*   11. *articles*
4. *foreign*   12. *tabernacle*
5. *rural*   13. *2 Corinthians 2 Cor.*
6. *Psalms*   14. *Philippians Phil.*
7. *Hosea*   15. *Philemon Philem.*
8. *Nahum*   16. *Revelation Rev.*

REVIEW WORDS

17. *nickel*   19. *Gospel*
18. *metal*   20. *deacon*

A. Sounds and Letters

> • Common spellings of /əl/ at the
> end of a word are *le, el, al,* and
> *il.* **artic<u>le</u>s nick<u>el</u> rur<u>al</u> penc<u>il</u>**

1. Add /əl/ as you write these spelling words.
   a. met___   d. artic___s
   b. Gosp___   e. tabernac___
   c. rur___   f. nick___
2. Also add /əl/ to these words.
   a. arriv___   e. jew___
   b. valuab___   f. electric___
   c. humb___   g. chann___
   d. penc___   h. apost___

fount/ən/

3. Which two NEW WORDS are spelled the same except for /əl/ at the end?

> • Common spellings of /ən/ at
> the end of a word are *an, en,*
> *on,* and *ain.* **Philippi<u>an</u> soft<u>en</u>**
> **pard<u>on</u> fount<u>ain</u>**
>
> • Other spellings of /ən/ are *eon*
> and *eign.* **pig<u>eon</u> for<u>eign</u>**

4. Write these words, spelling /ən/ correctly.
   a. fount___   d. pig___
   b. deac___   e. pard___
   c. Philem___   f. Revelati___

5. Write the two NEW WORDS that end with /ənz/ spelled *ans.* Both of these are derived from the names of people who lived in certain cities.

6. Write the spelling word that ends with /ən/ spelled *eign.* This spelling can be remembered by associating it with the word *reign.*

7. Which NEW WORDS have these spellings?
   a. final /ə/ spelled *a*
   b. /s/ spelled *ps*
   c. /əm/ spelled *um*

A. 28 points
1. a. metal
   b. Gospel
   c. rural
   d. articles
   e. tabernacle
   f. nickel
2. a. arrival
   b. valuable
   c. humble
   d. pencil
   e. jewel
   f. electrical
   g. channel
   h. apostle
3. principal, principle
4. a. fountain
   b. deacon
   c. Philemon
   d. pigeon
   e. pardon
   f. Revelation
5. 2 Corinthians, Philippians
6. foreign
7. a. Hosea
   b. Psalms
   c. Nahum

24

Test Sentences

1. *pardon*   Please *pardon* my interruption.
2. *pigeon*   A *pigeon* is sometimes called a dove.
3. *fountain*   Jesus is the *fountain* of living water.
4. *principal*   The school *principal* took me home.
5. *principle*   The *principle* of honesty is important.
6. *rural*   Do you live in a *rural* area?
7. *articles*   These *articles* do not belong here.
8. *tabernacle*   The Israelites took the *tabernacle* with them.
9. *foreign*   Solomon had many *foreign* wives.
10. *Hosea*   The prophet *Hosea* lived in the time of Hezekiah.
11. *Nahum*   The Book of *Nahum* has three chapters.
12. *Psalms*   Much of *Psalms* was written by David.

B. Using Your Words

1. *Principal* and *principle* are often confused.
   a. Which word means "most important"?
   b. Which means "an underlying rule"? (Associate its spelling with ru<u>le</u>.)
2. Write *principal* or *principle*.
   a. Nonresistance is based on the _____ of Christian love.
   b. The _____ reason for studying music is to improve our singing.
   c. The law of inertia is an important _____ in science.
3. Do not confuse *rural* with *urban* or *medal* with *metal*. Write the correct words.
   a. Air pollution is a serious problem in many (rural, urban) communities.
   b. Farming is a common occupation in (rural, urban) areas.
   c. Country people receive mail by a system called (rural, urban) free delivery.
   d. Tubal-cain was the first man known to work with (medal, metal).
   e. The soldier received a (medal, metal) for his bravery.
4. Write spelling words that are synonyms.
   a. forgive   c. tent
   b. dove   d. items

Dictionary Practice

5. *Tabernacle* may refer to the human body because the body is a _____ dwelling place of the soul.

C. Building Words

- **The long names of Bible books have abbreviations.**
  2 Corinthians—2 Cor.

1. Write the four NEW WORDS that are abbreviations for names of Bible books.
2. a. Which Bible book name has the suffix *-ation*?
   b. Is this name in a singular or a plural form?
3. *Psalms* is capitalized when it refers to the Book of Psalms or to certain psalms: Psalms 23 and 24. The word is not capitalized when it does not refer to a certain psalm: two psalms, a short psalm.

   Write the correct form of *Psalms* for each phrase.

   a. learning _____ 91 and 92
   b. reading a _____ every day
   c. the Bible book after _____
   d. memorized five _____
   e. discussing _____ 137
4. Add *-ed* and *-ing* to *pardon*. Divide one word between the root word and the suffix.
5. Write the two NEW WORDS that have the suffix *-al* but whose roots are not words that can stand alone.

Bible Thoughts

Use a spelling word to complete this Bible verse.
6. "Thou art a God ready to _____, gracious and merciful, slow to anger, and of great kindness" (Nehemiah 9:17).

25

B. 15 points

1. a. principal
   b. principle
2. a. principle
   b. principal
   c. principle
3. a. urban
   b. rural
   c. rural
   d. metal
   e. medal
4. a. pardon
   b. pigeon
   c. tabernacle
   d. articles
5. temporary

C. 16 points

1. 2 Cor., Phil., Philem., Rev.
2. a. Revelation
   b. singular
3. a. Psalms
   b. psalm
   c. Psalms
   d. psalms
   e. Psalm
4. pardoned, pardon/ing
5. rural, principal
6. pardon

For numbers 13–16, write the words *and* their abbreviations.
13. *2 Corinthians*   *2 Cor.*   Paul wrote *2 Corinthians* at Philippi.
14. *Philippians*   *Phil.*   He wrote to the *Philippians* from prison.
15. *Philemon*   *Philem.*   Paul's epistle to *Philemon* was a personal letter.
16. *Revelation*   *Rev.*   The Book of *Revelation* tells of John's visions.

   A *nickel* is made of *metal*.

   Philip was a *deacon* who preached the *Gospel*.

LESSON 11

NEW WORDS

1. design
2. annual
3. dying
4. museum
5. groan
6. recipe
7. beautifully
8. loneliness
9. bureau
10. funeral
11. capable
12. communicate
13. Messiah
14. Jehovah
15. supreme
16. grateful

REVIEW WORDS

17. increased
18. lightning
19. nephew
20. greetings

A. Sounds and Letters

- The /ā/ sound is commonly spelled *a, ai,* or *a-e.* **capable plains grateful**
- The /ē/ sound is commonly spelled *e, ea, ee,* or *e-e.* **museum increased greetings supreme** At the end of words, /ē/ is usually spelled *y.* **beauty**
- The /ī/ sound is commonly spelled *i, ie, y,* or *igh.* **Messiah lie dying lightning**

26

bur/ō/

- The /ō/ sound is commonly spelled *o, oa,* or *o-e.* **Jehovah groan loneliness**
  In a few words, /ō/ is spelled *eau.* **bureau**
- The /yōō/ sound is commonly spelled *u, ew,* or *u-e.* **funeral nephew cube**
  In a few words, /yōō/ is spelled *eau.* **beauty**

1. Write these spelling words, being sure to spell the long vowel sounds correctly.
   a. l/ī/tning
   b. gr/ō/n
   c. incr/ē/sed
   d. c/ā/pable
   e. supr/ēm/
   f. neph/yōō/
   g. communic/āt/
   h. des/ī/n
   i. mus/ē/um
   j. gr/ē/tings

2. a. In which NEW WORD is the French spelling *eau* pronounced /ō/?
   b. In which word is *eau* pronounced /yōō/?

3. Write the two spelling words of Hebrew origin that end with /ə/ spelled *ah.*

4. Write the NEW WORD in which *ie* was changed to *y* before *-ing* was added. Then write the one in which *y* was changed to *i* before *-ness* was added.

5. Which NEW WORD ends with /ē/, but the sound is spelled *e* instead of *y*?

6. Write the NEW WORDS in which /əl/ is spelled in these ways.
   a. le   b. al (2 words)   c. ul (2 words)

A. 22 points

1. a. lightning
   b. groan
   c. increased
   d. capable
   e. supreme
   f. nephew
   g. communicate
   h. design
   i. museum
   j. greetings
2. a. bureau
   b. beautifully
3. Messiah, Jehovah
4. dying; loneliness
5. recipe
6. a. capable
   b. annual, funeral
   c. beautifully, grateful

Test Sentences

1.	*museum*	A *museum* has many interesting things.
2.	*design*	This is a good *design* for the house.
3.	*dying*	The light was slowly *dying* out.
4.	*groan*	The wounded man uttered a *groan* of pain.
5.	*recipe*	Put the card in the *recipe* file.
6.	*funeral*	We attended the *funeral* yesterday.
7.	*bureau*	That *bureau* has many drawers.
8.	*beautifully*	The book was *beautifully* illustrated.
9.	*annual*	The board held its *annual* meeting.
10.	*communicate*	Telephones make it easy to *communicate.*
11.	*Jehovah*	The Lord *Jehovah* is our God.
12.	*Messiah*	The Jews waited for the *Messiah* to come.

B. Using Your Words

1. Write the correct homophones.
 a. Mrs. Lincoln was (dying, dyeing) the yarn she had spun.
 b. The last light of the day was (dying, dyeing) in the west.
 c. Corn is (groan, grown) in almost every state of the United States.
 d. The (groan, grown) of the hinges startled me.

2. Write spelling words for these definitions.
 a. Sadness from having no companionship.
 b. A place where interesting things are displayed.

3. Write spelling words to complete these comparisons.
 a. *Joy* is to *wedding* as *sorrow* is to _____.
 b. *Roar* is to *lion* as *thunder* is to _____.
 c. *House* is to *blueprint* as *pie* is to _____.
 d. *Aunt* is to *uncle* as *niece* is to _____.

4. Write the spelling word that could replace each underlined word.
 a. The cobbler <u>augmented</u> his income by making furniture to sell.
 b. The searchers' <u>paramount</u> concern was to find the child before dark.
 c. This wall must have been built by a <u>competent</u> bricklayer

Dictionary Practice

5. Write the two plural forms of *bureau*.
6. *Jehovah* comes from four Hebrew letters which in English are _____.

B. 16 points
 1. a. dyeing
  b. dying
  c. grown
  d. groan
 2. a. loneliness
  b. museum
 3. a. funeral
  b. lightning
  c. recipe
  d. nephew
 4. a. increased
  b. supreme
  c. capable
 5. bureaus, bureaux
 6. YHWH

C. Building Words

- Many words have one consonant sound between two vowel sounds. If the first vowel is short, the syllable division usually comes after the consonant: VC/V. If it is long, the division comes after the vowel: V/CV. **ref/uge na/tive**

- When two consonant sounds or two vowel sounds come together between syllables, the syllable division is made between them: VC/CV and CV/VC. **pub/lic mu/se/um**

- When a word ends with *le*, the preceding consonant is kept with *le* to form the last syllable. But words that end with *ckle* are divided

before *le*. **ca/pa/ble pick/les**
- Compound words are divided into syllables between their parts. **wind/mills here/to/fore**

1. Use slashes to syllabicate these words.
 a. nephew   d. beautifully
 b. annual   e. capable
 c. tickled   f. museum
2. Syllabicate these compound words.
 a. meanwhile   c. gentleman
 b. whatever   d. overlook

Bible Thoughts
Use a spelling word to complete this Bible verse.
3. "But to do good and to _____ [share] forget not" (Hebrews 13:16).

27

C. 11 points
 1. a. neph/ew
  b. an/nu/al
  c. tick/led
  d. beau/ti/ful/ly
  e. ca/pa/ble
  f. com/mu/ni/cate
 2. a. mean/while
  b. what/ev/er
  c. gen/tle/man
  d. o/ver/look
 3. communicate

13. *supreme*   God is the *Supreme* Being.
14. *grateful*   I am *grateful* for your help.
15. *capable*   He is a very *capable* boy.
16. *loneliness*   The prisoner endured much *loneliness*.

Has the number of *lightning* bugs *increased*?

My *nephew* sends his *greetings*.

LESSON 12

7	8	9	10	11
attack	industrial	testament	pardon	design
musical	misspell	furious	fountain	annual
automatic	embarrass	generous	pigeon	dying
domestic	government	Nazareth	foreign	museum
traffic	syllable	abundant	rural	groan
correction	synagogue	severe	Psalms	recipe
stock	customer	suggest	Hosea	beautifully
defective	gossip	currant	Nahum	loneliness
electrical	Gethsemane	according	principal	bureau
electricity	apostle	territory	principle	funeral
attic	inherit	religious	articles	capable
public	passover	chocolate	tabernacle	communicate
publication	chickenpox	et cetera etc.	2 Corinthians 2 Cor.	Messiah
successful	windmills	advertisement ad	Philippians Phil.	Jehovah
readily	everlasting	examination exam	Philemon Philem.	supreme
construction	quality	telephone phone	Revelation Rev.	grateful

A. Sounds and Letters Review

1. Write these spelling words, using the correct spellings of /k/. The last two are REVIEW WORDS from Lesson 7.
   a. defe/k/tive   c. /k/ingdom
   b. chi/k/enpox   d. stro/k/

2. Spell these words correctly.
   a. p/a/ssover   f. c/ā/pable
   b. r/e/dily   g. recip/ē/
   c. s/i/llable   h. d/ī/ing
   d. ap/o/stle   i. gr/ō/n
   e. c/u/stomer   j. m/yōō/seum

3. Add /ə/, /əl/, or /ən/ to each word.
   a. artic__s   d. rur__
   b. pig__   e. exam__nation
   c. fount__   f. for__

4. Add /əs/ to each word.
   a. religi__   c. gener__
   b. furi__   d. embarr__

5. Write the NEW WORDS that have these sounds. Lesson numbers are in parentheses.
   a. /u/ spelled *o* (8)
   b. two /ə/ sounds spelled *a* (9)
   c. /ämz/ spelled *alms* (10)
   d. /ī/ spelled *ig* (11)

A. 28 points
1. a. defective
   b. kingdom
   c. chickenpox
   d. stroke
2. a. passover
   b. readily
   c. syllable
   d. apostle
   e. customer
   f. capable
   g. recipe
   h. dying
   i. groan
   j. museum
3. a. articles
   b. pigeon
   c. fountain
   d. rural
   e. territory
   f. foreign
4. a. religious
   b. furious
   c. generous
   d. embarrass
5. a. government
   b. abundant
   c. Psalms
   d. design

28

See page 83 for test sentences.

B. Using Your Words Review

1. Write the correct word for each sentence.
   a. Some (currants, currents) grow wild in North America.
   b. Iron is one of the most important (medals, metals) used by man.
   c. Most apartment buildings are found in (rural, urban) communities.
   d. We can see the (principle, principal) of sowing and reaping in Jacob's life.
   e. Jesus' (dying, dyeing) words were, "It is finished."
   f. The traveler was startled by a low (grown, groan).

2. Which words are antonyms of these?
   a. basement (7)   c. unable (11)
   b. native (10)   d. thankless (11)

3. Write the word whose connotation suggests a greater degree or intensity.
   a. principal, important
   b. severe, bad
   c. angry, furious
   d. thriving, successful

4. Which spelling words have these double meanings?
   a. (1) farm animals
      (2) something kept in store
   b. (1) things; items
      (2) the words *a, an,* and *the*
   c. (1) vehicles moving along a road
      (2) buy and sell illegally
   d. (1) make a proposal
      (2) indicate indirectly

C. Building Words Review

1. Write words with these roots and suffixes.
   a. suggest + ion   d. natural + ly
   b. ready + ly   e. success + ful
   c. defect + ive   f. industry + al

2. Make two closed compounds by joining *home* with *work* and *stead.*

3. Write open compounds by joining *house* with *call* and *sparrow.*

4. Write the abbreviations for these.
   a. et cetera   d. Revelation
   b. Philemon   e. September
   c. February   f. 2 Corinthians

5. Write the shortened forms of *examination, telephone,* and *advertisement.*

6. Write the correct forms of *Psalms.*
   The Book of (a) _____ is not divided into chapters. Each portion in this book is a separate (b) _____. Probably the best known (c) _____ is (d) _____ 23.

7. Use slashes to syllabicate these words.
   a. readily   e. completing
   b. secret   f. publication
   c. passover   g. tiniest
   d. Hosea   h. principle

29

B. 18 points
1. a. currants
   b. metals
   c. urban
   d. principle
   e. dying
   f. groan
2. a. attic
   b. foreign
   c. capable
   d. grateful
3. a. principal
   b. severe
   c. furious
   d. thriving
4. a. stock
   b. articles
   c. traffic
   d. suggest

C. 31 points
1. a. suggestion
   b. readily
   c. defective
   d. naturally
   e. successful
   f. industrial
2. homework, homestead
3. house call, house sparrow
4. a. etc.
   b. Philem.
   c. Feb.
   d. Rev.
   e. Sept.
   f. 2 Cor.
5. exam, phone, ad
6. a. Psalms
   b. psalm
   c. psalm
   d. Psalm
7. a. read/i/ly
   b. se/cret
   c. pass/o/ver
   d. Ho/se/a
   e. com/plet/ing
   f. pub/li/ca/tion
   g. ti/ni/est
   h. prin/ci/ple

LESSON 13

r/ā/ndeer

NEW WORDS

1. league
2. deceive
3. grieve
4. weight
5. depot
6. ceiling
7. veil
8. reindeer
9. relief
10. apiece
11. cedar
12. shield
13. believed
14. unbeliever
15. medium
16. children's

REVIEW WORDS

17. breathe
18. secret
19. neither
20. height

A. Sounds and Letters

> • For words in which the vowel sound is spelled *ie* or *ei*, it is helpful to remember the following lines.
>
>   *I* before *e*, except after *c*,
>   Or when sounded like /ā/
>   As in *neighbor* and *weigh*.
>
> **shi<u>e</u>ld dec<u>ei</u>ve r<u>ei</u>ndeer**

1. Spell these words correctly, which are in the "*i* before *e*" category.
   a. gr/ē/ve   d. bel/ē/ved
   b. rel/ē/f   e. ap/ē/ce
   c. sh/ē/ld   f. unbel/ē/ver

2. These words are in the "except after *c*" category. Spell them correctly.
   a. c/ē/ling   c. dec/ē/ve
   b. conc/ē/t   d. rec/ē/pt

3. The word *neither* is an exception to the "*i* before *e*" pattern, but it can be associated with *either*. Write *neither* and *either*.

4. Which REVIEW WORD ends with /īt/ spelled *eight*? This word is another exception to the usual pattern.

5. These words have /ā/ spelled *ei*. Write them correctly.
   a. v__l   c. w__ght
   b. r__ndeer   d. r__gn

6. Write spelling words with these sounds.
   a. /ō/ spelled *ot*
   b. /ər/ spelled *ar*
   c. /g/ spelled *gue*
   d. /əm/ spelled *um*
   e. /k/ spelled *c*
   f. /ē/ spelled *ea* (2 words)
   g. final /z/ spelled *s*

7. Which spelling words are derived from these words? Observe how the original spellings influence the modern spellings.
   a. medius   c. legue
   b. depost   d. reindere

A. 29 points
   1. a. grieve
      b. relief
      c. shield
      d. believed
      e. apiece
      f. unbeliever
   2. a. ceiling
      b. conceit
      c. deceive
      d. receipt
   3. neither, either
   4. height
   5. a. veil
      b. reindeer
      c. weight
      d. reign
   6. a. depot
      b. cedar
      c. league
      d. medium
      e. secret
      f. league, breathe
      g. children's
   7. a. medium
      b. depot
      c. league
      d. reindeer

30

Test Sentences

1.	league	Joshua made a *league* with the Gibeonites.
2.	deceive	We must not *deceive* others.
3.	grieve	Do not *grieve* your parents.
4.	weight	The *weight* of the truck was ten tons.
5.	depot	We stopped at the bus *depot* in town.
6.	ceiling	Can you reach the *ceiling*?
7.	relief	It was a *relief* to hear your voice.
8.	apiece	The books cost one dollar *apiece*.
9.	shield	The Lord is my *shield* and buckler.
10.	veil	Moses put a *veil* over his face.
11.	cedar	The *cedar* tree is an evergreen.
12.	believed	They *believed* and were baptized.

B. Using Your Words

1. Write the spelling word that belongs with each group.
   a. elk, moose, caribou
   b. delude, mislead, beguile
   c. helmet, breastplate, greaves
   d. pine, cypress, spruce
   e. station, terminal, airport
2. Choose the correct homophones.
   a. A (vale, veil) of fog hung over the (vale, veil).
   b. I had to (wait, weight) a bit before the scale showed my correct (wait, weight).
   c. The boys were (ceiling, sealing) the cracks in the old (ceiling, sealing).

3. Do not confuse *apiece* with *a piece*. Choose the correct words.
   a. The ten servants in Jesus' parable received one pound (apiece, a piece).
   b. Darrel ate (apiece, a piece) of cake.
   c. The three boys picked five quarts of strawberries (apiece, a piece).

Dictionary Practice

4. What is an archaic spelling of *veil*?
5. *Neither* may be what three parts of speech?
6. Choose the letters of two correct pronunciations for *depot*.
   a. (dē′pō)   b. (dep′it)   c. (dep′ō)

C. Building Words

- The possessive form of singular nouns is made by adding *'s*. **my father's work** Plural nouns that do not end with *s* are also made possessive by adding *'s*. **the children's lessons**
- The possessive form of plural nouns that end with *s* is made by adding only an apostrophe. **two disciples' request the neighbors' houses**

1. Write the possessive forms of these singular nouns.
   a. clerk   d. unbeliever
   b. apostle   e. governor
   c. buffalo   f. customer
2. Write the possessive forms of these plural nouns.
   a. wolves   d. merchants
   b. ladies   e. children
   c. reindeer   f. gentlemen
3. "House of John" means "John's house." Rewrite each phrase in a similar way, using a possessive noun.
   a. time of Noah
   b. throne of David
   c. feathers of birds
   d. journey of a day
   e. worth of a dollar

Bible Thoughts

Use a spelling word to complete this Bible verse.

4. "Thou art my hiding place and my _____: I hope in thy word" (Psalm 119:114).

31

B. 20 points
1. a. reindeer
   b. deceive
   c. shield
   d. cedar
   e. depot
2. a. veil, vale
   b. wait, weight
   c. sealing, ceiling
3. a. apiece
   b. a piece
   c. apiece
4. vail
5. conjunction, adjective, pronoun (Accept abbreviations.)
6. a, c

C. 18 points
1. a. clerk's
   b. apostle's
   c. buffalo's
   d. unbeliever's
   e. governor's
   f. customer's
2. a. wolves'
   b. ladies'
   c. reindeer's
   d. merchants'
   e. children's
   f. gentlemen's
3. a. Noah's time
   b. David's throne
   c. birds' feathers
   d. day's journey
   e. dollar's worth
4. shield

---

13. *unbeliever*   An *unbeliever* will not enter heaven.
14. *medium*   Set it on *medium* heat.
15. *reindeer*   There are *reindeer* in Norway.
16. *children's*   The *children's* books are over here.

It is hard to *breathe* at this *height*.

Neither of these facts is a *secret*.

LESSON 14

NEW WORDS

1. surface
2. earnest
3. burden
4. courtesy
5. reverse
6. circulation
7. eternal
8. firmament

9. personality
10. research
11. current
12. reserve
13. furnace
14. merchant
15. servant
16. missionary

REVIEW WORDS

17. worst
18. alligators

19. sister's
20. worship

A. Sounds and Letters

- Common spellings of /ûr/ are *er*, *ur* or *urr*, and *ir*. **eternal burden current firmament** Other spellings are *ear* and *our*. **earnest courtesy** After *w*, /ûr/ is often spelled *or*. **worship**

1. The /ûr/ sound is spelled *er* in each of these NEW WORDS. Write them correctly.
   a. res__ve
   b. m__chant
   c. rev__se
   d. s__vant
   e. et__nal
   f. p__sonality

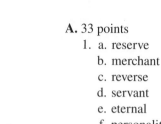

b/ûr/den

2. Write these words, using *ur* or *urr* to spell /ûr/.
   a. b__den
   b. c__ent
   c. t__tle
   d. f__nace
   e. f__ther
   f. s__face

3. Use *our* to spell /ûr/ as you write these.
   a. c__tesy
   b. c__age
   c. j__ney
   d. sc__ge

4. Write these words correctly.
   a. /ûr/nest
   b. wh/ûr/l
   c. l/ûr/ned
   d. c/ûr/culation
   e. res/ûr/ch
   f. f/ûr/mament

5. Use *or* to spell /ûr/ as you write these.
   a. w__st
   b. w__ker
   c. w__ms
   d. w__thy
   e. w__ship
   f. w__ldly

6. Write the NEW WORD that has /sh/ spelled *ssi* and final /ē/ spelled *y*.

7. Write the spelling words that end with these sounds.
   a. /ərz/ spelled *ors*
   b. /chənt/ spelled *chant*
   c. /ərz/ spelled *er's*

8. Which NEW WORD is derived from *court*, but the /ôr/ sound is changed to /ûr/?

A. 33 points
1. a. reserve
   b. merchant
   c. reverse
   d. servant
   e. eternal
   f. personality
2. a. burden
   b. current
   c. turtle
   d. furnace
   e. further
   f. surface
3. a. courtesy
   b. courage
   c. journey
   d. scourge
4. a. earnest
   b. whirl
   c. learned
   d. circulation
   e. research
   f. firmament
5. a. worst
   b. worker
   c. worms
   d. worthy
   e. worship
   f. worldly
6. missionary
7. a. alligators
   b. merchant
   c. sister's
8. courtesy

32

Test Sentences

1. *surface* — A whale must *surface* for air.
2. *burden* — Jesus is our *burden* bearer.
3. *courtesy* — Please show *courtesy* to your guests.
4. *earnest* — He is an *earnest* young man.
5. *circulation* — Grandmother's *circulation* is poor.
6. *eternal* — We have God's *eternal* Word.
7. *firmament* — The *firmament* was made on the second day.
8. *personality* — Her *personality* seems very pleasant.
9. *research* — Have you done your *research* properly?
10. *current* — The *current* is strong close to the shore.
11. *reverse* — You must *reverse* your thinking.
12. *reserve* — Please *reserve* this seat.

B. Using Your Words

1. Write a spelling word that is a synonym of the underlined word in each sentence.
   a. The Lord created the <u>heavens</u>.
   b. An Israelite girl worked as a <u>domestic</u> for Naaman's wife.
   c. We must <u>venerate</u> the Lord alone.
   d. Mr. Gray showed remarkable <u>civility</u> in spite of his customer's insults.
2. Write the correct word for each sentence.
   a. The children went into the woods to look for (currants, currents).
   b. Stoicism was a (currant, current) philosophy in Paul's day.
3. Write the spelling words that are synonyms of these but have better connotations.

   a. oppress   c. peddler
   b. slave   d. fanatical
4. Which words have these definitions?
   a. Something set aside.
   b. Investigation.
   c. The characteristics that make each person an individual.
   d. Reptiles similar to crocodiles.

Dictionary Practice

5. Look up *earnest*[1], and copy the boldface idiom that means "determined; serious."
6. *Burden* has two entries. Write the number of the entry that matches each use below.
   a. The donkey carried a heavy <u>burden</u>.
   b. Father told us the <u>burden</u> of the letter.

C. Building Words

- Do not confuse plural forms with possessive forms. A possessive noun shows ownership. A plural noun simply indicates more than one person, place, or thing.
  Possessive: my sister's room
  Plural: my two sisters

1. Write the plural form of each word.
   a. burden   c. personality
   b. reverse   d. courtesy
2. Write the possessive forms of these.
   a. merchant   c. missionary
   b. calf   d. class
3. Write the correct plural or possessive form of each word in parentheses.
   a. my (mother) wishes
   b. many (reserve) for wild animals

   c. three (copy) of the book
   d. a (carpenter) skills
4. In each sentence, one underlined noun should be plural and one should be possessive. Write the correct forms.
   a. My <u>cousin</u> mow my <u>grandfather</u> lawn.
   b. These <u>tool</u> are the <u>company</u> equipment.
   c. One <u>rabbit</u> babies are hiding in the <u>bush</u>.
   d. The <u>toy</u> are in the <u>children</u> room.

Bible Thoughts

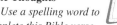

Use a spelling word to complete this Bible verse.
5. "Fight the good fight of faith, lay hold on _____ life" (1 Timothy 6:12).

33

B. 17 points
1. a. firmament
   b. servant
   c. worship
   d. courtesy
2. a. currants
   b. current
3. a. burden
   b. servant
   c. merchant
   d. earnest
4. a. reserve
   b. research
   c. personality
   d. alligators
5. in earnest
6. a. 1
   b. 2

C. 21 points
1. a. burdens
   b. reverses
   c. personalities
   d. courtesies
2. a. merchant's
   b. calf's
   c. missionary's
   d. class's
3. a. mother's
   b. reserves
   c. copies
   d. carpenter's
4. a. cousins, grandfather's
   b. tools, company's
   c. rabbit's, bushes
   d. toys, children's
5. eternal

13. *furnace*   The *furnace* is hot.
14. *missionary*   I like to read *missionary* stories.
15. *merchant*   That is a *merchant* ship.
16. *servant*   The minister is a *servant* of God.

Is man the *worst* enemy of *alligators?*

My *sister's* class will *worship* here.

LESSON 15

NEW WORDS

min/ər/s

1. tailor
2. instructor
3. observation
4. reference
5. regularly
6. permission
7. embroidery
8. ignorant
9. miners
10. deliveries
11. failure
12. debtor
13. reverence
14. scholarship
15. governor
16. international

REVIEW WORDS

17. customer
18. battery
19. factories
20. oyster

A. Sounds and Letters

• The /ûr/ sound occurs in accented syllables, and the /ər/ sound in unaccented syllables. Common spellings of /ər/ are er, ar, and or.
ref<u>er</u>ence regul<u>ar</u>ly ign<u>or</u>ant

1. Write these words, spelling /ər/ correctly.
a. oyst__   f. fact__ies
b. regul__ly   g. rev__ence
c. obs__vation h. schol__ship
d. p__mission   i. batt__y
e. deliv__ies

34

2. Add er to the first column and or to the second column.
a. oyst__   d. tail__
b. min__s   e. instruct__
c. custom__   f. debt__

3. The /ər/ at the end of each word comes from a comparative suffix. Spell the words correctly.
a. happi/ər/   c. pretti/ər/
b. swift/ər/   d. strong/ər/

• The /yər/ sound is usually spelled ure or ior. **fail<u>ure</u> jun<u>ior</u>**

4. Add /yər/ to the end of each word.
a. fail__   c. super__
b. jun__   d. fig__

5. Write the three spelling words that end with /ē/ spelled y.

6. Write the NEW WORDS with these sounds.
a. /sk/ spelled sch
b. final /s/ spelled ce (2 words)
c. final /əl/ spelled al

7. Which NEW WORD has two /ər/ sounds, one spelled er and one spelled or?

8. Write the NEW WORD with which ignore will help you to spell /ər/ correctly.

A. 32 points
1. a. oyster
   b. regularly
   c. observation
   d. permission
   e. deliveries
   f. factories
   g. reverence
   h. scholarship
   i. battery
2. a. oyster
   b. miners
   c. customer
   d. tailor
   e. instructor
   f. debtor
3. a. happier
   b. swifter
   c. prettier
   d. stronger
4. a. failure
   b. junior
   c. superior
   d. figure
5. regularly, embroidery, battery
6. a. scholarship
   b. reference reverence
   c. international
7. governor
8. ignorant

Test Sentences

1. international — This is an *international* airport.
2. instructor — The flight *instructor* is here.
3. observation — We stood on the *observation* deck.
4. reference — He brought a *reference* book.
5. regularly — The planes are inspected *regularly*.
6. tailor — This suit was made by a *tailor*.
7. embroidery — That is good *embroidery* work.
8. deliveries — There will not be many *deliveries* today.
9. failure — There was a power *failure* yesterday.
10. debtor — The *debtor* could not pay what he owed.
11. permission — Do you have *permission* to leave?
12. reverence — Always show *reverence* in church.

B. Using Your Words

1. Which spelling words have these double meanings?
   a. (1) A person who makes clothing to order.
   (2) Make (something) suitable.
   b. (1) A person who rules.
   (2) A device that regulates the speed of a machine.
   c. (1) A person who can recommend someone.
   (2) The calling of attention to something.

2. Do not confuse *miner* and *minor*. Write the correct words.
   a. Many coal (miners, minors) work more than two hundred feet underground.
   b. Thousands of (miners, minors) flocked to California to look for gold.
   c. A ten-year-old boy is a (miner, minor).
   d. Only (miner, minor) damage was done to the car.

3. Write spelling words that are antonyms.
   a. pupil   d. wise
   b. creditor   e. success
   c. infrequently   f. prohibition

Dictionary Practice

4. A battery may be a group of things that are (similar, different).

C. Building Words

- Prefixes and suffixes are added to many words to make derived forms. Spelling changes are sometimes made when these affixes are attached.
  in + regular = irregular
  observe + ation = observation

1. Write words with these roots and affixes.
   a. custom + er   e. embroider + y
   b. debt + or   f. refer + ence
   c. permit + ion   g. mine + er + s
   d. fail + ure   h. inter + nation + al

2. Which spelling word with *-or* does not have a root that can stand alone as a word with a related meaning?

3. Write spelling words that are derived forms of the underlined words.
   a. Coal <u>mine</u> no longer need to work as hard as they once did.
   b. There may be serious consequences for <u>fail</u> to listen carefully.
   c. Airplanes are inspected <u>regular</u> to keep them in safe flying condition.

4. Change the suffix in each word to the suffix before that pair.
   a. *-ance*: ignorant, observant
   b. *-ent*: reverence, dependence
   c. *-ity*: regularly, electrical

Bible Thoughts

Use a spelling word to complete this Bible verse.

5. "God is . . . to be had in _____ of all them that are about him" (Psalm 89:7).

35

B. 14 points
   1. a. tailor
      b. governor
      c. reference
   2. a. miners
      b. miners
      c. minor
      d. minor
   3. a. instructor
      b. debtor
      c. regularly
      d. ignorant
      e. failure
      f. permission
   4. similar

C. 19 points
   1. a. customer
      b. debtor
      c. permission
      d. failure
      e. embroidery
      f. reference
      g. miners
      h. international
   2. tailor
   3. a. miners
      b. failure
      c. regularly
   4. a. ignorance, observance
      b. reverent, dependent
      c. regularity, electricity
   5. reverence

13.	*ignorant*	Jonathan was *ignorant* of Saul's command.
14.	*governor*	He is the *governor* of our state.
15.	*miners*	The coal *miners* work hard.
16.	*scholarship*	His work shows good *scholarship*.

Show the *customer* a *battery*.

These *factories* make *oyster* crackers.

LESSON 16

NEW WORDS

1. *approach*
2. *cheerful*
3. *adventure*
4. *channel*
5. *Scripture*
6. *butcher*
7. *dispatch*
8. *charity*
9. *stretch*
10. *manufacturing*
11. *fortunate*
12. *moisture*
13. *natural*
14. *disappear*
15. *disappointed*
16. *independence*

REVIEW WORDS

17. *Christian*
18. *choice*
19. *engineer*
20. *Redeemer*

A. Sounds and Letters

- The /ch/ sound is usually spelled *ch* at the beginning of a word or after a long vowel sound. **choice appro<u>ch</u>**
  After a short vowel, /ch/ is often spelled *tch*. **bu<u>tch</u>er stre<u>tch</u>**
  Sometimes /ch/ is spelled *t* or *ti*. **for<u>t</u>unate Chris<u>ti</u>an**

1. Write these words, spelling /ch/ correctly.
   a. __arity
   b. approa__
   c. __eerful
   d. mer__ant
   e. __annel
   f. sear__
   g. __oice
   h. or__ard

36

bu/ch/er

2. In these words, /ch/ comes after short vowels. Write them correctly.
   a. dispa/ch/
   b. wa/ch/
   c. stre/ch/
   d. swi/ch/
   e. bu/ch/er
   f. ca/ch/
3. Write the spelling words with which the root words *fortune* and *Christ* will help you to spell /ch/ correctly.

- The /chər/ sound is usually spelled *tur* or *ture*. **na<u>tur</u>al mois<u>ture</u>**

4. Write these words, spelling /chər/ correctly.
   a. Scrip__
   b. mois__
   c. na__al
   d. lec__
   e. manufac__ing
   f. adven__
5. These spelling words contain /ə/, /ər/, and /əl/. Write them correctly.
   a. dis__ppear
   b. butch__
   c. __pproach
   d. m__chant
   e. Redeem__
   f. eng__neer
   g. natur__
   h. dis__ppointed
6. Which NEW WORD has four syllables and four *e*'s?
7. Knowing how to spell *engine* will help you to spell /ə/ in which REVIEW WORD?

A. 32 points
  1. a. charity
     b. approach
     c. cheerful
     d. merchant
     e. channel
     f. search
     g. choice
     h. orchard
  2. a. dispatch
     b. watch
     c. stretch
     d. switch
     e. butcher
     f. catch
  3. fortunate, Christian
  4. a. Scripture
     b. moisture
     c. natural
     d. lecture
     e. manufacturing
     f. adventure
  5. a. disappear
     b. butcher
     c. approach
     d. merchant
     e. Redeemer
     f. charity
     g. natural
     h. disappointed
  6. independence
  7. engineer

Test Sentences

1.	*approach*	We could not *approach* the horse.
2.	*adventure*	They had an *adventure* today.
3.	*channel*	The *channel* looks deep.
4.	*manufacturing*	This is a *manufacturing* state.
5.	*Scripture*	The *Scripture* is God's Word.
6.	*butcher*	Father worked in a *butcher* shop.
7.	*stretch*	It is refreshing to *stretch*.
8.	*dispatch*	Will you *dispatch* this message?
9.	*charity*	Show *charity* to all.
10.	*cheerful*	He sang a *cheerful* song.
11.	*fortunate*	That is a *fortunate* man.
12.	*moisture*	The *moisture* on the grass soon dried up.

B. Using Your Words

1. Write the synonym in the spelling list that has a better connotation than the underlined word in each phrase.
   a. an <u>uncomplaining</u> worker
   b. a <u>lucky</u> man
   c. an exciting <u>escapade</u>
   d. a <u>carnal</u> desire
2. Which spelling word is another name for
   a. Jesus?   c. a believer in Jesus?
   b. the Bible?
3. Write spelling words for these definitions. Each has a prefix that means *not* or *out*.
   a. Go out of sight.
   b. Send out.
   c. Not receiving what was expected.
   d. The state of not relying on others for support.

4. Write spelling words to complete these comparisons.
   a. *Store* is to *selling* as *factory* is to ____.
   b. *Airplane* is to *pilot* as *train* is to ____.
   c. *Faith* is to *belief* as *love* is to ____.
   d. *Bread* is to *baker* as *meat* is to ____.
   e. *Defend* is to *defense* as *choose* is to ___.
5. Write spelling words with these meanings.
   a. slight wetness
   b. a narrow sea

Dictionary Practice

6. *Scripture* comes from a Latin word with the idea of (drawing, painting, writing).

C. Building Words

- Not all words with affixes have roots that can stand alone as English words. The root of such a word is a word in the language from which it came.
  ad (Latin prefix for *to*) + prope (Latin word for *near*) = appropiare (Latin source of approach)

1. Write words with these roots and affixes.
   a. Christ + ian   c. nature + al
   b. engine + eer   d. fortune + ate
2. Write the spelling words that are composed of these word parts.
   a. **char** (from *carus*, dear) + **ity**
   b. **dis** (not) + **patch** (from *peechier*, hinder)

   c. **ad** (to) + **vent** (from *venire*, come) + **ure**
   d. **in** (not) + **de** (down) + **pend** (from *pendere*, hang) + **ence**
3. Write the derived forms indicated.
   a. moist + ure   c. adventure + ous
   b. cheer + ful   d. Scripture + al
4. Write correctly each noun that should be a plural or possessive form.
   a. a butcher work
   b. many channel of assistance
   c. three important dispatch

Bible Thoughts
Use a spelling word to complete this Bible verse.
5. "And above all things have fervent ____ among yourselves" (1 Peter 4:8).

37

B. 19 points
1. a. cheerful
   b. fortunate
   c. adventure
   d. natural
2. a. Redeemer
   b. Scripture
   c. Christian
3. a. disappear
   b. dispatch
   c. disappointed
   d. independence
4. a. manufacturing
   b. engineer
   c. charity
   d. butcher
   e. choice
5. a. moisture
   b. channel
6. writing
C. 16 points
1. a. Christian
   b. engineer
   c. natural
   d. fortunate
2. a. charity
   b. dispatch
   c. adventure
   d. independence
3. a. moisture
   b. cheerful
   c. adventurous
   d. Scriptural
4. a. butcher's
   b. channels
   c. dispatches
5. charity

13. *natural*   Jesus used *natural* illustrations.
14. *disappear*   How could it *disappear* so quickly?
15. *disappointed*   I was *disappointed* in the book.
16. *independence*   U.S. *independence* was won in 1783.

The *Christian* trusts in his *Redeemer*.

The *engineer* had to make a *choice*.

LESSON 17

NEW WORDS

1. insurance
2. assure
3. machinery
4. patience
5. delicious
6. appreciate
7. congregation
8. especially
9. stationary
10. stationery
11. situation
12. combination
13. definition
14. publish
15. fashion
16. generation

REVIEW WORDS

17. anxious
18. shelter
19. invitation
20. penmanship

deli/sh/ous

a. machine   c. special
b. sure (2 words)

3. Change the underlined letters in these words to letters that spell /sh/.
  a. pub<u>lic</u>   d. <u>m</u>elter
  b. al<u>l</u>ure   e. fa<u>ct</u>ion
  c. <u>fl</u>ower   f. cra<u>mp</u>

> • The /shən/ sound is spelled *tion*, *shion*, and *ssion*. defini<u>tion</u> <u>fashion</u> permis<u>sion</u>

4. Write these words, spelling /shən/ correctly.
  a. sta__ary   d. combina__
  b. fa__   e. sta__ery
  c. loca__   f. mi__ary

5. Change the final *te* in each word to letters that spell /shən/.
  a. generate   d. definite
  b. situate   e. congregate
  c. devote   f. populate

6. Write NEW WORDS with these sounds.
  a. /ch/ spelled *t* in the first syllable
  b. final /s/ spelled *ce* (2 words)

7. Write the spelling word in which /ng/ before /sh/ is spelled *n*.

A. Sounds and Letters

> • Common spellings of /sh/ are *sh*, *ti*, and *ci*. **publi<u>sh</u> pa<u>ti</u>ence deli<u>ci</u>ous** Other spellings of /sh/ are *c*, *ch*, *s*, *ss*, and *xi*. **appre<u>c</u>iate ma<u>ch</u>inery in<u>s</u>urance a<u>ss</u>ure an<u>xi</u>ous**

1. Add /sh/ as you write these words.
  a. pa__ence   d. penman__ip
  b. appre__ate   e. deli__ous
  c. an__ous   f. invita__on

2. Write the NEW WORDS whose /sh/ spellings can be remembered by association with these words.

38

A. 32 points
  1. a. patience
     b. appreciate
     c. anxious
     d. penmanship
     e. delicious
     f. invitation
  2. a. machinery
     b. insurance, assure
     c. especially
  3. a. publish
     b. assure
     c. shower
     d. shelter
     e. fashion
     f. crash
  4. a. stationary
     b. fashion
     c. location
     d. combination
     e. stationery
     f. missionary
  5. a. generation
     b. situation
     c. devotion
     d. definition
     e. congregation
     f. population
  6. a. situation
     b. insurance, patience
  7. anxious

Test Sentences

1.	insurance	Carefulness is good *insurance* against accidents.
2.	assure	Let me *assure* you that you are correct.
3.	machinery	The *machinery* was very noisy.
4.	patience	Have *patience* till he comes.
5.	delicious	That was a *delicious* meal.
6.	appreciate	We *appreciate* your help.
7.	especially	The night seemed *especially* cold.
8.	congregation	The *congregation* knelt to pray.
9.	stationery	I took *stationery* along to write letters.
10.	stationary	He crashed into a *stationary* vehicle.
11.	situation	This *situation* is not good.
12.	combination	The *combination* to the safe is lost.

B. Using Your Words

1. Write the spelling word that belongs with each group.
   a. church, brotherhood, assembly
   b. English, spelling, composition
   c. savory, tasteful, delectable
   d. compound, union, joining
   e. entry word, phonetic spelling, etymology
2. Write spelling words that could replace the underlined words.
   a. Paul learned to be content in whatever circumstances he was.
   b. Coal and waterpower are important in the production of electricity.
   c. The children were concerned because Father still had not come home.
3. Write the correct word for each sentence.

   a. A (stationary, stationery) automobile is seldom involved in a serious accident.
   b. Construction paper was sold at the (stationary, stationery) counter.
   c. The earth appears to be (stationary, stationery), but it is moving swiftly.
   d. This doctor is not accepting any new (patience, patients).
   e. The Israelites sorely tested the (patience, patients) of Moses.
   f. Difficult experiences develop our (patience, patients).

Dictionary Practice

4. When land *appreciates*, it becomes more (fertile, useful, valuable).

C. Building Words

- When words are divided into syllables, their structure is considered. Derived and inflected forms are divided between root words and affixes. Compound words are divided between their parts. **in/sur/ance reach/ing pen/man/ship**

- Other patterns are used for other syllable divisions.
  VC/V: **pig/eon**   V/CV: **na/ture**
  VC/CV: **pub/lish**   CV/VC: **li/on**

1. Show only the division indicated for each group.
   Between parts of the compound
   a. everlasting   b. fainthearted
   Between the suffix and the rest of the word
   c. cheerful   e. stationary
   d. connected   f. stiffness
   Between the prefix and the rest of the word
   g. unbeliever   i. international
   h. disappear   j. reassure
2. Show only the division indicated by the pattern before each word.
   a. VC/V: definition
   b. V/CV: patience
   c. VC/CV: insurance
   d. CV/VC: appreciate

Bible Thoughts
Use a spelling word to complete this Bible verse.
3. "Thou hast been a _____ for me, and a strong tower from the enemy" (Psalm 61:3).

39

B. 15 points
1. a. congregation
   b. penmanship
   c. delicious
   d. combination
   e. definition
2. a. situation
   b. generation
   c. anxious
3. a. stationary
   b. stationery
   c. stationary
   d. patients
   e. patience
   f. patience
4. valuable

C. 15 points
1. a. ever/lasting
   b. faint/hearted
   c. cheer/ful
   d. connect/ed
   e. station/ary
   f. stiff/ness
   g. un/believer
   h. dis/appear
   i. inter/national
   j. re/assure
2. a. def/inition
   b. pa/tience
   c. in/surance
   d. appreci/ate
3. shelter

13. *definition*   What is the *definition* of this word?
14. *fashion*   The *fashion* of the world will perish.
15. *generation*   This is the *generation* of them that seek Thee.
16. *publish*   Can you *publish* this book?

We gave *shelter* to the *anxious* man.

The *penmanship* on this *invitation* is beautiful.

LESSON 18

13	14	15	16	17
league	surface	tailor	approach	insurance
deceive	earnest	instructor	manufacturing	assure
grieve	burden	observation	adventure	machinery
weight	courtesy	reference	channel	patience
depot	reverse	regularly	Scripture	delicious
ceiling	circulation	permission	butcher	appreciate
veil	eternal	embroidery	dispatch	congregation
reindeer	firmament	ignorant	charity	especially
relief	personality	miners	stretch	stationary
apiece	research	deliveries	cheerful	stationery
cedar	current	failure	fortunate	situation
shield	reserve	debtor	moisture	combination
believed	furnace	reverence	natural	definition
unbeliever	merchant	scholarship	disappear	publish
medium	servant	governor	disappointed	fashion
children's	missionary	international	independence	generation

A. Sounds and Letters Review

1. Write these Lesson 13 words, using
ie or *ei* to spell the missing vowel
sounds.

    a. gr__ve   c. c__ling

    b. w__ght   d. ap__ce

2. Add /ûr/ as you write these Lesson 14
words.

    a. c__tesy   d. res__ve

    b. f__nace   e. __nest

    c. f__mament   f. c__ent

3. Use *ior* or *ure* to add /yər/ to each
word.

    a. fail__   b. jun__

4. Add /ch/ as you write these words.

    a. __eerful   c. for__unate

    b. dispa__   d. approa__

5. Add /chər/ to these words.

    a. na__al   c. mois__

    b. Scrip__   d. manufac__ing

6. Add /sh/ as you write these words.

    a. a/sh/ure   d. ma/sh/inery

    b. permi/sh/on   e. deli/sh/ous

    c. publi/sh/   f. pa/sh/ence

7. Add /shən/ to these words.

    a. fa__   b. circula__

A. 28 points

  1. a. grieve

     b. weight

     c. ceiling

     d. apiece

  2. a. courtesy

     b. furnace

     c. firmament

     d. reserve

     e. earnest

     f. current

  3. a. failure

     b. junior

  4. a. cheerful

     b. dispatch

     c. fortunate

     d. approach

  5. a. natural

     b. Scripture

     c. moisture

     d. manufacturing

  6. a. assure

     b. permission

     c. publish

     d. machinery

     e. delicious

     f. patience

  7. a. fashion

     b. circulation

See page 84 for test sentences.

B. Using Your Words Review

1. From each pair, copy the word with the more favorable connotation.
   a. atheist, unbeliever
   b. patience, toleration
   c. deceive, misinform
   d. uneducated, ignorant

2. Tell whether the words in each pair are synonyms or antonyms.
   a. mourn, grieve
   b. credited, believed
   c. disappointed, satisfied
   d. delicious, delectable
   e. earnest, halfhearted

3. Write the correct word for each sentence.
   a. The apples were selling for twenty-five cents (apiece, a piece).

   b. A (veil, vale) divided the tabernacle into two parts.
   c. Try not to cause others to (weight, wait) unnecessarily.
   d. Christians avoid following (currant, current) fads.
   e. Sulfur (minors, miners) do not need to work underground.
   f. It takes (patients, patience) to wait calmly.
   g. The cold front became a (stationary, stationery) front.

4. Write two words from Lesson 16 that could fit in this blank.
   A narrow _____ of water separated the island from the mainland.

C. Building Words Review

1. Write the plural of each noun.
   a. reserve   c. reference
   b. stretch   d. delivery

2. Write the possessive forms of these.
   a. tailor   c. butcher
   b. miners   d. patients

3. One underlined noun in each sentence should be plural, and one should be possessive. Write the correct forms.
   a. After what seemed like many <u>failure</u>, the <u>missionary</u> efforts were fruitful at last.
   b. The <u>enemy</u> of Jesus had to obtain the <u>governor</u> permission crucify Him.

4. Write the words that have these parts.
   a. situate + ion   c. station + ary
   b. nature + al   d. observe + ation

5. Write words with these roots and prefixes.
   a. dis + appointed   c. re + search
   b. inter + national   d. in + dependent

6. Use the VC/CV pattern to divide these words into syllables.
   a. burden   c. surface
   b. moisture   d. channel

7. Also syllabicate these words.
   a. cedar   c. scholarship
   b. merchant   d. reindeer

41

B. 18 points
   1. a. unbeliever
      b. patience
      c. misinform
      d. uneducated
   2. a. synonyms
      b. synonyms
      c. antonyms
      d. synonyms
      e. antonyms
   3. a. apiece
      b. veil
      c. wait
      d. current
      e. miners
      f. patience
      g. stationary
   4. channel, stretch

C. 28 points
   1. a. reserves
      b. stretches
      c. references
      d. deliveries
   2. a. tailor's
      b. miners'
      c. butcher's
      d. patients'
   3. a. failures, missionary's
      b. enemies, governor's
   4. a. situation
      b. natural
      c. stationary
      d. observation
   5. a. disappointed
      b. international
      c. research
      d. independent
   6. a. bur/den
      b. mois/ture
      c. sur/face
      d. chan/nel
   7. a. ce/dar
      b. mer/chant
      c. schol/ar/ship
      d. rein/deer

LESSON 19

NEW WORDS

1. *irrigate*
2. *pier*
3. *miracles*
4. *sincere*
5. *heretofore*
6. *materials*
7. *swear*
8. *preparing*
9. *affair*
10. *guard*
11. *aware*
12. *heir*
13. *radar*
14. *who'd*
15. *who'll*
16. *garbage*

REVIEW WORDS

17. *contrary*
18. *declare*
19. *weren't*
20. *appeared*

A. Sounds and Letters

> • The /är/ sound is usually spelled *ar*. **radar** It may also be spelled *uar*. **guard**

1. Add /är/ as you write these NEW WORDS.
   a. rad__ b. g__bage c. g__d

2. Add /är/ spelled *ar* as you write these.
   a. h__bor d. al__m
   b. c__penter e. ch__ge
   c. d__kness f. sp__k

/îr/igate

> • Common spellings of /îr/ are *ir* or *irr*, *er* or *ere*, *ier*, *ear*, and *eer*.
> **mi<u>r</u>acles i<u>rr</u>igate mat<u>er</u>ials sinc<u>ere</u> p<u>ier</u> app<u>ear</u>ed reind<u>eer</u>**

3. Write these words, spelling /îr/ correctly.
   a. sinc/îr/ d. ch/îr/ful
   b. mat/îr/ials e. h/îr/tofore
   c. disapp/îr/ f. s/îr/ious

4. Make spelling words by changing the underlined letters to letters that spell /îr/.
   a. <u>pa</u>re c. m<u>iti</u>gate
   b. m<u>a</u>nacles d. app<u>all</u>ed

> • Common spellings of /âr/ or /er/ are *air*, *ar* or *are*, *ear*, and *eir*. **aff<u>air</u> contr<u>ar</u>y aw<u>are</u> sw<u>ear</u> th<u>eir</u>**

5. Add /âr/ or /er/ as you write these spelling words.
   a. sw__ d. aff__
   b. h__ e. aw__
   c. contr__y f. decl__

6. In one NEW WORD, /âr/ is usually spelled *are*, but *e* was dropped to add *-ing*. Write this word.

7. Write spelling words with these sounds.
   a. /ûr/ spelled *ere*
   b. /h/ spelled *wh* (2 words)
   c. final /ij/ spelled *age*

A. 30 points

1. a. radar
   b. garbage
   c. guard
2. a. harbor
   b. carpenter
   c. darkness
   d. alarm
   e. charge
   f. spark
3. a. sincere
   b. materials
   c. disappear
   d. cheerful
   e. heretofore
   f. serious
4. a. pier
   b. miracles
   c. irrigate
   d. appeared
5. a. swear
   b. heir
   c. contrary
   d. affair
   e. aware
   f. declare
6. preparing
7. a. weren't
   b. who'd, who'll
   c. garbage

42

Test Sentences

1.	*pier*	The *pier* was covered with water.
2.	*irrigate*	We must *irrigate* this field.
3.	*miracles*	Jesus did many *miracles* there.
4.	*sincere*	We must be *sincere* and honest.
5.	*heretofore*	Nothing *heretofore* had been like this.
6.	*materials*	The building *materials* have arrived.
7.	*preparing*	I am *preparing* dinner.
8.	*swear*	Do not *swear* at all.
9.	*aware*	I am *aware* of that.
10.	*heir*	Isaac was *heir* to Abraham.
11.	*affair*	The whole *affair* was a misunderstanding.
12.	*radar*	The pilot watched his *radar* screen.

B. Using Your Words

1. The words *heir, air,* and *err* are homophones. Write the correct word for each sentence.
   a. To _____ is part of being human.
   b. Isaac was Abraham's _____.
   c. Causing a little child to _____ is a serious matter.
   d. The _____ around us is composed mostly of nitrogen.
   e. A Christian is an _____ of eternal life.
2. Write the spelling word that belongs with each group.
   a. trash, junk, rubbish
   b. marvels, wonders, signs
   c. honest, genuine, earnest
   d. isn't, aren't, wasn't
   e. dock, wharf, quay
3. Write spelling words with these meanings.
   a. Before this time.
   b. To cleanse with a stream of water.
   c. Matter; business.
   d. Having knowledge; perceiving.

Dictionary Practice

4. The word *radar* is an *acronym*; it comes from the beginning letters of a five-word phrase. What is that phrase?
5. *Contrary* may be pronounced (kən trâr′ ē) when it is (a noun, an adjective, an adverb).

C. Building Words

- A contraction may be considered a closed compound from which one or more letters have been dropped. An apostrophe replaces the omitted letters. **cannot—can't who will—who'll**
- Some contractions are combinations of verbs with *not*, or of pronouns with *will, had,* or *would*. **weren't I'll she'll who'd**

1. Join these verbs with *not* to form contractions.
   a. is   d. were
   b. have   e. was
   c. does   f. could

2. Make contractions by joining these pronouns with *will*.
   a. we   d. you
   b. he   e. who
   c. she   f. they
3. Write a contraction that could be used in each sentence.
   a. Soon you will see.
   b. I cannot come.
   c. I wonder who would do that.
   d. They do not care.

Bible Thoughts

Use a spelling word to complete this Bible verse.

4. "Above all things, . . . _____ not, neither by heaven, neither by the earth" (James 5:12).

43

B. 16 points
1. a. err
   b. heir
   c. err
   d. air
   e. heir
2. a. garbage
   b. miracles
   c. sincere
   d. weren't
   e. pier
3. a. heretofore
   b. irrigate
   c. affair
   d. aware
4. radio detecting and ranging
5. an adjective

C. 17 points
1. a. isn't
   b. haven't
   c. doesn't
   d. weren't
   e. wasn't
   f. couldn't
2. a. we'll
   b. he'll
   c. she'll
   d. you'll
   e. who'll
   f. they'll
3. a. you'll
   b. can't
   c. who'd
   d. don't
4. swear

13. *guard*   We must *guard* against lying.
14. *garbage*   Put the *garbage* in the bag.
15. *who'd*   There was no one *who'd* seen it.
16. *who'll*   Can you find someone *who'll* go?

On the *contrary,* we *weren't* late at all.

He *appeared* to *declare* the truth.

LESSON 20

NEW WORDS

1. overalls
2. laundry
3. abroad
4. lawyer
5. dawn
6. author
7. faucet
8. what's
9. ore
10. mortal
11. ordain
12. quarrel
13. glorify
14. source
15. how's
16. where's

REVIEW WORDS

17. automatic
18. orchard
19. territory
20. moss

m/ô/ss

A. Sounds and Letters

- Common spellings of /ô/ are *a, au, aw, o,* and *oa.* **overalls faucet dawn moss abroad** The /ô/ sound may also be spelled *augh* or *ough.* **taught sought**

1. Add /ô/ spelled *au* as you write these words.
   a. __thor
   b. l__ndry
   c. f__cet
   d. p__se
   e. __tomatic
   f. __dience

2. Also spell /ô/ as you write these words.
   a. l/ô/yer
   b. m/ô/ss
   c. abr/ô/d
   d. d/ô/n
   e. over/ô/lls
   f. withdr/ô/
   g. gl/ô/ssy
   h. inst/ô/ll

- The /ôr/ or /ōr/ sound is usually spelled *or* or *ore.* **mortal more** Other spellings of /ôr/ or /ōr/ are *oar* and *our.* **board source** After /w/, /ôr/ or /or/ is often spelled *ar* or *arr.* **reward quarrel**

3. Write these words, spelling /ôr/ correctly.
   a. __dain
   b. m__tal
   c. rest__
   d. s__ce
   e. gl__ify
   f. heretof__
   g. __chard
   h. territ__y

4. Which NEW WORD has no sound other than /ôr/?

5. Spell these words correctly, in which /ôr/ or /or/ follows /w/.
   a. w__ning
   b. qu__el
   c. dw__f
   d. qu__y
   e. w__ior
   f. qu__ter

6. Which NEW WORDS have these sounds?
   a. /âr/ spelled *ere*
   b. /ou/ spelled *ow*
   c. /o/ spelled *a* after /hw/
   d. final /yər/ spelled *yer*

A. 33 points

1. a. author
   b. laundry
   c. faucet
   d. pause
   e. automatic
   f. audience
2. a. lawyer
   b. moss
   c. abroad
   d. dawn
   e. overalls
   f. withdraw
   g. glossy
   h. install
3. a. ordain
   b. mortal
   c. restore
   d. source
   e. glorify
   f. heretofore
   g. orchard
   h. territory
4. ore
5. a. warning
   b. quarrel
   c. dwarf
   d. quarry
   e. warrior
   f. quarter
6. a. where's
   b. how's
   c. what's
   d. lawyer

Test Sentences

1.	overalls	These *overalls* are dirty.
2.	abroad	He was *abroad* for a month.
3.	lawyer	A *lawyer* wanted to tempt Jesus.
4.	dawn	The *dawn* of the day is here.
5.	laundry	Take the *laundry* outside.
6.	author	Christ is the *author* of eternal salvation.
7.	faucet	The *faucet* is leaking.
8.	ore	The iron *ore* was melted down.
9.	mortal	We are *mortal* creatures.
10.	ordain	The church will *ordain* a minister.
11.	source	Christ is the *source* of living water.
12.	quarrel	Abraham would not *quarrel* with Lot.

B. Using Your Words

1. The words *ore, or,* and *oar* are homophones. Write the correct word for each sentence.

   a. It was hard to row the boat straight because I had only one _____.

   b. A metal is usually not found pure, but in an _____.

   c. Which is saltier, the Great Salt Lake _____ the ocean?

   d. Some copper _____ also contains gold.

2. Do not confuse *abroad* with *aboard* or *mortal* with *moral*. Write the correct words.

   a. For most of his time (abroad, aboard), the president stayed in England.

   b. "All (abroad, aboard)!" called the sailor.

   c. There was a rumor (abroad, aboard) that the store was selling contaminated food.

   d. This story has a good (mortal, moral).

   e. Ahab died of a (mortal, moral) wound.

3. Write the spelling word that belongs with each group.

   a. dispute, argue, fight

   b. producer, composer, creator

   c. doctor, architect, professor

   d. garden, vineyard, field

   e. praise, worship, honor

Dictionary Practice

4. *Automatic* comes from the Greek word *automatos,* which means "_____."

C. Building Words

> • Some contractions are made by joining pronouns or interrogative words with forms of *be* or *have*.
> **we're what's you're how's**

1. Make contractions by joining each pronoun with *is* or *are*.

   a. you   d. she

   b. it   e. that

   c. they   f. someone

2. Also make contractions by joining these words with *is*.

   a. how   c. where

   b. what   d. who

3. Form contractions from these phrases.

   a. I have, they have

   b. she has, what has

   c. you had, he had

4. Think of "it's here" and "it's come." The *'s* in a contraction can replace the word _____ or the word _____.

5. Write the contraction for each phrase.

   a. I am   d. they will

   b. were not   e. there is

   c. she had   f. where has

Bible Thoughts

Use a spelling word to complete this Bible verse.

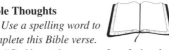

6. "God is not the _____ of confusion, but of peace" (1 Corinthians 14:33).

45

B. 15 points

  1. a. oar

     b. ore

     c. or

     d. ore

  2. a. abroad

     b. aboard

     c. abroad

     d. moral

     e. mortal

  3. a. quarrel

     b. author

     c. lawyer

     d. orchard (*or* territory)

     e. glorify

  4. self-acting

C. 25 points

  1. a. you're

     b. it's

     c. they're

     d. she's

     e. that's

     f. someone's

  2. a. how's

     b. what's

     c. where's

     d. who's

  3. a. I've, they've

     b. she's, what's

     c. you'd, he'd

  4. is, has

  5. a. I'm

     b. weren't

     c. she'd

     d. they'll

     e. there's

     f. where's

  6. author

13. *glorify*   Christ came to *glorify* the Father.

14. *how's*   But *how's* that going to work?

15. *what's*   I wonder *what's* in this box.

16. *where's*   Now *where's* my screwdriver?

    Was there *moss* in the old *orchard?*

    He had an *automatic* right to the *territory.*

LESSON 21

NEW WORDS

1. bulletin   9. reducing
2. mature   10. develop
3. jewel   11. produced
4. influence   12. including
5. bruise   13. propeller
6. Jerusalem   14. admitted
7. assured   15. attempt
8. procured   16. preferred

REVIEW WORDS

17. believed   19. introduced
18. approved   20. losing

A. Sounds and Letters

- Common spellings of /o͞o/ and /yo͞o/ are *u, ui, u-e, o-e, oo,* and *ew.* **infl**u**ence br**ui**se ref**u**se appr**o**ve foren**oo**n f**ew**

1. Write these words, spelling /o͞o/ correctly.
   a. incl__ding   e. appr__ved
   b. j__el   f. Jer__salem
   c. l__sing   g. gl__my
   d. br__se   h. infl__ence

br/o͞o/se

2. In these words, the missing vowel sound may be pronounced /o͞o/ or /yo͞o/, and it is spelled *u, ue,* or *ew.* Write the words.
   a. red__cing   d. st__ard
   b. prod__ced   e. aven__
   c. ren__   f. subd__

- The /o͞o/ and /yo͞o/ sounds are commonly spelled *u* or *oo.* **b**u**lletin proc**u**red overl**oo**k**

3. Add /o͞o/ as you write these words. One word does not follow the rule.
   a. ass__red   e. w__lves
   b. j__ry   f. g__dness
   c. br__k   g. b__lletin
   d. b__tcher   h. withst__d

4. Write these words, adding letters that spell /o͞ord/ or /yo͞ord/ at the end.
   a. mat__   c. end__
   b. proc__   d. sec__

5. Write spelling words with these sounds.
   a. /ûr/ spelled *err*
   b. three consonant sounds at the end
   c. /sh/ spelled *ss*
   d. final /əp/ spelled *op*
   e. /ē/ spelled *ie*
   f. final /ər/ spelled *er*

46

A. 32 points

1. a. including
   b. jewel
   c. losing
   d. bruise
   e. approved
   f. Jerusalem
   g. gloomy
   h. influence
2. a. reducing
   b. produced
   c. renew
   d. steward
   e. avenue
   f. subdue
3. a. assured
   b. jury
   c. brook
   d. butcher
   e. wolves
   f. goodness
   g. bulletin
   h. withstood
4. a. matured
   b. procured
   c. endured
   d. secured
5. a. preferred
   b. attempt
   c. assured
   d. develop
   e. believed
   f. propeller

Test Sentences

1. *mature*   A *mature* person is not quickly offended.
2. *bulletin*   We rearranged the *bulletin* board.
3. *jewel*   A valuable *jewel* was stolen.
4. *bruise*   There was a *bruise* under his eye.
5. *Jerusalem*   Jesus went to *Jerusalem* often.
6. *influence*   Do not let evil men *influence* you.
7. *assured*   He *assured* me that he was all right.
8. *procured*   Two disciples *procured* a colt for Jesus.
9. *reducing*   Are you *reducing* your fractions?
10. *produced*   The fields have *produced* abundantly.
11. *including*   Many people, *including* Jacob, went to Egypt.
12. *admitted*   David *admitted* that he had sinned.

B. Using Your Words

1. Write spelling words that are synonyms of the underlined words.
   a. The Lord <u>sanctioned</u> David's desire to build a house of worship.
   b. The guide suggested <u>curtailing</u> our activities in the afternoon.
   c. Some of the settlers <u>obtained</u> salt by trading with the Indians.
   d. The magicians managed to keep the king under their <u>sway</u>.
2. Write spelling words that are antonyms.
   a. doubted   c. excluding
   b. unripe   d. gaining
3. Write spelling words with these meanings.
   a. A brief public statement.
   b. A shaft with slanted blades.
   c. Liked better.
   d. The capital of Israel.
   e. A black-and-blue injury.
4. Write two NEW WORDS that could fit in the following blank.
   It takes many years for a sapling to _____ into a full-grown tree.

Dictionary Practice

5. Which is *not* a correct pronunciation of *mature*?
   a. (mə to͞or′)   c. (mə to͞or′)
   b. (mə tyo͞or′)   d. (mə cho͞or′)

C. Building Words

- When a verb ends with e, the final e is dropped to add *-es*, *-ed,* or *-ing.*
  reduce + es = reduces
  assure + ed = assured
  mature + ing = maturing
- To add a suffix beginning with a vowel to a one-syllable word ending with a single vowel and then a single consonant, the final consonant is doubled.
  step + ed = stepped
- Such a final consonant is also doubled in a two-syllable word if the last syllable is accented.
  prefer + ed = preferred
  propel + er = propeller

1. Add *-es* and *-ing* to these verbs.
   a. influence   c. introduce
   b. lose   d. bruise
2. Add *-ed* to each of these.
   a. ship   c. plan
   b. trot   d. stop
3. Add *-ing* to these. For one word you will not double the final consonant.
   a. admit   c. defeat
   b. rebel   d. prefer
4. For what *two* reasons does *developed* have only one *p*?
   a. The last syllable is accented.
   b. The last syllable is unaccented.
   c. The word has more than one syllable.

Bible Thoughts
Use a spelling word to complete this Bible verse.
5. "The lips of knowledge are a precious _____" (Proverbs 20:15).

47

B. 16 points
  1. a. approved
     b. reducing
     c. procured
     d. influence
  2. a. believed
     b. mature
     c. including
     d. losing
  3. a. bulletin
     b. propeller
     c. preferred
     d. Jerusalem
     e. bruise
  4. mature, develop
  5. c
C. 19 points
  1. a. influences, influencing
     b. loses, losing
     c. introduces, introducing
     d. bruises, bruising
  2. a. shipped
     b. trotted
     c. planned
     d. stopped
  3. a. admitting
     b. rebelling
     c. preferring
     d. defeating
  4. b, c
  5. jewel

---

13. *preferred*   Daniel was *preferred* above other rulers.
14. *propeller*   The plane's *propeller* has stopped.
15. *develop*   A bad cold can *develop* into pneumonia.
16. *attempt*   Do not *attempt* to do that alone.

He *introduced* an idea that few people *believed*.

The captain *approved* the plan without *losing* any time.

LESSON 22

NEW WORDS

1. division
2. garage
3. measure
4. encounter
5. announce
6. bough
7. devout
8. foul
9. nowadays
10. bound
11. account
12. driven
13. stole
14. sought
15. shone
16. fowl

b/ou/

REVIEW WORDS

17. doubt
18. drown
19. pronounce
20. usually

A. Sounds and Letters

- The /zh/ sound is usually spelled *s*. **usually** Its most common spelling at the end of a word is *ge*. **garage**

1. Add /zh/ spelled *s* as you write these words.
   a. u__ually   b. ca__ual   c. A__ia
2. Each /zh/ or /j/ sound at the end of these words has the same spelling. Write the words correctly.
   a. gara__   c. barra__
   b. mira__   d. massa__

- The /zhən/ ending is usually spelled *sion*. **division**

3. Add /zhən/ spelled *sion* as you write these words.
   a. divi__   d. deci__
   b. explo__   e. occa__
   c. confu__   f. provi__

- The /zhər/ ending usually spelled *sure*. **measure**

4. Add /zhər/ as you write these words.
   a. trea__   c. mea__
   b. lei__   d. clos__
5. In two English words, final /zhər/ is spelled *zure*. Write those words.
   a. sei/zhər/   b. a/zhər/

- The /ou/ sound is spelled *ou*, *ow*, and *ough*. **announce dr<u>ow</u>n b<u>ough</u>**

6. Add /ou/ spelled *ou* as you write these spelling words.
   a. dev__t   e. ann__nce
   b. b__nd   f. enc__nter
   c. f__l   g. acc__nt
   d. d__bt   h. pron__nce
7. Make spelling words by changing the underlined letters to /ou/ spelled *ow* or *ough*.
   a. dr<u>ai</u>n   b. f<u>ee</u>l   c. b<u>o</u>y
8. Which three-syllable word has /ou/ spelled *ow*?

48

A. 31 points
1. a. usually
   b. casual
   c. Asia
2. a. garage
   b. mirage
   c. barrage
   d. massage
3. a. division
   b. explosion
   c. confusion
   d. decision
   e. occasion
   f. provision
4. a. treasure
   b. leisure
   c. measure
   d. closure
5. a. seizure
   b. azure
6. a. devout
   b. bound
   c. foul
   d. doubt
   e. announce
   f. encounter
   g. account
   h. pronounce
7. a. drown
   b. fowl
   c. bough
8. nowadays

Test Sentences

1.	division	These problems in *division* are not hard.
2.	garage	The *garage* should be cleaned out.
3.	measure	Did you *measure* that correctly?
4.	encounter	Jacob had an *encounter* with God.
5.	announce	An angel came to *announce* Jesus' birth.
6.	bough	Absalom was caught by the *bough* of an oak.
7.	devout	Simeon was a *devout* man.
8.	foul	The river had a *foul* smell.
9.	fowl	A creature that has feathers is a *fowl*.
10.	nowadays	Smallpox is not a threat *nowadays*.
11.	account	Every man must someday give *account* to God.
12.	bound	Samson was *bound* and taken away.

B. Using Your Words

1. Write the correct homophone for each sentence.
   a. The (bou) was loaded with apples.
   b. "Let us worship and (bou) down."
   c. The Lord created (foul) on the fifth day.
   d. My first strike was a (foul) ball.
   e. The air was (foul) with smoke.
   f. The Christians' faces (shōn) with joy.
   g. Have I ever (shōn) you this picture?
   h. The sun (shōn) brightly all day.
2. Write the spelling words that are synonyms of the underlined words, but which have less favorable connotations.
   a. the improper deed
   b. took some money
   c. motivated by greed

d. a meeting with the adversary
3. Write spelling words to complete these comparisons.
   a. *John* is to *love* as *Thomas* is to ____.
   b. *Ship* is to *harbor* as *car* is to ____.
   c. *Scales* is to *fish* as *feathers* is to ____.
   d. *Airplane* is to *flown* as *truck* is to ____.

Dictionary Practice

4. *Bound* has four entries. Write the number of the entry that matches each use below.
   a. The deer bounded away.
   b. Paul was bound with chains.
   c. Paul was bound for Rome.
   d. Nevada bounds California.

C. Building Words

- The suffix *-ed* is used to make the past forms of most verbs. Some past forms are made in other ways. **measure—measured bind—bound drive—driven**

- When a verb ends with a consonant and then *y*, the *y* is changed to *i* before *-ed* is added. Final *y* is kept when *-ing* is added or when a vowel comes before the *y*. **reply—replied, replying play—played, playing**

1. Write the past form of each verb.
   a. account   c. pronounce
   b. doubt   d. measure
2. Write the past form of the REVIEW WORD that has a final *n*. This form is

pronounced (dround), not (droun' did).
3. Give the present, past, and past participle forms of each verb. For *ride* you would write *ride, rode, ridden*.
   a. drive   b. steal   c. seek
4. Add *-ed* to each verb.
   a. envy   c. journey
   b. vary   d. employ
5. Add *-ing* to these.
   a. copy   c. reply
   b. supply   d. delay

Bible Thoughts

Use a spelling word to complete this Bible verse.
6. "Simeon . . . was just and ____, waiting for the consolation of Israel" (Luke 2:25).

49

B. 20 points
1. a. bough
   b. bow
   c. fowl
   d. foul
   e. foul
   f. shone
   g. shown
   h. shone
2. a. foul
   b. stole
   c. driven
   d. encounter
3. a. doubt
   b. garage
   c. fowl
   d. driven
4. a. 2
   b. 1
   c. 4
   d. 3
C. 23 points
1. a. accounted
   b. doubted
   c. pronounced
   d. measured
2. drowned
3. a. drive, drove, driven
   b. steal, stole, stolen
   c. seek, sought, sought
4. a. envied
   b. varied
   c. journeyed
   d. employed
5. a. copying
   b. supplying
   c. replying
   d. delaying
6. devout

13. *driven*   The car was *driven* a thousand miles.
14. *shone*   The sun *shone* brightly.
15. *sought*   The shepherd *sought* his lost sheep.
16. *stole*   "Let him that *stole* steal no more."

People do not *usually drown* in shallow water.

I *doubt* that you can *pronounce* all Hebrew words.

LESSON 23

NEW WORDS

1. adjustment   9. jury
2. baggage   10. injury
3. series   11. heroes
4. hedge   12. scissors
5. hygiene   13. buffalo
6. percentage   14. basis
7. journey   15. salesman
8. pajamas   16. gentlemen

REVIEW WORDS

17. pigeon   19. generous
18. suggest   20. voyage

A. Sounds and Letters

- The /j/ sound is usually spelled *j* or *g*. **jury hygiene**

1. Add /j/ spelled *j* as you write these words.
   a. __ourney   e. pa__amas
   b. en__oy   f. in__ury
   c. __ury   g. pro__ect
   d. __ustice   h. __anitor

2. Add /j/ spelled *g* as you write these.
   a. sug__est   d. reli__ious
   b. hy__iene   e. pi__eon
   c. __enerous   f. __entlemen

50

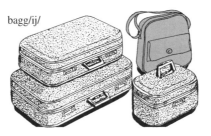

bagg/ij/

3. In which NEW WORD is /j/ spelled *dj*?

- Final /j/ in a one-syllable word is commonly spelled *dge* after a short vowel. **hedge**

4. Spell /j / correctly as you write each word.
   a. he/j/   c. do/j/
   b. bri/j/   d. ju/j/

- Final /ij/ is commonly spelled *age*. **baggage**

5. Add final /ij/ as you write each word.
   a. voy__   d. percent__
   b. bagg__   e. aver__
   c. post__   f. cour__

6. Final /ij/ may also be spelled *ege*. Use that spelling in these words.
   a. coll__   b. privil__

7. Write the three NEW WORDS in which double letters occur after a short vowel in the first syllable.

8. Which NEW WORDS have these sounds?
   a. /ā/ in the first syllable (2 words)
   b. final /ōz/ spelled *oes*
   c. /ē/ spelled *ie* (2 words)
   d. /ûr/ spelled *our*

A. 36 points

1. a. journey
   b. enjoy
   c. jury
   d. justice
   e. pajamas
   f. injury
   g. project
   h. janitor
2. a. suggest
   b. hygiene
   c. generous
   d. religious
   e. pigeon
   f. gentlemen
3. adjustment
4. a. hedge
   b. bridge
   c. dodge
   d. judge
5. a. voyage
   b. baggage
   c. postage
   d. percentage
   e. average
   f. courage
6. a. college
   b. privilege
7. baggage, scissors, buffalo
8. a. basis, salesman
   b. heroes
   c. series, hygiene
   d. journey

Test Sentences

1.	*adjustment*	Make an *adjustment* on this chair.
2.	*hedge*	The Lord keeps a *hedge* around His people.
3.	*hygiene*	Good *hygiene* helps to keep us healthy.
4.	*percentage*	A large *percentage* of the crop was destroyed.
5.	*baggage*	He left his *baggage* on the train.
6.	*journey*	That was a long *journey* for you.
7.	*jury*	Most criminals receive a *jury* trial.
8.	*injury*	He suffered not one *injury* in the accident.
9.	*heroes*	Hebrews 11 lists many *heroes* of the faith.
10.	*buffalo*	The *buffalo* belongs to the cattle family.
11.	*scissors*	Have you seen my *scissors* today?
12.	*series*	We had a *series* of meetings last week.

B. Using Your Words

1. Write three spelling words that match each description.
   a. Something alive that is not a person.
   b. More than one person.
2. Write spelling words that are synonyms.
   a. foundation
   b. bison
   c. trip
   d. proportion
   e. hint
   f. succession
   g. liberal
   h. shears
3. Write the spelling word that belongs with each group.
   a. healthfulness, cleanliness, sanitation
   b. judge, lawyer, witness
   c. nightgown, slippers, bathrobe
   d. fence, wall, railing
   e. damage, wound, harm
4. Write the same spelling word (or a form of it) for both blanks.
   a. Arthur _____ when his father asked him about the gap in the _____.
   b. The sailor had often _____ across the sea, but this _____ was different.

Dictionary Practice

5. The second *a* in *pajamas* may be pronounced (ā, ä, a, ô). (Choose two.)
6. What is another spelling of *pajamas*?

C. Building Words

- Most nouns are made plural simply by adding *-s* or *-es*. Other plurals are formed in different ways. **pigeon—pigeons hero—heroes injury—injuries calf—calves salesman—salesmen reindeer—reindeer**

- A few nouns are always plural in form. Some of these always take a plural verb, some always take a singular verb, and some take a singular or plural verb according to the meaning intended. **These scissors are sharp. The news is good. This species is common. These species are common.**

1. Write the plural of each noun.
   a. injury
   b. journey
   c. salesman
   d. hero

2. One NEW WORD is an animal name whose plural can be spelled in three different ways. Write these three forms.
3. Write *is* or *are* for each sentence.
   a. The scissors _____ in the drawer.
   b. This series _____ rather unusual.
   c. The other two series _____ common.
   d. Your pajamas _____ in the laundry.
4. a. Write the plural form of *basis*.
   b. The second syllable in this plural form is pronounced (sēz, sez, siz).

Bible Thoughts

Use a spelling word to complete this Bible verse.

5. "The way of the slothful man is as an _____ of thorns: but the way of the righteous is made plain" (Proverbs 15:19).

51

13. *gentlemen*   Show these *gentlemen* to their room.
14. *salesman*   We had a *salesman* at the house.
15. *basis*   On what *basis* do you judge him?
16. *pajamas*   Put the *pajamas* in the drawer.

You were *generous* to *suggest* it.

Did the *pigeon* go along on the *voyage?*

LESSON 24

19	20	21	22	23
irrigate	overalls	bulletin	division	adjustment
pier	laundry	mature	garage	baggage
miracles	abroad	jewel	measure	series
sincere	lawyer	influence	encounter	hedge
heretofore	dawn	bruise	announce	hygiene
materials	author	Jerusalem	bough	percentage
swear	faucet	assured	devout	journey
preparing	what's	procured	foul	pajamas
affair	ore	reducing	nowadays	jury
guard	mortal	develop	bound	injury
aware	ordain	produced	account	heroes
heir	quarrel	including	driven	scissors
radar	glorify	propeller	stole	buffalo
who'd	source	admitted	sought	basis
who'll	how's	attempt	shone	salesman
garbage	where's	preferred	fowl	gentlemen

A. Sounds and Letters Review

1. Spell /är/ and /îr/ in these Lesson 19 spelling words.
  a. m/îr/acles   c. g/är/d
  b. g/är/bage   d. mat/îr/ials

2. Add /âr/ as you write these words.
  a. aw__   c. prep__ing
  b. sw__   d. anywh__

3. Spell these Lesson 20 words correctly.
  a. l/ô/yer   c. /ô/thor
  b. m/ôr/tal   d. s/ôr/ce

4. Spell /o͞o/ or /yo͞o/ correctly in these words.
  a. ren__   c. subd__
  b. prod__ced   d. introd__ced

5. Add /zh/ as you write these words.
  a. gara__   c. u__ually
  b. mea__ure   d. divi__on

6. Write words from Lesson 22.
  a. /ou/ = *ough*
  b. /ô/ = *ough*
  c. /k/ = *cc*
  d. /ou/ = *ow* (2 words)

7. Add /j/ or /ij/ as you write these Lesson 23 words.
  a. pa__amas   d. he__
  b. hy__iene   e. bagg__
  c. in__ury   f. percent__

52

A. 31 points
1. a. miracles
   b. garbage
   c. guard
   d. materials
2. a. aware
   b. swear
   c. preparing
   d. anywhere
3. a. lawyer
   b. mortal
   c. author
   d. source
4. a. renew
   b. produced
   c. subdue
   d. introduced
5. a. garage
   b. measure
   c. usually
   d. division
6. a. bough
   b. sought
   c. account
   d. nowadays, fowl
7. a. pajamas
   b. hygiene
   c. injury
   d. hedge
   e. baggage
   f. percentage

See page 85 for test sentences.

B. Using Your Words Review

1. Write the correct words.
  a. The news about the healing spread rapidly (aboard, abroad).
  b. Be careful about associating with people of low (morals, mortals).
2. Write the correct spelling of each word in parentheses.
  a. When the (âr) of the vineyard came, the wicked husbandmen killed him.
  b. Aluminum (ôr) is called bauxite.
  c. One (ôr) in the boat was broken.
  d. For the Feast of Tabernacles, shelters were made with leafy (bouz).
  e. Fatted (foul) was served at Solomon's table every day.
  f. Do not (foul) the creek with garbage.
  g. After the teacher had (shōn) the solution, the problem seemed simple.

3. Write spelling words with these meanings. Lesson numbers are in parentheses.
  a. Business; matter. (19)
  b. Clothing that has been washed. (20)
  c. Sincerely religious. (22)
  d. A cutting tool with two blades. (23)
  e. A group that decides whether an accused person is guilty or innocent. (23)
4. Write the words whose connotations suggest a greater intensity.
  a. The men (disagreed, quarreled) about how the land should be divided.
  b. Such a rumor was an (injury, outrage) to Mr. Bond's reputation for honesty.

C. Building Words Review

1. Write the contraction for each phrase.
  a. she will   c. have not
  b. we are   d. that is
2. Write two meanings for each contraction.
  a. it's   c. who'd
  b. how's   d. they'd
3. Add *-ing* to each verb.
  a. prefer   b. develop
4. Change each verb to its past form.
  a. irrigate   d. deal
  b. lose   e. ordain
  c. glorify   f. enjoy

5. Write the present, past, and past participle forms of these.
  a. drive   b. steal
6. Write the plurals of these nouns.
  a. injury   d. approach
  b. journey   e. shelf
  c. belief   f. laundry
7. Also write the plurals of these.
  a. basis   d. hero
  b. buffalo   e. series
  c. salesman   f. garage

53

B. 16 points
  1. a. abroad
     b. morals
  2. a. heir
     b. ore
     c. oar
     d. boughs
     e. fowl
     f. foul
     g. shown
  3. a. affair
     b. laundry
     c. devout
     d. scissors
     e. jury
  4. a. quarreled
     b. outrage

C. 38 points
  1. a. she'll
     b. we're
     c. haven't
     d. that's
  2. a. it has, it is
     b. how has, how is
     c. who had, who would
     d. they had, they would
  3. a. preferring
     b. developing
  4. a. irrigated
     b. lost
     c. glorified
     d. dealt
     e. ordained
     f. enjoyed
  5. a. drive, drove, driven
     b. steal, stole, stolen
  6. a. injuries
     b. journeys
     c. beliefs
     d. approaches
     e. shelves
     f. laundries
  7. a. bases
     b. buffalos, buffaloes, *or* buffalo
     c. salesmen
     d. heroes
     e. series
     f. studios

LESSON 25

NEW WORDS

1. assemble
2. prophecy
3. satisfactory
4. disciples
5. grease
6. practice
7. audience
8. happiest
9. necessary
10. prophesy
11. expensive
12. recently
13. fierce
14. serious
15. further
16. prettiest

REVIEW WORDS

17. embarrass
18. furious
19. mercies
20. reference

grea/s/

A. Sounds and Letters

- Common spellings of /s/ are *s, c, ss,* and *sc.* **prophe*sy* re*c*ently a***ss*emble di*s*ciples**

For exercises 1–4, write words that have:

1. /s/ spelled *s.*
  a. expen__ive   e. in__ide
  b. furiou__   f. prophe__/ī/
  c. happie__t   g. con__ented
  d. __eriou__   h. __ati__factory

2. /s/ spelled *ss.*
  a. a__emble   d. gue__ed
  b. blo__om   e. le__ons
  c. po__ible   f. me__enger

3. /s/ spelled *c.*
  a. re__ently   d. prophe__/ē/
  b. __itizen   e. con__ern
  c. mer__ies   f. __elebrate

4. /s/ spelled *sc.*
  a. di__iples   d. __ience
  b. __enery   e. de__end
  c. mu__le   f. __issors

- Final /s/ is usually spelled *ss, se,* or *ce.* **embarra*ss* grea*se* fier*ce***

For exercises 5–7, write words that have:

5. final /s/ spelled *ss.*
  a. progre__   c. embarra__
  b. busine__   d. compa__

6. final /s/ spelled *se.*
  a. grea__   c. increa__
  b. rever__   d. conden__

7. final /s/ spelled *ce.*
  a. practi__   c. audien__
  b. fier__   d. referen__

8. Write the NEW WORD with two /s/ sounds, one spelled *c* and one spelled *ss.*

54

Test Sentences

1.	assemble	The people will *assemble* here.
2.	prophecy	Moses spoke a *prophecy* about Christ.
3.	prophesy	The mob challenged Jesus to *prophesy* to them.
4.	disciples	The twelve *disciples* followed Jesus.
5.	audience	Peter preached to a large *audience*.
6.	practice	Regular *practice* will improve your skill.
7.	grease	There is *grease* on the floor.
8.	satisfactory	Your work is *satisfactory* to me.
9.	necessary	Is this a *necessary* item?
10.	expensive	The rich man wore *expensive* clothes.
11.	serious	Saul made a *serious* mistake.
12.	fierce	Daniel was protected from the *fierce* lions.

Lesson 25—67 points

A. 39 points

1. a. expensive
  b. furious
  c. happiest
  d. serious
  e. inside
  f. prophesy
  g. consented
  h. satisfactory
2. a. assemble
  b. blossom
  c. possible
  d. guessed
  e. lessons
  f. messenger
3. a. recently
  b. citizen
  c. mercies
  d. prophecy
  e. concern
  f. celebrate
4. a. disciples
  b. scenery
  c. muscle
  d. science
  e. descend
  f. scissors
5. a. progress
  b. business
  c. embarrass
  d. compass
6. a. grease
  b. reverse
  c. increase
  d. condense
7. a. practice
  b. fierce
  c. audience
  d. reference
8. necessary

B. Using Your Words

1. Do not confuse *prophecy* and *prophesy*. (*Prophecy* has a *c,* and its last syllable sounds like the name of the letter *c.*) Write the correct words.
   a. Revelation is a book of (prophecy, prophesy).
   b. The soldiers challenged Jesus to (prophecy, prophesy) which one of them had struck Him.
   c. The (prophecies, prophesies) of a true prophet always comes to pass.
   d. Micah (prophecied, prophesied) that Jesus would be born in Bethlehem.
2. Write a spelling word that could replace each underlined word.
   a. Please <u>lubricate</u> this bearing for me.
   b. The <u>somber</u> expression on Father's face showed his deep concern.
   c. Jesus' enemies could not <u>disconcert</u> Him with crafty questions.
3. Write spelling words that are antonyms.
   a. cheap   c. unsuitable
   b. disperse   d. needless
4. There is a slight difference in the use of *farther* and *further*. *Farther* is preferred when actual distance is meant, and *further* when a more figurative meaning is intended. Write the preferred forms.
   a. Please explain _____ what you mean.
   b. Drive the nail _____ into the wood.

Dictionary Practice

5. When *grease* is used as a verb, it may be pronounced
   a. (grāz).   b. (grez).   c. (grēz).

C. Building Words

- Adjectives and adverbs may have three degrees of comparison: positive (no comparing), comparative (comparing two things), and superlative (comparing three or more things). The suffixes -er and -est are used to form the comparative and superlative degrees of many modifiers. **old, older, oldest**

- When -er or -est is added, final e may be dropped, final y may be changed to i, or the final consonant may be doubled. **fierce—fiercer happy—happiest big—bigger**

1. Write -er and -est forms of each word.
   a. thin   c. happy
   b. fierce   d. pretty
2. Write the NEW WORD that is a comparative form made by changing the vowel and adding -ther instead of just -er.
3. For most modifiers of two or more syllables, the words *more* and *most* are used to show comparison: *expensive, more expensive, most expensive.* Write the comparative and superlative forms of these.
   a. recently   b. serious

Bible Thoughts
Use a spelling word to complete this Bible verse.
4. "I have esteemed the words of his mouth more than my _____ food" (Job 23:12).

55

B. 14 points
1. a. prophecy
   b. prophesy
   c. prophecies
   d. prophesied
2. a. grease
   b. serious
   c. embarrass
3. a. expensive
   b. assemble
   c. satisfactory
   d. necessary
4. a. further
   b. farther
5. c

C. 14 points
1. a. thinner, thinnest
   b. fiercer, fiercest
   c. happier, happiest
   d. prettier, prettiest
2. further
3. a. more recently, most recently
   b. more serious, most serious
4. necessary

13. *happiest*   We are the *happiest* when we obey.
14. *prettiest*   These are the *prettiest* flowers in the garden.
15. *further*   We will discuss the plans *further*.
16. *recently*   They have *recently* moved here.

His *furious* anger did not *embarrass* her.

David made *reference* to God's *mercies*.

LESSON 26

NEW WORDS

1. *business*
2. *baptism*
3. *baptized*
4. *dessert*
5. *composition*
6. *unpleasant*
7. *exactly*
8. *example*
9. *blizzard*
10. *disease*
11. *opposite*
12. *vice-president*
13. *citizen*
14. *advertised*
15. *there's*
16. *theirs*

REVIEW WORDS

17. *poison*
18. *puzzle*
19. *they're*
20. *represented*

A. Sounds and Letters

- Common spellings of /z/ are z, ze, zz, s, se, and ss. ci**t**i**z**en bapti**z**e bli**zz**ard di**s**ea**s**e de**ss**ert

1. Add the correct spelling of /z/ as you write these NEW WORDS.
   a. oppo__ite   d. compo__ition
   b. citi__en   e. vice-pre__ident
   c. their__   f. unplea__ant
2. Also add /z/ as you write these words.
   a. bree__   d. __ebra
   b. de__ign   e. sci__ors
   c. po__itive   f. Na__areth

56

de/z/ert

3. Write spelling words with these sounds.
   a. /iz/ spelled *usi*
   b. /z/ spelled *ss*
   c. /z/ spelled *s* and /z/ spelled *se*

4. For each description, write spelling words according to the number in parentheses.
   a. The /z/ sound is spelled *zz* after a short vowel (2).
   b. A suffix causes a final /d/ sound (3).
   c. The first sound is /th/. (3)

- The /gz/ sound is usually spelled x. e**x**ample

5. Write the two NEW WORDS that have /gz/ spelled *x*.

6. Spell these words correctly.
   a. e/gz/ist   d. e/gz/amination
   b. e/gz/hort   e. e/gz/aggerate
   c. e/gz/alt   f. e/gz/emption

7. Write these words, being especially careful to spell the last syllables correctly.
   a. blizz/ərd/   d. baptis/əm/
   b. pois/ən/   e. unpleas/ənt/
   c. puzz/əl/   f. oppos/it/

A. 37 points
1. a. opposite
   b. citizen
   c. theirs
   d. composition
   e. vice-president
   f. unpleasant
2. a. breeze
   b. design
   c. positive
   d. zebra
   e. scissors
   f. Nazareth
3. a. business
   b. dessert
   c. disease
4. a. blizzard, puzzle
   b. baptized, advertised, represented
   c. there's, theirs, they're
5. exactly, example
6. a. exist
   b. exhort
   c. exalt
   d. examination
   e. exaggerate
   f. exemption
7. a. blizzard
   b. poison
   c. puzzle
   d. baptism
   e. unpleasant
   f. opposite

Test Sentences

1.	*business*	This is a *business* street.
2.	*baptism*	Jesus' *baptism* was an example for us.
3.	*baptized*	He was *baptized* in the Jordan River.
4.	*composition*	This *composition* is well written.
5.	*unpleasant*	We had an *unpleasant* experience.
6.	*exactly*	Do *exactly* as I showed you.
7.	*example*	Be an *example* to others.
8.	*dessert*	Do you want your *dessert* later?
9.	*blizzard*	A *blizzard* was raging outside.
10.	*citizen*	Paul was a Roman *citizen*.
11.	*disease*	Naaman had the *disease* of leprosy.
12.	*vice-president*	Our *vice-president* is in Washington.

B. Using Your Words

1. Write the spelling word that belongs with each group.
   a. salad, main dish, vegetable
   b. ours, hers, yours
   c. president, secretary, treasurer
   d. hurricane, thunderstorm, tempest
   e. Communion, feet washing, anointing with oil

2. The words in parentheses may be confused with each other. Write the correct ones.
   a. A person's (decease, disease) is his death.
   b. Smallpox was a dreaded (decease, disease) for hundreds of years.
   c. Which car is (theirs, there's)?
   d. Father said (theirs, there's) an important reason for the tail rotor on a helicopter.
   e. Not all (deserts, desserts) are covered with sand.
   f. Mother does not serve (desert, dessert) at the end of every meal.

3. Write spelling words that are synonyms.
   a. precisely   d. illness
   b. symbolized   e. disagreeable
   c. contrary   f. perplex

Dictionary Practice

4. In British use, *dessert* is _____ or _____ served after sweets at the end of a meal.

5. The word *disease* comes from *dis-* and *ease*, which together mean "___ ___ ___."

C. Building Words

- Pronouns show possession by a change in form. They do not show possession by use of the apostrophe. **he—his I—my it—its**
- Only in contractions are apostrophes used in connection with pronouns. **he is—he's it is—it's**

1. Write spelling words that could replace the underlined words.
   a. These books are the books belonging to them.
   b. They are all written by the same author.
   c. There is much information in the books.

2. Write the correct words.
   a. (Whose, Who's) the man (whose, who's) coat is missing?
   b. (There's, Theres) much work to do.
   c. These trays are (ours, our's), but those are (yours, your's).
   d. (Its, It's) too early for this tree to be losing (its, it's) leaves.
   e. Is (your, you're) car like (theirs, there's)?

3. For *one*, the possessive form is *one's* and the plural form is *ones*. Write the correct form for each sentence.
   a. Losing (ones, one's) way is distressing.
   b. Were those the largest (ones, one's)?

Bible Thoughts

Use a spelling word to complete this Bible verse.

4. "I have given you an _____, that ye should do as I have done to you" (John 13:15).

57

B. 20 points
   1. a. dessert
      b. theirs
      c. vice-president
      d. blizzard
      e. baptism
   2. a. decease
      b. disease
      c. theirs
      d. there's
      e. deserts
      f. dessert
   3. a. exactly
      b. represented
      c. opposite
      d. disease
      e. unpleasant
      f. puzzle
   4. fruit, nuts
   5. not at ease
C. 15 points
   1. a. theirs
      b. They're
      c. There's
   2. a. Who's, whose
      b. There's
      c. ours, yours
      d. It's, its
      e. your, theirs
   3. a. one's
      b. ones
   4. example

13. *advertised*   The book was *advertised* here.
14. *opposite*   You do the *opposite* of what I do.
15. *there's*   She said *there's* a box in here.
16. *theirs*   The money was *theirs* to keep.

They're using *poison* to kill the weeds.

The *puzzle represented* nothing at all.

LESSON 27

NEW WORDS

1. brook
2. clerk
3. pickles
4. qualified
5. acquaint
6. occur
7. connected
8. court
9. kerosene
10. choir
11. instruction
12. qualities
13. equipment
14. respectable
15. overlook
16. yourselves

REVIEW WORDS

17. electrical
18. quarrel
19. according
20. securing

broo/k/

c. conne__ted   e. instru__tion
d. respe__table   f. a__ording

> • When final /k/ follows a short vowel in a one-syllable word or in an accented syllable, it is usually spelled *ck*. **stack pickles** Such a final /k/ is usually spelled *k* when it follows a vowel that is not short. **brook hearken**

4. Use *k* or *ck* to spell /k/ in these words.
   a. pi__les   d. overloo__
   b. broo__   e. wre__age
   c. atta__   f. remar__
5. Write the REVIEW WORD in which /k/ follows a short vowel in an accented syllable, but the spelling is *c* instead of *ck*.

> • The /kw/ sound at the beginning of a word is usually spelled *qu*. **qualities** Other spellings of /kw/ are *cqu* and *ch*. **acquaint choir**

6. Spell /kw/ as you write these words.
   a. /kw/alified   e. e/kw/ipment
   b. /kw/oir   f. /kw/alities
   c. s/kw/ash   g. in/kw/ire
   d. a/kw/aint   h. /kw/arrel
7. Write the NEW WORD that has
   a. /o͞or/ spelled *our*.
   b. /ôr/ spelled *our*.
   c. final /sēn/ spelled *sene*.

A. Sounds and Letters

> • The /k/ sound is usually spelled *c* or *k* at the beginning of a word. **court kerosene** Within a word, /k/ may be spelled *c* or *cc*. **direct occur**

1. Write the three NEW WORDS that begin with /k/ spelled *c* (not *ch*).
2. The NEW WORD that begins with /k/ spelled *k* is derived from the Greek word *keros* (wax). Write this NEW WORD.
3. Add /k/ as you write these words.
   a. se__uring   b. o__ur

58

A. 28 points
1. clerk, connected, court
2. kerosene
3. a. securing
   b. occur
   c. respectable
   d. connected
   e. instruction
   f. according
4. a. pickles
   b. brook
   c. attack
   d. overlook
   e. wreckage
   f. remark
5. electrical
6. a. qualified
   b. choir
   c. squash
   d. acquaint
   e. equipment
   f. qualities
   g. inquire
   h. quarrel
7. a. yourselves
   b. court
   c. kerosene

Test Sentences

1. *brook*   That *brook* is deep.
2. *clerk*   The *clerk* sold a broom.
3. *pickles*   Do you want *pickles* on your sandwich?
4. *choir*   The *choir* sang to the old people.
5. *acquaint*   Please *acquaint* me with your plans.
6. *equipment*   Did you bring your *equipment* along?
7. *qualified*   He is a *qualified* surgeon.
8. *qualities*   Honesty and courtesy are two important *qualities*.
9. *occur*   Did this ever *occur* before?
10. *connected*   The wire is not *connected* to the box.
11. *instruction*   The Bible contains much *instruction* for us.
12. *court*   The *court* will decide who is guilty.

B. Using Your Words

1. Write spelling words with these meanings.
a. Vegetables, especially cucumbers, preserved in salt water and spices.
b. Tools and supplies for doing work.
c. Good but not extraordinary.
d. Fail to notice.
e. A person who keeps records for a business or in court.

2. Which spelling word is a homophone for *quire*?

3. Write spelling words to complete these comparisons.
a. *Mine* is to *thine* as *ourselves* is to ___.
b. *Foreman* is to *crew* as *judge* is to ___.
c. *Milk* is to *cream* as *petroleum* is to ___.
d. *Exact* is to *precise* as *happen* is to ___.
e. *Working* is to *crew* as *singing* is to ___.

4. Write the same spelling word (or a form of it) for both blanks in each sentence.
a. A _____ product has many good _____.
b. The boys hoped to make their supplies _____ by _____ them to a high branch.
c. The man who _____ death by climbing a skyscraper was brought into _____.
d. The believers were of one _____, and they walked _____ to the truth.

Dictionary Practice

5. Write whether each pronunciation fits the *noun* or the *verb* meaning of *overlook*.
a. (ō′vər lŏŏk′)　　b. (ō′vər lŏŏk′)

C. Building Words

- Compound words ending with *like, ache,* or *self* are spelled solid. **rooflike headache yourself**
- When compounds referring to relatives begin with *great* or end with *in-law,* they are spelled with hyphens. **great-grandmother brother-in-law**

1. Form compounds by combining the boldface words with the words after them.
a. **like:** floor, home
b. **ache:** tooth, head
c. **self:** my, her
d. **selves:** our, them
e. **great:** uncle, aunt
f. **in-law:** father, mother

2. Make closed compounds from these words.
a. pass + over
b. run + away
c. sales + clerk
d. light + house
e. under + take
f. choir + master

3. Write closed compounds that have these meanings. For "light from the moon" you would write *moonlight*.
a. a book of stories
b. a fighter of fires
c. a beat of the heart
d. men operating businesses

Bible Thoughts
Use a spelling word to complete this Bible verse.
4. "Hear the _____ of thy father, and forsake not the law of thy mother" (Proverbs 1:8)

59

B. 21 points
1. a. pickles
   b. equipment
   c. respectable *or* qualified
   d. overlook
   e. clerk
2. choir
3. a. yourselves
   b. court
   c. kerosene
   d. occur
   e. choir
4. a. quality, qualities
   b. secure, securing
   c. courted, court
   d. accord, according
5. a. noun
   b. verb

C. 22 points
1. a. floorlike, homelike
   b. toothache, headache
   c. myself, herself
   d. ourselves, themselves
   e. great-uncle, great-aunt
   f. father-in-law, mother-in-law
2. a. passover
   b. runaway
   c. salesclerk
   d. lighthouse
   e. undertake
   f. choirmaster
3. a. storybook
   b. firefighter
   c. heartbeat
   d. businessmen
4. instruction

13. *kerosene*　　The jug is full of *kerosene.*
14. *respectable*　　She led a very *respectable* life.
15. *overlook*　　God will not *overlook* sin.
16. *yourselves*　　You *yourselves* know what happened.

According to him, they had a *quarrel.*

The man is *securing* the *electrical* wire.

(Teacher: Tell the students to place a comma in one of the sentences.)

LESSON 28

NEW WORDS

1. *width*
2. *weapon*
3. *forwarding*
4. *accept*
5. *accident*
6. *whirl*
7. *worthy*
8. *express*
9. *watchful*
10. *exclaimed*
11. *expedition*
12. *experience*
13. *excess*
14. *meanwhile*
15. *whatever*
16. *elsewhere*

REVIEW WORDS

17. *whether*
18. *weigh*
19. *exercise*
20. *excitement*

A. Sounds and Letters

- The /w/ sound is usually spelled *w.* **worthy**

1. Write these spelling words correctly.
   a. /wûr/thy
   b. /woch/ful
   c. /wep/on
   d. /wā/
   e. for/wərd/ing
   f. /wid/th

2. The /w/ sound is sometimes spelled *u.* Use that spelling in the words below.
   a. lang/w/age
   b. pers/w/ade

e/ks/ercise

- The /hw/ sound is usually spelled *wh.* **elsewhere**

3. Write the spelling words with /hw/ that are
   a. compound words (3).
   b. not compound words (2).

- The /ks/ sound is commonly spelled *x,* especially after /e/. **ex̲ercise** When a syllable division occurs between /k/ and /s/, the spelling is often *xc* or *cc.* **ex̲cess** **ac̲cident**

4. Write the five NEW WORDS that begin with /eks/ or /iks/.

5. Use *x* to spell these words correctly.
   a. e/ks/tend
   b. fi/ks/ture
   c. e/ks/it
   d. refle/ks/
   e. e/ks/pensive
   f. e/ks/ecute

6. Write the two NEW WORDS in which /ks/ is spelled *cc* after *a.*

7. Use *cc* to spell /ks/ in these words.
   a. a/ks/ess
   b. a/ks/ent
   c. a/ks/elerate
   d. va/ks/inate

8. Write the REVIEW WORD that has
   a. /ks/ spelled *xc.*
   b. /ks/ spelled *x.*

9. Write NEW WORDS with these sounds.
   a. /e/ spelled *ea*
   b. /ā/ spelled *ai*

A. 34 points
   1. a. worthy
      b. watchful
      c. weapon
      d. weigh
      e. forwarding
      f. width
   2. a. language
      b. persuade
   3. a. meanwhile, whatever, elsewhere
      b. whirl, whether
   4. express, exclaimed, expedition, experience, excess
   5. a. extend
      b. fixture
      c. exit
      d. reflex
      e. expensive
      f. execute
   6. accept, accident
   7. a. access
      b. accent
      c. accelerate
      d. vaccinate
   8. a. excitement
      b. exercise
   9. a. weapon
      b. exclaimed

60

Test Sentences

1.	*width*	We measured the *width* of the room.
2.	*weapon*	David's *weapon* was a sling.
3.	*watchful*	"Be *watchful,*" the Bible tells us.
4.	*forwarding*	I am *forwarding* this letter to you.
5.	*exclaimed*	"What?" *exclaimed* Father.
6.	*expedition*	The *expedition* was successful.
7.	*experience*	I do not have *experience* in that work.
8.	*excess*	There was an *excess* of noise.
9.	*accept*	Will you *accept* this gift?
10.	*accident*	They had an *accident* today.
11.	*express*	Let me *express* my thanks.
12.	*meanwhile*	There was a delay, so, *meanwhile,* I read.

B. Using Your Words

1. Choose the correct words.
   a. All the answers (accept, except) one were correct.
   b. Learn to (accept, except) compliments gracefully.
   c. The little ones were (accepted, excepted) from the rule about wearing shoes.
   d. Warm (weather, whether) will soon be here.
   e. I could hardly decide (weather, whether) to go or stay.
   f. Christians have (access, excess) to God through prayer.
   g. Father sold the (access, excess) corn.

2. Write spelling words that are antonyms.
   a. reject   c. undeserving
   b. calmness   d. scarcity
3. Which spelling words have these double meanings?
   a. (1) Go through.
      (2) Knowledge and skill gained by direct contact.
   b. (1) Revolve rapidly.
      (2) A confused state.

Dictionary Practice
4. *Express* may be used as what three parts of speech?

C. Building Words

- Cardinal number names from 21 to 99 are spelled with hyphens. **forty-two**
- Ordinal names derived from these numbers are also spelled with hyphens. **forty-second**
- When the name of a fraction is spelled out, a hyphen is placed between the numerator and the denominator unless one of the two already has a hyphen. **five-sixths fifteen thirty-seconds**

1. Spell out the names of these numbers.
   a. 52   c. 83
   b. 98   d. 79
2. Spell out the ordinal number names derived from these.
   a. 34   c. 69
   b. 26   d. 57

3. Spell out the names of these fractions.
   a. $\frac{3}{4}$ c. $\frac{9}{16}$
   b. $\frac{5}{9}$ d. $\frac{17}{36}$
4. Make closed compounds by combining these words.
   a. mean + while   c. express + way
   b. else + where   d. what + ever
5. Make derived forms as indicated.
   a. accept + ance   c. accident + al
   b. excess + ive   d. express + ion

Bible Thoughts
Use a spelling word to complete this Bible verse.
6. "Thou art _____, O Lord, to receive glory and honour and power" (Revelation 4:11).

61

13. *whatever*   You should do *whatever* he does.
14. *elsewhere*   Please move this box *elsewhere*.
15. *whirl*   Watch the top *whirl* around.
16. *worthy*   I am not *worthy* of your kindness.

Do you know *whether* we should do this *exercise?*

In his *excitement* he failed to *weigh* the matter.

B. 16 points
   1. a. except
      b. accept
      c. excepted
      d. weather
      e. whether
      f. access
      g. excess
   2. a. accept
      b. excitement
      c. worthy
      d. excess
   3. a. experience
      b. whirl
   4. verb, noun, adjective
      (Accept abbreviations.)
C. 21 points
   1. a. fifty-two
      b. ninety-eight
      c. eighty-three
      d. seventy-nine
   2. a. thirty-fourth
      b. twenty-sixth
      c. sixty-ninth
      d. fifty-seventh
   3. a. three-fourths
      b. five-ninths
      c. nine-sixteenths
      d. seventeen thirty-sixths
   4. a. meanwhile
      b. elsewhere
      c. expressway
      d. whatever
   5. a. acceptance
      b. excessive
      c. accidental
      d. expression
   6. worthy

LESSON 29

NEW WORDS

1. *accurate*
2. *volume*
3. *companion*
4. *universal*
5. *knowledge*
6. *kneel*
7. *onion*
8. *beyond*
9. *humble*
10. *honestly*
11. *honesty*
12. *bushel bu.*
13. *peck pk.*
14. *milligram mg*
15. *millimeter mm*
16. *boulevard blvd.*

REVIEW WORDS

17. *lawyer*
18. *heir*
19. *failure*
20. *regularly*

A. Sounds and Letters

- A few words begin with *h* or *k* but have no /h/ or /k/ sound. The initial *h* or *k* was pronounced at one time, but it is now silent. **<u>h</u>onesty <u>k</u>nowledge**

1. Write these spelling words correctly.
   a. (nol'ij)   d. (âr)
   b. (on'is tē)   e. (hum'bəl)
   c. (nēl)   f. (on'ist lē)

2. Write the words for the phonetic spellings in these sentences.
   a. The plane flew at a speed of five

on/yən/

hundred miles per (our).
   b. Some (ûrbz) are useful as medicines.
   c. Who (nokt) on the door?
   d. Sharp tools such as (nīvz) and scissors must be used carefully.

- The /y/ sound is usually spelled *y*. **<u>b</u>eyond** When /y/ helps to form the /yōō/sound, the most common spelling is *u*. **<u>u</u>niversal**

3. Add /y/ or /yōō/ as you write each word.
   a. law__er   c. __niversal
   b. vol__me   d. be__ond

- The usual spelling of /yən/ is *ion*, and of /yər/ is *ur* or *ure*. **on<u>ion</u> acc<u>ur</u>ate fail<u>ure</u>**

4. Add /yən/ or /yər/ as you write these.
   a. on__   c. acc__ate
   b. fail__   d. compan__

5. Which REVIEW WORD
   a. ends with /yər/ but not *ure*?
   b. has /lər/ spelled *lar*?

6. Write NEW WORDS with these sounds.
   a. final /əl/ spelled *el*
   b. /ōōl/ spelled *oul*
   c. final /k/ spelled *ck*
   d. /l/ spelled *ll* (2 words)
   e. final /ij/ spelled *edge*

A. 26 points

1. a. knowledge
   b. honesty
   c. kneel
   d. heir
   e. humble
   f. honestly
2. a. hour
   b. herbs
   c. knocked
   d. knives
3. a. lawyer
   b. volume
   c. universal
   d. beyond
4. a. onion
   b. failure
   c. accurate
   d. companion
5. a. lawyer
   b. regularly
6. a. bushel
   b. Boulevard
   c. peck
   d. milligram, millimeter
   e. knowledge

Test Sentences

1.	*volume*	Find the *volume* of this box.
2.	*accurate*	Be sure to do *accurate* work.
3.	*kneel*	The Hebrews would not *kneel* to the image.
4.	*knowledge*	Solomon had *knowledge* about many things.
5.	*onion*	Put an *onion* in the stew.
6.	*companion*	His only *companion* was a book.
7.	*universal*	Father replaced the *universal* joint.
8.	*beyond*	We must live *beyond* what we see.
9.	*honesty*	Your *honesty* is refreshing.
10.	*humble*	Moses was a *humble* man.
11.	*honestly*	The statement was *honestly* made.

B. Using Your Words

1. Write the spelling word that belongs with each group.
   a. fairness, uprightness, integrity
   b. garlic, horseradish, chive
   c. wisdom, understanding, perception
   d. stand, lie, sit
   e. friend, associate, comrade
2. Write spelling words that are synonyms of the underlined words.
   a. The attempt to raise corn in the desert was a <u>fiasco</u>.
   b. The report must have been <u>correct</u>, for several people said the same thing.
3. Write spelling words with these meanings.
   a. A book; also, the space occupied by something.

b. Having to do with all people.
c. Farther on than.
d. A person who inherits or will inherit something.
e. In a fair and truthful manner.

4. Both *humble* and *humiliate* mean "reduce the pride of," but *humiliate* has a connotation of shame and embarrassment. Write the correct word for each sentence.
   a. Sharon felt (humbled, humiliated) by the insult.
   b. It is (humbling, humiliating) to consider the greatness of God's creation.

Dictionary Practice

5. Write *knowledge,* and use a slash to divide it into syllables.

C. Building Words

- Except for metric units of measure, most abbreviations are followed by periods. If the full word is capitalized, the abbreviation is also capitalized.
  peck—pk. millimeter—mm Lincoln Boulevard—Lincoln Blvd.
- A few abbreviations contain capital letters even though the full words are not capitalized. Such an abbreviation has no space after the internal period. **before Christ—B.C. post meridiem—P.M.**

1. Write these measures with abbreviations.

   a. 7 pecks   c. 20 millimeters
   b. 12 bushels   d. 175 milligrams
2. Write out these measures in full.
   a. 46 kg   c. 32 lb.
   b. 135 mi.   d. 150 g
3. Write *Oak Boulevard* in abbreviated form.
4. Rewrite each expression, using *A.M., P.M.,* or *B.C.*
   a. 2:45 in the afternoon
   b. 7 hr. 30 min. beyond midnight
   c. 750 years before Christ was born

Bible Thoughts

Use a spelling word to complete this Bible verse.

5. "Whosoever shall exalt himself shall be abased; and he that shall _____ himself shall be exalted" (Matthew 23:12).

63

B. 15 points
1. a. honesty
   b. onion
   c. knowledge
   d. kneel
   e. companion
2. a. failure
   Teacher: Encourage students to use classroom dictionary.
   b. accurate
3. a. volume
   b. universal
   c. beyond
   d. heir
   e. honestly
4. a. humiliated
   b. humbling
5. knowl/edge

C. 13 points
1. a. 7 pk.
   b. 12 bu.
   c. 20 mm
   d. 175 mg
2. a. 46 kilograms
   b. 135 miles
   c. 32 pounds
   d. 150 grams
3. Oak Blvd.
4. a. 2:45 P.M.
   b. 7:30 A.M.
   c. 750 B.C.
5. humble

For numbers 12–16, write the words *and* their abbreviations.

12. *peck*   *pk.*   We bought a *peck* of apples.
13. *bushel*   *bu.*   We needed a *bushel* of potatoes too.
14. *millimeter* *mm*   A *millimeter* is a small measurement.
15. *milligram*   *mg*   Every day we need one *milligram* of vitamin B_1.
16. *Boulevard*   *Blvd.*   Jeffrey lives along the *boulevard* where the pink dogwoods bloom.

The *lawyer* must know who the *heir* will be.

Failure is *regularly* caused by poor planning.

LESSON 30

25	26	27	28	29
assemble	business	brook	width	accurate
prophecy	baptism	clerk	weapon	volume
satisfactory	baptized	pickles	forwarding	companion
disciples	composition	qualified	accept	universal
grease	dessert	acquaint	accident	knowledge
practice	unpleasant	occur	whirl	kneel
audience	exactly	connected	worthy	onion
happiest	example	court	express	beyond
necessary	blizzard	kerosene	watchful	humble
prophesy	disease	choir	exclaimed	honestly
expensive	opposite	instruction	expedition	honesty
recently	vice-president	qualities	experience	bushel bu.
fierce	citizen	equipment	excess	peck pk.
serious	advertised	respectable	meanwhile	milligram mg
further	there's	overlook	whatever	millimeter mm
prettiest	theirs	yourselves	elsewhere	boulevard blvd.

A. Sounds and Letters Review

1. Write Lesson 25 words with these sounds.
  a. /s/ = sc   c. final /is/ = ice
  b. final /s/ = se   d. /səs/ = cess

2. Add /z/ or /gz/ as you write these words from Lesson 26.
  a. bapti__m   c. citi__en
  b. di__ea__   d. e__ample

3. Write Lesson 27 words with these sounds.
  a. /k/ spelled ck
  b. /kw/ spelled ch
  c. /kwip/ spelled quip

4. Write Lesson 28 words with these sounds.
  a. /wûr/ spelled wor
  b. /wo/ spelled wa
  c. /wep/ spelled weap

5. Spell these Lesson 28 words correctly.
  a. /hw/atever   c. e/ks/claimed
  b. e/ks/ess   d. a/ks/ident

6. Add the initial silent letters as you write these words from Lesson 29.
  a. __neel   c. __onestly
  b. __onesty   d. __nowledge

7. Spell these Lesson 29 words correctly.
  a. /yo͞o/niversal   b. compan/yən/

A. 24 points
  1. a. disciples
     b. grease
     c. practice
     d. necessary
  2. a. baptism
     b. disease
     c. citizen
     d. example
  3. a. pickles
     b. choir
     c. equipment
  4. a. worthy
     b. watchful
     c. weapon
  5. a. whatever
     b. excess
     c. exclaimed
     d. accident
  6. a. kneel
     b. honesty
     c. honestly
     d. knowledge
  7. a. universal
     b. companion

See page 86 for test sentences.

B. Using Your Words Review

1. Write the correct word for each sentence.

a. One (prophecy, prophesy) about Christ is found in Deuteronomy 18.

b. David had a black eye but no (farther, further) injuries.

c. Cholera is a serious (decease, disease).

d. Before his (decease, disease), Peter wrote an epistle to exhort the believers.

e. We had cake for (desert, dessert).

f. See if (theirs, there's) time for that.

g. Job had learned to (accept, except) whatever the Lord allowed to happen.

h. To be temperate means to avoid (access, excess) in all things.

i. God allows hardships as a way to (humble, humiliate) us.

j. The (weather, whether) has been rainy.

2. Write whether the words in each pair are *synonyms, antonyms,* or *homophones.*

a. deserving, worthy

b. choir, quire

c. prophesy, foretell

d. local, universal

e. stationary, stationery

f. divided, connected

3. Write spelling words with these meanings. Lesson numbers are in parentheses.

a. Needful; essential (25)

b. Not enjoyable. (26)

c. Fairly good; acceptable. (27)

d. An instrument for fighting. (28)

e. Exactly according to truth. (29)

C. Building Words Review

1. Write the comparative and superlative forms of each word.

a. slim   c. fierce

b. strong   d. pretty

2. Form these compounds correctly.

a. leaf + like

b. her + self

c. great + uncle

d. son + in-law

e. sixty + nine

f. five + thirty-sixths

3. Also write these as compound words.

a. court + house   d. what + ever

b. vice + president   e. mean + while

c. over + looked   f. else + where

4. Write the abbreviated form of each expression.

a. 86 bushels

b. 55 gallons

c. 18 pecks

d. 250 millimeters

e. 400 milligrams

f. Adams Boulevard

g. 458 years before Christ's birth

h. 8:25 in the morning

5. Write the shorter forms of these.

a. Doctor Evans

b. Mister Lake

c. pages 157–162

d. pen, ink, and so on

65

B. 21 points

1. a. prophecy
   b. further
   c. disease
   d. decease
   e. dessert
   f. there's
   g. accept
   h. excess
   i. humble
   j. weather

2. a. synonyms
   b. homophones
   c. synonyms
   d. antonyms
   e. homophones
   f. antonyms

3. a. necessary
   b. unpleasant
   c. respectable
   d. weapon
   e. accurate

C. 32 points

1. a. slimmer, slimmest
   b. stronger, strongest
   c. fiercer, fiercest
   d. prettier, prettiest

2. a. leaflike
   b. herself
   c. great-uncle
   d. son-in-law
   e. sixty-nine
   f. five thirty-sixths

3. a. courthouse
   b. vice-president
   c. overlooked
   d. whatever
   e. meanwhile
   f. elsewhere

4. a. 86 bu.
   b. 55 gal.
   c. 18 pk.
   d. 250 mm
   e. 400 mg
   f. Adams Blvd.
   g. 458 B.C.
   h. 8:25 A.M.

5. a. Dr. Evans
   b. Mr. Lake
   c. pp. 157–162
   d. pen, ink, etc.

LESSON 31

NEW WORDS

1. parable
2. amendment
3. iniquity
4. practicing
5. grammar
6. strength
7. column
8. effect
9. additional
10. calendar
11. jealous
12. advanced
13. continued cont.
14. Galatians Gal.
15. Ephesians Eph.
16. Song of Solomon
    Song of Sol.

REVIEW WORDS

17. industrial
18. fierce
19. basis
20. governor

A. Sounds and Letters

1. Write NEW WORDS with these spellings.
   a. /ak/ = ac   c. /al/ = al
   b. /am/ = amm   d. /ans/ = anc
2. Write NEW WORDS with these spellings.
   a. /ekt/ = ect   c. /eng/ = eng
   b. /el/ = eal   d. /end/ = end
3. Add /i/ as you write the following words.
   a. __n__quity   c. __ffect
   b. bas__s   d. __phesians

(kal′ən dər) = calendar

MAY						
S	M	T	W	T	F	S
		1	2	2	4	5
6	7	8	9	10	11	12
13	14	15	16	17	18	19
20	21	22	23	24	25	26
27	28	29	30	31		

4. Write these words, using o to add /o/.
   a. c__lumn   b. Song of S__lomon
5. Add /u/ as you write these words.
   a. ind__strial   b. g__vernor
6. Add /ər/ as you write these.
   a. gramm__   c. gov__n__
   b. calend__
7. Write the spelling words that have these sounds.
   a. /bəl/ spelled *ble*
   b. /ənz/ spelled *ans* (2 words)
   c. final /m/ spelled *mn*
   d. /ir/ spelled *ier*
   e. final /mən/ spelled *mon*
   f. /f/ spelled *ff*
8. Write these spelling words correctly.
   a. ini/kw/ity   d. practi/s/ing
   b. a/dish/onal   e. jeal/əs/
   c. advan/st/   f. contin/yo͞od/
9. Write the REVIEW WORD that has
   a. /ē/ spelled *i*.
   b. two /s/ sounds.
   c. final /s/ spelled *ce*.

Lesson 31—72 points

A. 35 points
1. a. practicing
   b. grammar
   c. calendar
   d. advanced
2. a. effect
   b. jealous
   c. strength
   d. amendment
3. a. iniquity
   b. basis
   c. effect
   d. Ephesians
4. a. column
   b. Song of Solomon
5. a. industrial
   b. governor
6. a. grammar
   b. calendar
   c. governor
7. a. parable
   b. Galatians, Ephesians
   c. column
   d. fierce
   e. Song of Solomon
   f. effect
8. a. iniquity
   b. additional
   c. advanced
   d. practicing
   e. jealous
   f. continued
9. a. industrial
   b. basis
   c. fierce

Test Sentences

1. *effect* — What *effect* did this have on you?
2. *column* — Write the numbers in a straight *column*.
3. *amendment* — Congress passed a Constitutional *amendment*.
4. *parable* — Do you know the *parable* of the lost sheep?
5. *iniquity* — The *iniquity* of Sodom was great.
6. *strength* — The Lord is my *strength* and shield.
7. *grammar* — Your *grammar* lesson is finished.
8. *practicing* — I am *practicing* this song.
9. *calendar* — The *calendar* says it is time for full moon.
10. *additional* — Do an *additional* lesson today.
11. *jealous* — God is a *jealous* God.
12. *advanced* — The old man was *advanced* in years.

B. Using Your Words

1. *Affect* is used only as a verb. *Effect* is usually a noun, but it can also be a verb. Write the correct word for each sentence.
   a. How will the new law (affect, effect) Christian schools?
   b. One (affect, effect) of the telegraph was greater safety in railroad travel.
   c. The death of Lazarus (affected, effected) Jesus strongly.
   d. By studying more, Nelson (affected, effected) an improvement in his grades.

2. Write spelling words that are synonyms.
   a. pillar   e. sin
   b. savage   f. extra
   c. envious   g. allegory
   d. improvement   h. force

3. Which NEW WORDS have these meanings?
   a. Went on after a pause.
   b. The principles that govern the correct usage of a language.
   c. A table showing months, weeks, and days.
   d. Doing often as a custom.

4. *Jealous* and *zealous* both come from the Greek word *zēlos* (zeal), but the English words are distinctly different. Which word has the more favorable connotation?

Dictionary Practice

5. *Iniquity* comes from a Latin word that means (not equal, not right, not straight).

C. Building Words

1. Write the abbreviation for each word.
   a. continued   c. Song of Solomon
   b. Galatians   d. Ephesians

2. Change each word in parentheses so that it shows the correct degree of comparison.
   a. A leopard is one of the (fierce) animals in the world.
   b. Judah seemed to be (jealous) of Joseph than Reuben was.
   c. Which kind of math is (advanced): arithmetic, algebra, or calculus?

3. Show only the syllable division indicated by the pattern before each word.
   a. VC/V: calendar
   b. CV/VC: situation
   c. VC/CV: advancing

   d. root/suffix: amendment

4. Write the plural of *strength*. That is the longest English word with only one syllable and one vowel.

5. Make derived forms as indicated.
   a. enlarge + ment   d. type + ist
   b. instruct + or   e. effect + ive
   c. addition + al   f. fierce + ly

Bible Thoughts

Use a spelling word to complete this Bible verse.

6. "The work of righteousness shall be peace; and the _____ of righteousness quietness and assurance for ever" (Isaiah 32:17).

67

B. 18 points
  1. a. affect
     b. effect
     c. affected
     d. effected
  2. a. column
     b. fierce
     c. jealous
     d. amendment
     e. iniquity
     f. additional
     g. parable
     h. strength
  3. a. continued
     b. grammar
     c. calendar
     d. practicing
  4. zealous
  5. not equal

C. 19 points
  1. a. cont.
     b. Gal.
     c. Song of Sol.
     d. Eph.
  2. a. fiercest
     b. more jealous
     c. most advanced
  3. a. cal/endar
     b. situ/ation
     c. ad/vancing
     d. amend/ment
  4. strengths
  5. a. enlargement
     b. instructor
     c. additional
     d. typist
     e. effective
     f. fiercely
  6. effect

For numbers 13–16, write the words *and* their abbreviations.
13. *continued*   *cont.*   The story was *continued.*
14. *Song of Solomon*   *Song of Sol.* *Song of Solomon* has beautiful poetry.
15. *Galatians*   *Gal.*   *Galatians* 5 lists the fruit of the Spirit.
16. *Ephesians*   *Eph.*   The armor of God is described in *Ephesians* 6.

He is the *governor* of an *industrial* state.

Saul's *fierce* anger had no *basis*.

LESSON 32

NEW WORDS

1. *education*
2. *valuable*
3. *arrival*
4. *honorable*
5. *mirror*
6. *estimate*
7. *quotation*
8. *immediately*
9. *humanity*
10. *scenery*
11. *society*
12. *data*
13. *community*
14. *destination*
15. *description*
16. *believing*

REVIEW WORDS

17. *museum*
18. *approach*
19. *beautifully*
20. *deliveries*

A. Sounds and Letters

1. Spell these NEW WORDS correctly.
   a. quot/ā/tion   c. educ/ā/tion
   b. estim/āt/   d. destin/ā/tion
2. Add /ē/ as you write these spelling words.
   a. deliver__s   d. imm__d__atel__
   b. sc__ner__   e. beautifull__
   c. humanit__   f. bel__ving
3. Write the two NEW WORDS that have /ī/ spelled *i*.

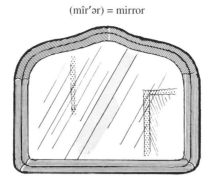

(mîr′ər) = mirror

4. Spell these words correctly.
   a. h/ī/giene   d. suppl/īd/
   b. scr/īb/   e. ch/wī/r
   c. d/ī/ing   f. exerc/īz/
5. Spell /ō/ correctly as you write these.
   a. appr__ch   c. (byo͞or′ō)
   b. qu__tation   d. (dē′pō)
6. Spell /yo͞o/ correctly as you write these spelling words.
   a. h__manity   c. comm__nity
   b. m__seum   d. b__tifully
7. Spell /ə/ or /ər/ correctly as you write these spelling words.
   a. dat__   d. hon__/ə/ble
   b. mirr__   e. est__mate
   c. s__ci__ty   f. __pproach
8. Write NEW WORDS that end with these syllables.
   a. /əl/ spelled *al*
   b. /əl/ spelled *le* (2 words)
9. Write NEW WORDS that have these sounds.
   a. initial /s/ spelled *sc*
   b. /îr/ spelled *irr*
   c. initial /ej/ spelled *ed*

68

Lesson 32—85 points

A. 38 points
1. a. quotation
   b. estimate
   c. education
   d. destination
2. a. deliveries
   b. scenery
   c. humanity
   d. immediately
   e. beautifully
   f. believing
3. arrival, society
4. a. hygiene
   b. scribe
   c. dying *or* dyeing
   d. supplied
   e. choir
   f. exercise
5. a. approach
   b. quotation
   c. bureau
   d. depot
6. a. humanity
   b. museum
   c. community
   d. beautifully
7. a. data
   b. mirror
   c. society
   d. honorable
   e. estimate
   f. approach
8. a. arrival
   b. valuable, honorable
9. a. scenery
   b. mirror
   c. education

Test Sentences

1. *education*   Our *education* includes everything that we learn.
2. *arrival*   We had a new *arrival* today.
3. *valuable*   Time is too *valuable* to waste.
4. *honorable*   You must do the *honorable* thing.
5. *mirror*   He looked in the *mirror*.
6. *estimate*   *Estimate* your answer before computing it.
7. *community*   That is a *community* park.
8. *immediately* He left *immediately* afterward.
9. *scenery*   The *scenery* is beautiful.
10. *society*   In our *society,* the handshake is a common greeting.
11. *quotation*   Romans 3:12 is a *quotation* from Psalms.
12. *humanity*   Christ's *humanity* is plainly taught in the Bible.

B. Using Your Words

1. Write spelling words that are antonyms.
   a. departure
   b. worthless
   c. disgraceful
   d. collections
   e. unattractively
   f. doubting

2. Write spelling words that could replace the underlined words.
   a. Some of the paintings in that <u>gallery</u> are worth thousands of dollars.
   b. Be very careful when you clean the <u>speculum</u> of a reflecting telescope.
   c. Disease and death are common experiences of <u>mankind</u>.
   d. The <u>panorama</u> before us was almost too beautiful to describe.

3. Write the spelling words suggested by these phrases. The numbers in parentheses show how many words you should write.
   a. a group of people (3)
   b. something spoken or written (2)
   c. highly esteemed (2)

Dictionary Practice

4. The first *a* in *data* may be pronounced (ā, a, ä, â). (Choose three.)

5. a. *Data* is actually (singular, plural), but it is often considered (singular, plural).
   b. What is the other form of *data*?

C. Building Words

1. Write these as open, hyphenated, or closed compounds. Numbers in parentheses give the lessons where you can find help.
   a. type + writer (5)
   b. chicken + pox (8)
   c. et + cetera (9)
   d. here + to + fore (19)
   e. gentle + men (23)
   f. vice + president (26)

2. Rewrite these phrases, using possessive nouns.
   a. society of today
   b. mirror belonging to Mother

3. Write the spelling words that are derived from these root words.
   a. scene
   b. arrive
   c. educate
   d. describe

4. Write the NEW WORD that is a verb with an inflectional suffix.

5. Write two spelling words that contain each suffix.
   a. *-ly*   b. *-ity*   c. *-able*

6. Change the suffix in each word to the suffix in parentheses.
   a. education (*-or*)
   b. scenery (*-ic*)
   c. description (*-ive*)
   d. destination (*-y*)

Bible Thoughts

Use a spelling word to complete this Bible verse.

7. "Now the God of hope fill you with all joy and peace in _____" (Romans 15:13).

69

B. 23 points
1. a. arrival (*or* approach)
   b. valuable
   c. honorable
   d. deliveries
   e. beautifully
   f. believing
2. a. museum
   b. mirror
   c. humanity
   d. scenery
3. a. humanity, society, community
   b. quotation, description (*or* data)
   c. valuable, honorable
4. ā, a, ä
5. a. plural, singular
   b. datum

C. 24 points
1. a. typewriter
   b. chickenpox
   c. et cetera
   d. heretofore
   e. gentlemen
   f. vice-president
2. a. today's society
   b. Mother's mirror
3. a. scenery
   b. arrival
   c. education
   d. description
4. believing
5. a. immediately, beautifully
   b. humanity, community
   c. valuable, honorable
6. a. educator
   b. scenic
   c. descriptive
   d. destiny
7. believing

LESSON 33

NEW WORDS

1. auditorium
2. eternity
3. gnawing
4. expression
5. vary
6. constantly
7. announcement
8. discontinued
9. godliness
10. moderate
11. transfer
12. happiness
13. connection
14. enforce
15. afford
16. whence

REVIEW WORDS

17. bulletin
18. bough
19. currant
20. disappointed

A. Sounds and Letters

1. Write these spelling words correctly.
   a. transf/ûr/
   b. b/ou/
   c. c/ûr/ant
   d. ann/ou/ncement
   e. disapp/oi/nted
   f. et/ûr/nity
2. Also spell these words correctly.
   a. v/oi/age
   b. av/oi/d
   c. cr/ou/n
   d. occ/ûr/
3. Add /är/ or /îr/ as you write these words.
   a. g__d
   b. l__gely
   c. sev__
   d. disapp__

(ik spresh′ən) = expression

4. Add /âr/ as you write these words. Similar spellings are in pairs: *a–b, c–d,* and so on.
   a. aff__
   b. desp__
   c. v__y
   d. prep__ing
   e. aw__
   f. decl__
   g. sw__
   h. forb__
5. Spell each word correctly.
   a. f/ô/lt
   b. aff/ôr/d
   c. ind/ôr/s
   d. enf/ôr/ce
   e. /ô/ffered
   f. gn/ô/ing
6. Write the NEW WORD that contains both /ô/ and /ôr/.
7. Write two NEW WORDS that contain
   a. a final /shən/ sound.
   b. final /s/ spelled *ss.*
   c. final /s/ spelled *ce.*
8. Write one spelling word for each description.
   a. The last syllable is /it/ or /āt/.
   b. The last syllable is /yōod/ spelled *ued.*
   c. Initial /n/ is spelled *gn.*
   d. The /ōol/ sound is spelled *ull.*
   e. The last syllable is /əm/ spelled *um.*

Lesson 33—80 points
A. 40 points
1. a. transfer
    b. bough
    c. currant
    d. announcement
    e. disappointed
    f. eternity
2. a. voyage
    b. avoid
    c. crown
    d. occur
3. a. guard
    b. largely
    c. severe
    d. disappear
4. a. affair
    b. despair
    c. vary
    d. preparing
    e. aware
    f. declare
    g. swear
    h. forbear
5. a. fault
    b. afford
    c. indoors
    d. enforce
    e. offered
    f. gnawing
6. auditorium
7. a. expression, connection
    b. godliness, happiness
    c. enforce, whence
8. a. moderate
    b. discontinued
    c. gnawing
    d. bulletin
    e. auditorium

Test Sentences

1.	*eternity*	The length of *eternity* is awesome.
2.	*auditorium*	The *auditorium* was cleaned.
3.	*gnawing*	There was a *gnawing* sound in the wall.
4.	*expression*	Read with *expression* and meaning.
5.	*vary*	Your answers will *vary* greatly.
6.	*afford*	Can you *afford* to lose?
7.	*enforce*	Policemen must *enforce* the law.
8.	*announcement*	Make the *announcement* today.
9.	*transfer*	You may *transfer* to the other bus.
10.	*discontinued*	That service has been *discontinued*.
11.	*whence*	You cannot see *whence* it cometh.
12.	*moderate*	There was a *moderate* rise in temperature.

B. Using Your Words

1. Write spelling words to complete these comparisons.
  a. *River* is to *tributary* as *tree* is to _____.
  b. *Hand* is to *gesture* as *face* is to _____.
  c. *Woodpecker* is to *drilling* as *mouse* is to _____.
  d. *Tree* is to *cherry* as *bush* is to _____.
  e. *Knowledge* is to *omniscience* as *time* is to _____.

2. Write the same spelling word (or a form of it) for both blanks in each sentence.
  a. My _____ will let me _____ from plane to bus travel.
  b. Kathy _____ her loud voice and spoke in a more _____ tone.
  c. The officer posted the _____ on the _____ board.
  d. A car would _____ a means of travel, but Father could not _____ to buy one.

3. Write *vary* or *very* for each sentence, changing forms as needed.
  a. The price of gasoline has _____ over the years.
  b. Some changes have been _____ rapid.
  c. Researchers find that people's opinions _____ widely.
  d. This is the _____ book I need.

Dictionary Practice

4. Find *constant*. Write the adverb form and its definition.

C. Building Words

1. Write the contraction for each phrase.
  a. we will   c. should not
  b. they are   d. where is

2. Add *-ing* to each word.
  a. transfer   c. compel
  b. gnaw   d. submit

3. Write correctly the noun in each sentence that should be a possessive form.
  a. The disciples were comforted by the Masters words.
  b. I like to read my oldest sisters book about flowers.
  c. These drawings are two pupils work.

4. Form spelling words by joining these roots and affixes.
  a. *-ion*: connect, express
  b. *dis-*: continued, appointed
  c. *-ness*: godly, happy

5. Write NEW WORDS that are different forms of these.
  a. disconnect   c. variance
  b. auditor   d. announcer

Bible Thoughts

Use a spelling word to complete this Bible verse.

6. "For bodily exercise profiteth little: but _____ is profitable unto all things" (1 Timothy 4:8).

71

13. *godliness*   "*Godliness* with contentment is great gain."
14. *happiness*   Joy and *happiness* are not the same.
15. *connection*   This *connection* seems loose.
16. *constantly*   He is *constantly* helping someone.

  I was *disappointed* by the *bulletin*.

  The *bough* crushed the *currant* bush.

B. 18 points
  1. a. bough
     b. expression
     c. gnawing
     d. currant
     e. eternity
  2. a. transfer, transfer
     b. moderated, moderate
     c. bulletin, bulletin
     d. afford, afford
  3. a. varied
     b. very
     c. vary
     d. very
  4. archaic

C. 22 points
  1. a. we'll
     b. they're
     c. shouldn't
     d. where's
  2. a. transferring
     b. gnawing
     c. compelling
     d. submitting
  3. a. Master's
     b. sister's
     c. pupils'
  4. a. connection, expression
     b. discontinued, disappointed
     c. godliness, happiness
  5. a. connection
     b. auditorium
     c. vary
     d. announcement
  6. godliness

LESSON 34

31	**32**	**33**
parable	education	auditorium
amendment	valuable	eternity
iniquity	arrival	gnawing
practicing	honorable	expression
strength	mirror	vary
grammar	estimate	constantly
column	quotation	announcement
effect	immediately	discontinued
additional	humanity	godliness
calendar	scenery	moderate
jealous	society	transfer
advanced	data	happiness
continued cont.	community	connection
Galatians Gal.	destination	enforce
Ephesians Eph.	description	afford
Song of Solomon Song of Sol.	believing	whence

A. Sounds and Letters Review

1. Write the spelling word with each spelling. Lesson numbers are in parentheses.

a. /e/ = *ea* (31) d. /ē/ = *ie* (32)

b. /f/ = *ph* (31) e. /ej/ = *ed* (32)

c. /sī/ = *ci* (32) f. /it/ or /āt/ = *ate* (33)

2. Write the spelling word that begins with

a. silent *h* (32). b. silent *g* (33).

3. For each sound spelled by double letters, write two words that have that spelling.

a. /m/ = *mm* (32) c. /n/ = *nn* (33)

b. /r/ = *rr* (32) d. /s/ = *ss* (33)

4. In which Lesson 33 word does *ss* help to spell /sh/ rather than /s/?

5. Which words begin with these consonant blends?

a. gr (31) b. pr (31) c. tr (33)

6. Write the words with these initial sounds.

a. /kw/ spelled *qu* (32)

b. /s/ spelled *sc* (32)

c. /ô/ spelled *au* (33)

d. /hw/ spelled *wh* (33)

7. Write the words with these final sounds.

a. /əm/ spelled *umn* (31)

b. /ôrs/ spelled *orce* (33)

72

A. 26 points

1. a. jealous
   b. Ephesians
   c. society
   d. believing
   e. education
   f. moderate
2. a. honorable
   b. gnawing
3. a. immediately, community
   b. arrival, mirror
   c. announcement, connection
   d. godliness, happiness
4. expression
5. a. grammar
   b. practicing
   c. transfer
6. a. quotation
   b. scenery
   c. auditorium
   d. whence
7. a. column
   b. enforce

See page 84 for test sentences.

B. Using Your Words Review

1. Write *synonyms, antonyms, homophones,* or *connotations* for each description.
   a. Words that have opposite meanings.
   b. Meanings or feelings suggested in addition to actual meanings.
   c. Words that sound alike but are not spelled alike.
   d. Words that have similar meanings.
2. Write the correct words.
   a. The improvement (affected, effected) more efficient use of fuel.
   b. Gravity (affects, effects) everything that is near the earth.
   c. The (affects, effects) of Galileo's discoveries continue to this day.
   d. Apples (vary, very) in color and shape.
   e. King Saul made some (vary, very) serious mistakes.
3. Write the spelling words that have these double meanings.
   a. (1) A glass that gives a reflection.
      (2) Show very clearly.
   b. (1) The reaching of a destination.
      (2) A person who comes.
   c. (1) Cause (something) to pass from one person to another.
      (2) A design that can be conveyed to another surface.
   d. (1) A change for the better.
      (2) An addition to an official document.

C. Building Words Review

1. Write the full word for each abbreviation.
   a. Eph.   c. blvd.
   b. cont.   d. pk.
2. Write the correct word for each sentence.
   a. (Its, It's) time to go home.
   b. Where is (your, you're) book?
   c. I wonder (whose, who's) calling me.
   d. Do you like (museums, museum's)?
3. Write the past form of each verb. If there are two different past forms, write both.
   a. vary   d. believe
   b. deal   e. steal
   c. drive   f. journey
4. Form closed compounds by joining each boldface word with the words after it.
   a. **light:** search, flash
   b. **wind:** mill, whirl
   c. **skin:** onion, sheep
   d. **sales:** clerk, man
5. Combine these roots and suffixes.
   a. vary + able   d. value + ation
   b. scene + ery   e. enforce + ment
   c. express + ly   f. estimate + ion
6. Write the spelling words that are roots of these derived forms.
   a. effectual (31)
   b. educational (32)
   c. transference (33)
   d. affordable (33)

73

B. 13 points
1. a. antonyms
   b. connotations
   c. homophones
   d. synonyms
2. a. effected
   b. affects
   c. effects
   d. vary
   e. very
3. a. mirror
   b. arrival
   c. transfer
   d. amendment

C. 34 points
1. a. Ephesians
   b. continued
   c. Boulevard
   d. peck
2. a. It's
   b. your
   c. who's
   d. museums
3. a. varied
   b. dealt
   c. drove, driven
   d. believed
   e. stole, stolen
   f. journeyed
4. a. searchlight, flashlight
   b. windmill, whirlwind
   c. onionskin, sheepskin
   d. salesclerk, salesman
5. a. variable
   b. scenery
   c. expressly
   d. valuation
   e. enforcement
   f. estimation
6. a. effect
   b. education
   c. transfer
   d. afford

Review Lesson 6—Test Sentences

1.	*degree*	The *degree* of damage was not known.
2.	*closet*	Paint the *closet* white.
3.	*pennies*	Ten *pennies* equal one dime.
4.	*agent*	An ambassador is an *agent* for his country.
5.	*greetings*	Paul sent *greetings* to the churches.
6.	*insects*	All *insects* have six legs.
7.	*search*	Did you *search* for your book?
8.	*couch*	We sat on a soft *couch*.
9.	*compass*	Take a *compass* with you on your hike.
10.	*taxes*	Publicans collected *taxes* for the Romans.
11.	*beef*	That farmer raises *beef* cattle.
12.	*voyage*	Paul's *voyage* to Rome was rough.
13.	*wolves*	False prophets are *wolves* in sheep's clothing.
14.	*vanity*	"All is *vanity*," said Solomon.
15.	*native*	This is our *native* land.
16.	*factories*	The *factories* are closed today.
17.	*delay*	The driver could not *delay* any longer.
18.	*poison*	Watch for *poison* ivy near that tree.
19.	*pavement*	The *pavement* on this road is new.
20.	*battery*	This *battery* is dead.
21.	*cliff*	The sheep had fallen over a *cliff*.
22.	*banking*	Father is *banking* the fire.
23.	*bull*	The *bull* was behind a strong fence.
24.	*tongue*	Guard your *tongue* carefully.
25.	*grief*	The prodigal son brought *grief* to his father.
26.	*drag*	Do not *drag* your chair.
27.	*lightning*	Franklin invented the *lightning* rod.
28.	*offer*	The men made no *offer* to help.
29.	*addressed*	Moses *addressed* the congregation.
30.	*credit*	Try to be a *credit* to your school.
31.	*leather*	The lineman wore *leather* boots.
32.	*priced*	This book is *priced* at five dollars.
33.	*assist*	Allow me to *assist* you.
34.	*breathe*	People with asthma cannot *breathe* well.
35.	*length*	The whale grew to a *length* of eighty feet.
36.	*required*	God *required* burnt offerings.
37.	*orchard*	The apple *orchard* was white with blossoms.
38.	*losing*	The clock seems to be *losing* time.
39.	*tickled*	Mother seemed *tickled* with her gift.
40.	*completing*	Jesus was *completing* God's will for Him.
41.	*nephew*	Paul's *nephew* warned him of danger.
42.	*chorus*	There was a sudden *chorus* of shouts.
43.	*introduced*	Have you been *introduced* yet?
44.	*contrary*	Jesus' life was *contrary* to the Pharisees'.
45.	*physical*	Doctors give *physical* examinations.
46.	*replying*	I am *replying* by telephone.
47.	*telegraph*	Samuel Morse invented the *telegraph*.
48.	*error*	There is an *error* in your spelling.
49.	*typewriter*	Put the *typewriter* on the table.
50.	*represented*	Candlesticks *represented* the seven churches.

Review Lesson 12—Test Sentences

1.	*attic*	The men were insulating the *attic*.
2.	*stock*	You may put *stock* in her words.
3.	*readily*	Jesus *readily* forgave the sinful woman.
4.	*public*	Zacchaeus made a *public* confession.
5.	*domestic*	The dog is a *domestic* animal.
6.	*construction*	Steel *construction* is strong.
7.	*defective*	Fred replaced a *defective* gear.
8.	*successful*	Paul's preaching was *successful*.
9.	*correction*	Make a *correction* in your books.
10.	*electricity*	Hand tools save *electricity*.
11.	*misspell*	Do you *misspell* many words?
12.	*quality*	The *quality* of your work is important.
13.	*industrial*	Ontario is an *industrial* province.
14.	*synagogue*	Jesus taught in the *synagogue*.
15.	*embarrass*	That did not *embarrass* her at all.
16.	*apostle*	Paul was an *apostle* of Jesus Christ.
17.	*chickenpox*	The baby has *chickenpox*.
18.	*inherit*	The meek will *inherit* the earth.
19.	*passover*	Christ is our *passover* today.
20.	*customer*	The *customer* returned the goods.
21.	*testament*	The lawyer wrote them a *testament*.
22.	*suggest*	May I *suggest* a book for you?
23.	*religious*	The Pharisees were a *religious* people.
24.	*generous*	Boaz was a *generous* man.
25.	*chocolate*	Do you have *chocolate* pie?
26.	*abundant*	Christ offers us *abundant* life.
27.	*territory*	That *territory* belongs to Canada.
28.	*currant*	We had *currant* jelly in our sandwiches.
29.	*principal*	The *principal* is not in school today.
30.	*pardon*	The prisoner received a *pardon*.
31.	*Psalms*	Asaph wrote *Psalms* 73 through 83.
32.	*rural*	A city is not a *rural* area.
33.	*fountain*	A *fountain* looks refreshing.
34.	*tabernacle*	The ark was in the *tabernacle*.
35.	*Nahum*	The Book of *Nahum* is very short.
36.	*foreign*	Have you visited a *foreign* land?
37.	*beautifully*	The birds sang *beautifully*!
38.	*museum*	A *museum* is always interesting.
39.	*groan*	There was a *groan* from the injured man.
40.	*bureau*	I keep that in a *bureau* drawer.
41.	*design*	Did you *design* this quilt?
42.	*Jehovah*	The Lord *Jehovah* is our God.
43.	*capable*	Mary is *capable* of helping you.
44.	*dying*	We watched the *dying* sunset.
45.	*supreme*	Jesus' sacrifice for sin was *supreme*.
46.	*annual*	We had our *annual* school picnic.

For numbers 47–50, write *only* the abbreviations or clipped forms.

47.	*exam*	*(examination)*	What day is our *examination?*
48.	*2 Cor.*	*(2 Corinthians)*	The minister read 2 *Corinthians* 5.
49.	*phone*	*(telephone)*	Our *telephone* is out of order.
50.	*Rev.*	*(Revelation)*	The last chapter in the Bible is *Revelation* 22.

Review Lesson 18—Test Sentences

1. *grieve*   "Do not *grieve* for me," Jesus said.
2. *league*   A *league* is an ancient measure of distance.
3. *depot*   The bus *depot* was crowded.
4. *veil*   Moses wore a *veil* over his face.
5. *ceiling*   Does the *ceiling* need to be painted?
6. *cedar*   Hiram sent *cedar* to Solomon.
7. *unbeliever*   Do not argue with an *unbeliever*.
8. *children's*   The *children's* boots are muddy.
9. *relief*   It is a *relief* to hear your voice.
10. *medium*   The color was *medium* brown.
11. *circulation*   Grandpa has poor *circulation*.
12. *burden*   The minister has a *burden* for his people.
13. *missionary*   The *missionary* came home.
14. *courtesy*   He had the *courtesy* to apologize.
15. *firmament*   God created the *firmament*.
16. *eternal*   We can trust God's *eternal* promises.
17. *furnace*   The *furnace* heated the house.
18. *merchant*   Is that a *merchant* ship?
19. *research*   You have done your *research* well.
20. *observation*   We watched from the *observation* deck.
21. *deliveries*   Our grocer makes *deliveries*.
22. *reserve*   The *reserve* has wild geese.
23. *scholarship*   This essay shows good *scholarship*.
24. *regularly*   We *regularly* pray before meals.
25. *tailor*   Is there a *tailor* in this town?
26. *failure*   There was a power *failure* last night.
27. *ignorant*   Sometimes we are *ignorant* of God's blessings.
28. *permission*   Sue has *permission* to leave.
29. *governor*   The *governor* was in town today.
30. *reverence*   Samuel showed *reverence* to God.
31. *channel*   The river *channel* is deep.
32. *natural*   Trees are a *natural* resource.
33. *adventure*   We had quite an *adventure* today.
34. *cheerful*   A *cheerful* smile is like a medicine.
35. *stretch*   Do not *stretch* the truth.
36. *fortunate*   They were *fortunate* to have heat.
37. *charity*   *Charity* is the love of God.
38. *disappointed*   I was *disappointed* not to go.
39. *moisture*   Fog is one form of *moisture* in the air.
40. *independence*   Panama gained *independence* in 1903.
41. *insurance*   The widow had no *insurance*.
42. *situation*   This *situation* is getting out of hand.
43. *delicious*   Mother serves *delicious* meals.
44. *machinery*   The *machinery* ran smoothly.
45. *publish*   Let us *publish* the Gospel to all.
46. *patience*   Your *patience* is appreciated.
47. *fashion*   Judy will *fashion* her clay into a cup.
48. *definition*   Which *definition* is correct?
49. *stationary*   A *stationary* object is not moving.
50. *appreciate*   I *appreciate* your help.

Review Lesson 24—Test Sentences

1. *pier* — From the *pier*, I can watch the boat.
2. *aware* — David was *aware* of God's presence.
3. *swear* — We must not *swear* oaths.
4. *irrigate* — The farmer plans to *irrigate* this field.
5. *radar* — *Radar* is used to check traffic speed.
6. *sincere* — Please accept my *sincere* apology.
7. *affair* — This *affair* does not concern you.
8. *who'd* — I saw the man *who'd* been sick.
9. *materials* — These *materials* are for my project.
10. *guard* — We must *guard* against envy.
11. *abroad* — The news of Christ's birth was spread *abroad*.
12. *ore* — Much copper *ore* is mined from open pits.
13. *source* — Christ is the *source* of true peace.
14. *lawyer* — A *lawyer* tried to trap Jesus.
15. *author* — God is the *author* of the Bible.
16. *glorify* — Our lives should *glorify* God.
17. *mortal* — We cannot trust in *mortal* man.
18. *what's* — Tell me *what's* wrong, and I'll help you.
19. *ordain* — The church plans to *ordain* a minister.
20. *quarrel* — Abram would not *quarrel* with Lot.
21. *mature* — She is *mature* for her age.
22. *jewel* — A *jewel* is a precious stone.
23. *bulletin* — Did you decorate the *bulletin* board?
24. *reducing* — *Reducing* cost increases profit.
25. *bruise* — These apples will *bruise* easily.
26. *Jerusalem* — The city of David is *Jerusalem*.
27. *preferred* — I would have *preferred* the other one.
28. *influence* — Do not let evil men *influence* you.
29. *produced* — More effort *produced* neater handwriting.
30. *develop* — Be careful not to *develop* bad habits.
31. *garage* — The *garage* door is open.
32. *division* — Do you think long *division* is hard?
33. *bough* — The *bough* of an oak caught Absalom.
34. *measure* — Be sure to *measure* carefully.
35. *nowadays* — Polio is rare *nowadays*.
36. *driven* — The snow was *driven* before the wind.
37. *devout* — Anna was a *devout* woman.
38. *shone* — The sun *shone* brightly through the window.
39. *account* — We must *account* for the lost apples.
40. *sought* — Jesus *sought* to save the lost.
41. *adjustment* — The *adjustment* screw was loose.
42. *baggage* — Take your *baggage* to that counter.
43. *series* — He asked a *series* of questions.
44. *hedge* — That *hedge* needs to be trimmed.
45. *buffalo* — The American *buffalo* is really a bison.
46. *journey* — Jacob made the long *journey* to Egypt.
47. *hygiene* — Good *hygiene* helps us stay well.
48. *scissors* — These *scissors* are sharp.
49. *basis* — On what *basis* did you conclude that?
50. *gentlemen* — Both *gentlemen* left early.

Review Lesson 30—Test Sentences

1.	*grease*	The pioneers often used bear *grease*.
2.	*further*	We plan to investigate *further* tomorrow.
3.	*prophecy*	Elisha's *prophecy* was fulfilled.
4.	*expensive*	That is too *expensive* for us.
5.	*disciples*	Then the *disciples* were glad indeed.
6.	*satisfactory*	Those plans are *satisfactory*.
7.	*audience*	Look at the *audience* as you speak.
8.	*fierce*	The devil is a *fierce* adversary.
9.	*necessary*	How much sugar is *necessary?*
10.	*prettiest*	Which do you think are the *prettiest* flowers?
11.	*baptism*	Glen was ready for *baptism*.
12.	*business*	This is called a *business* letter.
13.	*example*	Be a good *example* to others.
14.	*composition*	This *composition* is too short.
15.	*blizzard*	The *blizzard* came up very quickly.
16.	*unpleasant*	Present chastening is *unpleasant*.
17.	*dessert*	That *dessert* was delicious.
18.	*vice-president*	The *vice-president* of the board was absent.
19.	*disease*	Naaman had the *disease* of leprosy.
20.	*acquaint*	*Acquaint* yourself with truth.
21.	*theirs*	This table is *theirs* for today.
22.	*instruction*	Follow each *instruction* carefully.
23.	*clerk*	The *clerk* wrapped my package.
24.	*equipment*	Keep your *equipment* indoors.
25.	*kerosene*	We used a *kerosene* lamp.
26.	*pickles*	These *pickles* are too sour.
27.	*respectable*	He is a *respectable* person.
28.	*occur*	When did your accident *occur?*
29.	*yourselves*	You *yourselves* saw it happen.
30.	*weapon*	A bird can use its beak as a *weapon*.
31.	*court*	The basketball *court* was empty.
32.	*expedition*	The *expedition* leaves tomorrow.
33.	*elsewhere*	I was *elsewhere* at the time.
34.	*watchful*	A *watchful* person is careful.
35.	*accept*	Will you *accept* a suggestion?
36.	*forwarding*	He left a *forwarding* address.
37.	*excess*	The elephant weighed in *excess* of three tons.
38.	*worthy*	John did not feel *worthy* to baptize Jesus.
39.	*accident*	There was an *accident* last night.
40.	*volume*	Find the *volume* of this cube.
41.	*whatever*	I plan to be here *whatever* happens.
42.	*universal*	Smiling is a *universal* expression.
43.	*onion*	I like *onion* soup.
44.	*accurate*	That was an *accurate* statement.
45.	*beyond*	He worked *beyond* closing time.
46.	*knowledge*	I had no *knowledge* of that.
47.	*honesty*	*Honesty* helps friendships grow.
48.	*companion*	Love is a *companion* to kindness.

For numbers 49 and 50, write only the abbreviations.

49.	*mg*	*(milligrams)*	Medicine is measured in *milligrams*.
50.	*Blvd.*	*(Boulevard)*	The *boulevard* south of town is being repaved.

Review Lesson 34—Test Sentences

1. *effect* — The medicine had a bad *effect* on his heart.
2. *amendment* — Delete that last *amendment*.
3. *grammar* — We will not have a *grammar* lesson today.
4. *column* — He stood by a *column* of the old building.
5. *practicing* — I am *practicing* my penmanship.
6. *education* — A good *education* is important.
7. *parable* — Hear the *parable* of the sower.
8. *advanced* — He *advanced* by one step.
9. *iniquity* — God hates *iniquity*.
10. *calendar* — That *calendar* still shows March.
11. *Ephesians* — The Book of *Ephesians* is a letter.
12. *strength* — Samson had no *strength* left.
13. *additional* — I will give you an *additional* test.
14. *Song of Solomon* — *Song of Solomon* follows Ecclesiastes.
15. *valuable* — You are wasting *valuable* time.
16. *jealous* — Saul was *jealous* of David.
17. *Galatians* — *Galatians* tells of a special fruit.
18. *immediately* — Pam left *immediately*.
19. *arrival* — We waited for the *arrival* of the bus.
20. *community* — This *community* is new to me.
21. *scenery* — I watched the *scenery* from the window.
22. *honorable* — Joseph was an *honorable* person.
23. *mirror* — Please wipe the *mirror* for me.
24. *society* — Ants have a well-ordered *society*.
25. *estimate* — He will *estimate* the pig's weight.
26. *quotation* — That *quotation* is from Genesis.
27. *humanity* — We believe in Christ's *humanity*.
28. *believing* — The Israelites were *believing* a lie.
29. *destination* — Our *destination* is the same.
30. *eternity* — *Eternity* is immeasurable.
31. *data* — The scientist collected *data* about insects.
32. *discontinued* — His paper was *discontinued*.
33. *description* — Your *description* was helpful.
34. *vary* — Your answers may *vary* greatly.
35. *auditorium* — The *auditorium* was soon full.
36. *gnawing* — A rodent is a *gnawing* animal.
37. *constantly* — She was *constantly* helping.
38. *expression* — Do not use that *expression*.
39. *afford* — We cannot *afford* to become lazy.
40. *godliness* — *Godliness* includes many virtues.
41. *moderate* — The boy ate a *moderate* lunch.
42. *enforce* — The policeman must *enforce* the law.
43. *announcement* — I read the *announcement*.
44. *whence* — From *whence* did they come?
45. *connection* — This *connection* is loose.
46. *happiness* — Your *happiness* is important to me.
47. *continued* — The story is *continued* on page 34.
48. *transfer* — The bank agreed to *transfer* the money.

For numbers 49 and 50, write *only* the abbreviations.

49. *Eph.* (*Ephesians*) — *Ephesians* follows Galatians.
50. *cont.* (*continued*) — The story was *continued* on page 50.

Final Test—Test Sentences

1.	*copies*	Give two *copies* to your father.
2.	*tithe*	A *tithe* is a tenth.
3.	*oyster*	Lester's mother made *oyster* stew.
4.	*congress*	A *congress* makes new laws.
5.	*invoice*	That pink paper is the *invoice*.
6.	*tongue*	Christ's love is more than *tongue* can tell.
7.	*chorus*	We sang the *chorus* softly.
8.	*paragraph*	Indent each new *paragraph*.
9.	*wrestle*	Do not *wrestle* your problems alone.
10.	*attack*	Do not make an *attack* on his character.
11.	*automatic*	The plane has an *automatic* pilot.
12.	*pigeon*	There is a *pigeon* in the barn.
13.	*electrical*	An *electrical* storm lit up the sky.
14.	*bureau*	The *bureau* had four drawers.
15.	*syllable*	Pronounce each *syllable* distinctly.
16.	*everlasting*	He is the *everlasting* God.
17.	*believed*	The disciples *believed* and rejoiced.
18.	*principle*	Daniel was a man of *principle*.
19.	*reindeer*	Are there *reindeer* in America?
20.	*deceive*	We cannot *deceive* God.
21.	*surface*	On the *surface*, things seemed normal.
22.	*reverse*	His actions were the *reverse* of his words.
23.	*international*	All nations should obey *international* laws.
24.	*debtor*	Paul was *debtor* to both Jews and Gentiles.
25.	*dispatch*	I want to *dispatch* a telegram.
26.	*insurance*	The *insurance* building burned down.
27.	*especially*	That was *especially* kind of you.
28.	*guard*	The Jews set a *guard* at the tomb.
29.	*disappear*	Problems *disappear* through prayer.
30.	*who'll*	I don't know *who'll* come.
31.	*source*	God is the *source* of all good.
32.	*bruise*	There was a small *bruise* on her face.
33.	*hygiene*	We study *hygiene* in health class.
34.	*assured*	He has *assured* me that all is well.
35.	*percentage*	What *percentage* is my profit?
36.	*happiest*	He was the *happiest* one there.
37.	*choir*	The shepherds heard an angelic *choir*.
38.	*prophesy*	Did Isaiah *prophesy* of Christ?
39.	*vice-president*	The *vice-president* was busy.
40.	*exactly*	Do *exactly* as I tell you.
41.	*qualified*	She is well *qualified* for the job.
42.	*accept*	God did not *accept* Cain's sacrifice.
43.	*exclaimed*	"Help me!" *exclaimed* Frank.
44.	*calendar*	Please change the *calendar* page.
45.	*honestly*	We must make our living *honestly*.
46.	*auditorium*	The *auditorium* had three hundred fifty seats.

For numbers 47–50, write *only* the abbreviations or clipped forms.

47.	*etc.*	*(et cetera)*	The word *et cetera* means "and so forth."
48.	*Phil.*	*(Philippians)*	The pupils memorized *Philippians* 4:8.
49.	*exam*	*(examination)*	This *examination* is nearly over.
50.	*mm*	*(millimeter)*	The cardboard was one *millimeter* thick.

The Speller Dictionary

Full Pronunciation Key

Each entry word in the Speller Dictionary is followed by a phonetic spelling that shows its pronunciation. This pronunciation key lists all the symbols used in the phonetic spellings, and it shows how they should be pronounced.

A heavy accent mark is placed after the syllable that receives the primary accent. A light accent mark follows a syllable with a secondary accent. Observe the primary and secondary accents in the word *pronunciation*: (prə nun′sē ā′shən).

a	man, had	ô	fall, paw	
ā	ate, made	ôr	cord, or	
ä	ah, father	oi	oil, point	
är	park, star	o͝o	pull, took	
âr	care, fair	o͞o	blue, pool	
b	boy, tab	ou	loud, round	
ch	choose, such	p	pay, dip	
d	deer, lid	r	rod, near	
e	red, then	s	saw, gas	
ē	me, east	sh	she, dish	
f	for, if	t	top, wet	
g	girl, peg	th	thank, with	
h	have, his	th̲	the, weather	
i	it, dim	u	bud, sun	
ī	hide, wire	ûr	turn, herd	
îr	dear, deer	v	very, over	
j	jar, rejoice	w	we, away	
k	kin, week	y	you, canyon	
l	lot, deal	z	zone, daze	
m	my, some	zh	treasure, vision	
n	need, win			
ng	sing, rang	ə	represents *a* in *ago*,	
o	not, fox		*e* in *open*, *i* in *pencil*,	
ō	home, so		*o* in *wagon*, *u* in *cactus*	

Abbreviations

adj.	adjective
adv.	adverb
conj.	conjunction
interj.	interjection
n.	noun
prep.	preposition
pron.	pronoun
v.	verb
abbr.	abbreviation
cap.	capitalized
def.	definition
pl.	plural
sing.	singular
<	from
E	English
F	French
G	German
Gk.	Greek
Ital.	Italian
L	Latin
M	Middle
O	Old
Scand.	Scandinavian
Sp.	Spanish

A

a broad (ə brôd′), *adv., adj.* 1. Outside one's home country; in a foreign country: *He is traveling abroad.* 2. Outside one's home; outdoors: *You are too sick to be abroad.* 3. Widely; among many people: *Rumors spread abroad very quickly.*

a bun dant (ə bun′dənt), *adj.* More than enough; plentiful; ample. **—a bun′dant ly,** *adv.*

ac cept (ak sept′), *v.* 1. To take what is offered, usually with favor and gratitude: *Susan accepted the gift.* 2. To consent to; give an affirmative answer to: *I will gladly accept your invitation.* 3. To acknowledge as being true or satisfactory: *The teacher accepted Mark's answer.*

ac ci dent (ak′si dənt), *n.* 1. A harmful or unfortunate happening; mishap: *The man was injured in an automobile accident.* 2. An unplanned happening: *Gold was discovered in California by accident.*

ac cord ing (ə kôr′ding), *adj. Archaic.* In agreement; harmonizing. **—ac cord′ing ly,** *adv.* **—according to,** *prep.* 1. In agreement with: *The doctor's action was according to hospital rules.* 2. As stated or written by: *The Gospel according to Luke contains the story of the prodigal son.*

ac count (ə kount′), *n.* 1. A statement that explains something in detail; explanation. 2. Worth; value: *of little account.* 3. A record of money received and spent. **—v.** To consider; esteem: *Abraham is accounted a man of faith.* **—on account of,** *idiom.* Because of; for the sake of: *Many people were absent on account of the snowstorm.* **—take into account,** *idiom.* To make allowance for; consider: *You must take into account that a five-year-old does not have your experience.*

ac cu rate (ak′yər it), *adj.* Free from error; exactly according to the truth; correct:

accurate computation, an accurate thermometer. **—ac′cu rate ly,** *adv.*

ac quaint (ə kwānt′), *v.* To make familiar; cause to know well; inform.

ad (ad), *n.* An advertisement.

ad di tion (ə dish′ən), *n.* 1. The process of adding. 2. Something added, such as a room to a house. **—ad di′tion al,** *adj.* More; added; extra: *We took additional clothes along.* **—ad di′tion al ly,** *adv.*

ad dress (ə dres′, ad′res′), *n.* The writing on a letter or package that directs it to a certain person or company. **—v.** (ə dres′). 1. To write an address on (an envelope or a package). 2. To speak to, especially in a formal manner: *The president addressed the lawmakers.* 3. To devote energy to; apply (oneself) to: *Wayne addressed himself to solving the problem.*

ad just ment (ə just′mənt), *n.* A change made to cause something to fit, be suitable, or operate properly: *The mechanic made an adjustment on the engine.*

ad mit (ad mit′) *v.,* **ad mit ted, ad mit ting.** 1. To allow to enter. 2. To agree that something is true, often unwillingly; acknowledge: *Achan admitted that he had taken things from Jericho.*

ad vanced (ad vanst′), *adj.* 1. In front of others; ahead. 2. Well along, as in development, progress or age: *the advanced stage of a disease, advanced in years.*

ad ven ture (ad ven′chər), *n.* 1. A dangerous experience or undertaking: *Columbus's trip to America was quite an adventure.* 2. A difficult undertaking made exciting by the danger

adj.	adjective	*pl.*	plural
adv.	adverb	*prep.*	preposition
conj.	conjunction	*pron.*	pronoun
interj.	interjection	*sing.*	singular
n.	noun	*v.*	verb

it involves: *the adventure of climbing Mt. Everest.* **—ad ven′tur er,** *n.*

ad ver tise (ad′vər tīz′), *v.,* **ad ver tised, ad ver tis ing.** To give public notice of, as in a newspaper; announce. **—ad′ver tis′er,** *n.*

ad ver tise ment (ad′vər tīz′mənt, ad vûr′tis mənt), *n.* A public announcement, as in a newspaper; a printed notice.

af fair (ə fâr′), *n.* A thing that is done; matter; business: *Do not meddle into the affairs of other people.*

af ford (ə fôrd′), *v.* 1. To have sufficient time, money, or strength for: *Anyone can afford to be kind.* 2. To provide; give: *The food afforded Elijah the strength he needed.*

a gent (a′jənt), *n.* 1. One who has authority to act for a company or some other person; representative. 2. Any means by which something is done: *Water is an excellent cleaning agent.*

al li ga tor (al′i gā′tər), *n.* 1. A large, thick-skinned reptile that looks much like a crocodile. 2. Leather made from the skin of an alligator.

a mend ment (ə mend′mənt), *n.* 1. A change for the better; an improvement: *repentance and amendment of life.* 2. A change in or an addition to a law or other official document: *an amendment to the Constitution.*

an nounce (ə nouns′), *v.,* **an nounced, an nounc ing.** To make known publicly; proclaim. **—an nounc′er,** *n.*

an nounce ment (ə nouns′mənt), *n.* Something made known publicly; a proclamation.

an nu al (an′yoo əl), *adj.* 1. Happening once each year; yearly: *the annual flooding of the Nile River.* 2. Each year; per year: *Mr. Young's annual salary was $20,000.* 3. Living only one year: *The potato is an annual plant.* **—an′nu al ly,** *adv.*

anx ious (angk′shəs, ang′shəs), *adj.* 1. Troubled because of uncertainty; worried. 2. Bringing about or filled with uneasiness: *anxious hours.* **—anx′ious ly,** *adv.* **—anx′ious ness,** *n.*

a piece (ə pēs′), *adv.* For each one; each; individually: *five cents apiece.*

a pos tle (ə pos′əl), *n.* One of the early church leaders who had personally seen Jesus (1 Corinthians 9:1).

ap pear (ə pîr′), *v.* 1. To come into view; become visible. 2. To seem: *The corn appears to be growing well.* 3. To come before a public audience; present oneself: *The governor is to appear in town next week.*

ap pre ci ate (ə prē′shē āt′), *v.,* **ap pre ci at ed, ap pre ci at ing.** 1. To recognize the worth and importance of; value: *We can better appreciate good singing if we study music.* 2. To be thankful for: *I appreciate your thoughtfulness.* 3. To be aware of; discern; recognize: *appreciate delicate shades of meaning.* 4. To increase in value: *Real estate usually appreciates steadily.*

ap proach (ə prōch′), *v.* To move toward and come near to, in distance or time: *The plane approached the airport. We are approaching winter.* **—n.** 1. The act of coming nearer: *the approach of spring.* 2. A way by which to reach (something); access: *The approach to the house was overgrown with weeds.* 3. A method of dealing with a task or problem: *Your approach seems reasonable.*

ap prove (ə proov′), *v.,* **ap proved, ap prov ing.** 1. To consider favorably; be pleased with. 2. To agree to; consent to: *The board approved the plans.*

ar ri val (ə rī′vəl), *n.* 1. The act of arriving; the coming to a place: *the arrival of the visitors.*

2. A person or thing that arrives: *a bench for late arrivals.*

ar ti cle (är′ti kəl), *n.* 1. A thing; an item. 2. A composition printed in a book, newspaper, or magazine. 3. One of the words *a, an,* or *the,* used before nouns. *The* is the definitive article; *a* and *an* are indefinite articles.

as sem ble (ə sem′bəl), *v.,* **as sem bled, as sem bling.** 1. To come together for a meeting: *The Christians assembled in Mary's house.* 2. To bring together for a meeting: *The teachers assembled the students in the basement.* 3. To fit together the parts of; put together: *assemble a puzzle.*

as sist (ə sist′), *v.* To give help to; aid.

as sure (ə sho͞or′), *v.,* **as sured, as sur ing.** 1. To make sure; guarantee. 2. To state positively so as to convince: *The angels assured the women that Jesus had risen from the dead.*

at tack (ə tak′), *v.* 1. To set upon violently; assail. 2. To work at with vigor: *Charles attacked his homework immediately.* —*n.* 1. The act of attacking: assault. 2. A sudden onset, as of a disease: *an attack of malaria.* —**at tack′er,** *n.*

at tempt (ə tempt′), *v.* To put forth effort to accomplish; try; endeavor. —*n.* An effort to accomplish; a trying.

at tic (at′ik), *n.* The space between the upper story and the roof of a building.

au di ence (ô′dē əns), *n.* 1. A group of listeners. 2. A chance to be heard, especially in a formal manner before a person of high rank: *an audience with the king.*

au di to ri um (ô′di tôr′ē əm), *n.* A large room for public gatherings.

au thor (ô′thər), *n.* A person who brings something into being, especially something written.

au to mat ic (ô′tə mat′ik), *adj.* Happening or operating by itself: *an automatic reaction, an automatic transmission.* [from the Greek word

had, māde, stär, câre, red, mē, dim, hīde, not, hōme, ôr, oil, to͝ok, po͞ol, loud, sun, tûrn; ch, such; ng, sing; sh, she; th, with; <u>th</u>, the; zh, vision

ə represents *a* in *ago, e* in *open, i* in *pencil, o* in *wagon, u* in *cactus*

automatos (self-acting)] —**au′to mat′i cal ly,** *adv.*

a ware (ə wâr′), *adj.* Having knowledge; being conscious; perceiving. —**a ware′ness,** *n.*

B

bag gage (bag′ij), *n.* Bags, trunks, and other items that a traveler takes with him.

bank ing (bang′king), *n.* The business of accepting and protecting depositors' money, lending money, cashing checks, and so forth.

bap tism (bap′tiz′əm), *n.* 1. The application of water by which a person affirms his faith in Christ and becomes a member of a church. 2. An experience in which a believer identifies with Christ or with some aspect of Christianity: *the baptism of suffering.*

bap tize (bap tīz′, bap′tīz′), *v.,* **bap tized, bap tiz ing.** To apply water to (a person) as a sign of his faith in Christ and his acceptance into a Christian church.

ba sis (bā′sis), *n., pl.* **ba ses** (bā′sēz′). That upon which something rests; base; foundation: *the basis of a belief.*

bat ter y (bat′ə rē), *n., pl.* **bat ter ies.** 1. A cell or set of cells that store and supply electricity, as in a flashlight. 2. A group of similar things used together for one purpose; a set: *a battery of questions.*

beau ti ful (byo͞o′tə fəl), *adj.* Pleasing to see or hear; delightful. —**beau′ti ful ly,** *adv.*

beef (bēf), *n.* 1. The meat from an adult member of the cattle family. 2. *pl.* **beef** or **beeves** (bēvz). An adult member of the cattle family raised for its meat, as a cow, a steer, or a bull.

adj.	adjective	*pl.*	plural
adv.	adverb	*prep.*	preposition
conj.	conjunction	*pron.*	pronoun
interj.	interjection	*sing.*	singular
n.	noun	*v.*	verb

be lieve (bi lēv′), *v.,* **be lieved, be liev ing.** 1. To accept (something) as being true or real. 2. To accept the words of (someone) as truth: *I believe him.* 3. To have faith; trust: *believe in Jesus.*

be neath (bi nēth′), *adv.* Below; under; underneath: *the ground beneath. —prep.* Lower than; below: *beneath the tree.*

be yond (bi yond′), *adv.* Farther away, at or to a great distance: *He tried to hit the mark, but the arrow went beyond. —prep.* 1. On or to the far side of; farther on than, in distance or time: *beyond the house, beyond one hour.* 2. Over and above; out of the reach of: *beyond my understanding, beyond help.*

bind (bīnd), *v.,* **bound, bind ing.** 1. To tie together, as with string or rope. 2. To obligate, as with a promise: *A husband and wife are bound by their marriage vows.*

bliz zard (bliz′ərd), *n.* A severe snowstorm, usually with strong winds, blinding snow, and great cold.

blos som (blos′əm), *n.* A flower, especially on a food-producing plant: *bean blossoms, cherry blossoms. —v.* To open into flowers; bloom.

bor row (bor′ō), *v.* 1. To obtain (something) with the understanding that it will be returned. 2. To adopt and use as one's own, as a foreign word: *The word* sombrero *is borrowed from Spanish.* **—bor′row er,** *n.*

bough (bou), *n.* A branch of a tree, especially one of the main branches.

boul e vard (bool′ə värd′), *n.* A wide city street, often lined with trees. *Abbr.* **blvd.**

bound[1] (bound), *v.* Past tense of **bind.**

bound[2] (bound), *v.* 1. To spring, jump lightly: *He bounded across the floor.* 2. To spring back; bounce: *The ball bounded over my head. —n.* 1. A springing jump: *The dog cleared the creek in one bound.* 2. A springing back; bounce: *the ball's first bound.*

bound[3] (bound), *n.* A boundary; an edge. *—v.* To touch the boundary of; be next to: *Mexico bounds the United States.*

bound[4] (bound), *adj.* Going toward; on the way; destined: *bound for the promised land.*

breathe (brē<u>th</u>), *v.,* **breathed, breath ing.** 1. To draw air into the lungs and expel it again; inhale and exhale. 2. To send out; give as if by breathing: *Jesus' resurrection breathed new courage into the disciples.*

brook[1] (brŏŏk), *n.* A small stream; rivulet.

brook[2] (brŏŏk), *v.* To put up with; tolerate: *Saul would brook no rival for the throne.*

bruise (brōōz), *n.* An injury that does not break the skin, but causes a black-and-blue mark. *—v.,* **bruised, bruis ing.** 1. To cause a bruise. 2. To damage the outside of, as fruit: *Be careful not to bruise the peaches.*

buf fa lo (buf′ə lō′), *n., pl.* **buf fa los, buf fa loes,** or **buf fa lo.** 1. The bison of North America, a member of the cattle family that has a great shaggy head and short, curved horns. 2. One of several kinds of oxen that live in Asia and Africa, as the water buffalo.

bull[1] (bŏŏl), *n.* An adult male of the cattle family or of whales, seals, elephants, and other large mammals.

bull[2] (bŏŏl), *n.* An official document issued by a Catholic pope, usually a decree, and stamped with his official seal (bulla): *Martin Luther burned the bull that the pope had issued against him.*

bul le tin (bŏŏl′i tin), *n.* A brief public statement, especially of a news item.

burden

chocolate

bur den[1] (bûr′dən), *n*. A heavy load, either physical or mental. —*v*. To place a burden upon; load heavily; oppress: *The king burdened his subjects with many taxes.*

bur den[2] (bûr′dən), *n*. The prevailing idea; main thought; gist: *the burden of a sermon.*

bu reau (byŏŏr′ō), *n., pl*. **bu reaus** or **bu reaux** (byŏŏr′ōz). 1. A chest of drawers for clothing. 2. An office that provides a specific service: *a travel bureau.* 3. A government department: *the Census Bureau.*

bush el (bŏŏsh′əl), *n*. 1. A unit of dry measure equal to four pecks. 2. A unit of weight equal to the amount in a bushel: *A bushel of wheat is 60 pounds. Abbr.* **bu.**

busi ness (biz′nis), *n*. 1. What one is busy with; work; job. 2. Matter(s); affair(s): *Playing with fire is risky business. Do not meddle into other people's business.* 3. Buying and selling; trade: *Business is good today.* 4. A commercial operation, as a store or factory: *The business was destroyed by fire.* **—have no business,** *phrasal verb.* To have no right (to do something): *Achan had no business taking the silver.*

butch er (bŏŏch′ər), *n*. One who slaughters animals or sells meat. —*v*. 1. To kill (an animal) for its meat; slaughter. 1. To kill needlessly, cruelly, or in large numbers: *Haman planned to butcher the Jews.*

C

cab bage (kab′ij), *n*. A plant in the mustard family whose leaves grow tightly together in the form of a head; also, the head itself.

cal en dar (kal′ən dər), *n*. A table showing the months, weeks, and days of a year.

ca pa ble (kā′pə bəl), *adj*. Able, especially in an outstanding way: *capable of working, a capable seamstress.* **—ca′pa bly,** *adv.*

had, māde, stär, câre, red, mē, dim, hīde, not, hōme, ôr, oil, tŏŏk, pōōl, loud, sun, tûrn; ch, such; ng, sing; sh, she; th, with; <u>th</u>, the; zh, vision

ə represents *a* in *ago, e* in *open, i* in *pencil, o* in *wagon, u* in *cactus*

ce dar (sē′dər), *n*. 1. An evergreen tree in the pine family that has reddish, fragrant wood. 2. The wood of the cedar tree.

ceil ing (sē′ling), *n*. 1. The inside, overhead lining of a room. 2. The distance from the earth to the lowest layer of clouds: *a ceiling of 500 feet.* 3. An upper limit; a maximum, as a price: *The ceiling was $1,000.*

chan nel (chan′əl), *n*. 1. The bed of a stream or river. 2. A narrow sea that joins two larger bodies of water; a large strait: *the English Channel.* 3. The deepest part of a river, which carries the main volume of its flow and which ships can use: *The channel of the river was deepened.* 4. The means by which something is conveyed; avenue: *Prayer is a channel by which we can communicate with God.* —*v*. To convey as through a channel: *The gifts were channeled to needy people by various means.*

char i ty (char′i tē), *n., pl*. **char i ties.** 1. Christian love (1 Corinthians 13). 2. The giving of help to the poor; almsgiving; also, that which is given. 3. An organization that helps those in need.

cheer ful (chîr′fəl), *adj*. 1. Full of cheer; happy. 2. Willing; not grudging: *a cheerful helper.* **—cheer′ful ly,** *adv.* **—cheer′ful ness,** *n.*

chick en pox (chik′ən poks′), *n*. A contagious disease also called varicella. It usually affects children, and its symptoms are skin eruptions and a slight fever.

chil dren (chil′drən), *n., pl*. More than one child.

choc o late (chô′kə lit, chôk′lit, chok′lit), *n*. 1. A food made by roasting and grinding cacao

adj.	adjective	*pl.*	plural
adv.	adverb	*prep.*	preposition
conj.	conjunction	*pron.*	pronoun
interj.	interjection	*sing.*	singular
n.	noun	*v.*	verb

seeds, usually sweetened. 2. A drink made by mixing chocolate with water or milk and sugar: *hot chocolate.* —*adj.* Flavored with chocolate: *chocolate candy.*

choice (chois), *n.* 1. An act of choosing: *a wise choice.* 2. The person or thing chosen; selection: *Her choice was an apple.* 3. A variety from which to choose: *a wide choice of colors.* —*adj.* Of excellent character or quality: *Joseph was a choice young man.*

choir (kwīr), *n.* An organized group of singers; a chorus.

cho rus (kôr′əs), *n.* 1. The part of a song repeated after each stanza; refrain. 2. A simple, short, well-known song. 3. An organized group of singers; a choir. 4. An incident of many people speaking at the same time: *a chorus of approval.* —*v.* To Speak or sing all at the same time: *"Yes!" chorused the children.*

Chris tian (kris′chən), *n.* A person who believes in Christ and lives by His teachings. —*adj.* 1. In accordance with the teachings of Christ: *It is not Christian to hate one's enemy.* 2. Having to do with Christ or Christianity: *the Christian faith.*

cir cu la tion (sûr′kyə lā′shən), *n.* 1. A moving around or through in a circular manner: *the circulation of the blood.* 2. A spreading abroad, as of news or information: *the circulation of rumors.* 3. The number of copies distributed, as of a newspaper or magazine: *This magazine has a circulation of ten thousand.*

cit i zen (sit′i zən), *n.* A person who belongs to a certain nation, which he must support and honor and which gives him certain privileges: *a citizen of Canada.*

clerk (klûrk), *n.* 1. A person who sells goods in a store; salesperson. 2. A person who keeps records for a business, in court, etc.

cliff (klif), *n.* A high, steep slope of rock or clay; precipice.

clip[1] (klip), *v.*, **clipped, clip ping.** 1. To trim with scissors, clippers, or similar instruments; cut shorter. 2. To cut out, as from a newspaper or magazine. 3. *Informal.* To strike with a sharp blow.

clip[2] (klip), *n.* Something used to hold things together: *a paper clip.* —*v.*, **clipped, clip ping.** To hold or fasten together with a clip: *The teacher clipped a paper to each chart.*

clos et (kloz′it), *n.* 1. A small room in which clothing, household supplies, and other things are stored. 2. A small private room: *"Enter into thy closet"* (Matthew 6:6).

col umn (kol′əm), *n.* 1. A heavy post that supports a building, often made of stone; a pillar. 2. Anything slender and upright that resembles a column: *a column of numerals.* 3. A narrow, vertical section of print separated by blank space: *a column in a newspaper.*

com bi na tion (kom′bə nā′shən), *n.* 1. The act of joining or the state of being joined; union. 2. That which is formed by combining; compound. 3. The series of numbers that will open a combination lock.

com mu ni cate (kə myoō′ni kāt′), *v.*, **com mu ni cat ed, com mu ni cat ing.** To transmit ideas or knowledge to another person by words or other symbols.

com mu ni ty (kə myoō′ni tē′), *n., pl.* **com mu ni ties.** 1. The people living close together in a certain area. 2. Shared possession; common ownership: *The early church had a community of goods.*

com pan ion (kəm pan′yən), *n.* 1. One who accompanies someone; comrade. 2. One of a pair, as of shoes; mate: *Where is the companion to this glove?*

com pass (kum′pəs, kom′pəs), *n.* **1.** An instrument for determining direction. **2.** An instrument for drawing circles. **3.** The area within specified boundaries; range; scope: *There were five hundred people in the compass of his voice.* —*v.* **1.** To travel around (something); make a circuit of: *The Israelites compassed Jericho.* **2.** To hem in, surround: *The Roman army compassed Jerusalem.*

com plete (kəm plēt′), *adj.,* **com plet er, com plet est. 1.** Having all the necessary or normal parts; lacking nothing; entire. **2.** Wholly finished; done; concluded: *The plans are complete.* **3.** Thorough; perfect: *complete joy.* —*v.,* **com plet ed, com plet ing.** To finish; make complete: *Complete what you have started.* —**com plete′ly,** *adv.* —**com plete′ness,** *n.*

com po si tion (kom′pə zish′ən), *n.* **1.** The act of putting together to form a whole; also, that which is put together. **2.** Make-up; constitution: *The composition of water includes hydrogen and oxygen.* **3.** Something composed, especially a short written piece; essay.

con gre ga tion (kong′gri gā′shən), *n.* **1.** A coming together; assembly. **2.** A group of people assembled for a church service, especially the group that usually comes together for worship.

con gress (kong′gris), *n.* **1.** The lawmaking body of a nation, corresponding to the parliament of other nations. **2.** Any conference held to settle certain issues. **3. Congress.** The national lawmaking body of the United States, consisting of the Senate and the House of Representatives.

con nect (kə nekt′), *v.* **1.** To join to one another; fasten together. **2.** To relate, as a thought or action; associate: *We connect singing with worship.*

con nec tion (kə nek′shən), *n.* **1.** The act of joining or the state of being joined; union.

had, māde, stär, câre, red, mē, dim, hīde, not, hōme, ôr, oil, tŏŏk, pōōl, loud, sun, tûrn; ch, such; ng, sing; sh, she; th, with; t̲h̲, the; zh, vision

ə represents *a* in *ago, e* in *open, i* in *pencil, o* in *wagon, u* in *cactus*

2. Relationship; association: *Do you have any connection with that company?* **3.** A transfer in traveling, from one route or vehicle to another: *We could not make connections in that city.*

con stant (kon′stənt), *adj.* Without stopping; unceasing, continuous. —**con′stant ly,** *adv.* Very often; regularly: *He is constantly forgetting his books.*

con struc tion (kən struk′shən), *n.* **1.** The act of building or putting together; also, something that is built. **2.** A method or quality of building: *a house of excellent construction.* **3.** The arrangement of words and phrases in a sentence: *How should this construction be diagramed?*

con tin ue (kən tin′yōō), *v.,* **con tin ued, con tin u ing. 1.** To keep on without stopping. **2.** To go on after a pause; carry on: *The teacher continued reading the story the next afternoon. Abbr.* **cont.**

con trar y (kon′trer′ē), *adj.* **1.** Opposite: *The meaning of* despondent *is contrary to that of* joyful. **2.** (*also* kən trâr′ē). Inclined to oppose and contradict: *A contrary person is hard to work with.* —*n., pl.* **con trar ies.** The reverse; the opposite: *He did the contrary of what he was told.* —**con′trar′i ly,** *adv.* —**con′trar′i ness,** *n.* [< ME *contrarie* < L *contrarius* : *contra* opposite]

cop y (kop′ē), *n., pl.* **cop ies. 1.** A thing made exactly like another thing, as a picture, a printed page, or a piece of furniture; a duplicate. **2.** A single book, magazine, newspaper, etc., of those produced in one printing: *a copy of* Pilgrim's Progress. —*v.,* **cop ied, cop y ing.**

adj.	adjective	*pl.*	plural
adv.	adverb	*prep.*	preposition
conj.	conjunction	*pron.*	pronoun
interj.	interjection	*sing.*	singular
n.	noun	*v.*	verb

1. To make a copy of; reproduce. 2. To follow the example of; imitate: *Children often copy their parents.*

Co rin thi ans (kə rin′thē ənz), *n.* One of two books in the New Testament, each consisting of a letter written by Paul to the believers at Corinth. *Abbr.* **1 Cor., 2 Cor.**

cor rect (kə rekt′), *adj.* Free from errors; right: *a correct answer.* —*v.* 1. To change so as to be correct; make right: *Myron corrected his mistake.* 2. To take action to bring about improvement: *"Correct thy son, and he shall give thee rest" (Proverbs 29:17).* **—cor rect′ly,** *adv.* **—cor rect′ness,** *n.*

cor rec tion (kə rek′shən), *n.* 1. The act of correcting mistakes; also, an item corrected: *Several corrections need to be made.* 2. Discipline; chastisement.

couch (kouch), *n.* A piece of furniture, usually upholstered, upon which to sit or recline; a sofa. —*v.* To put into words; phrase: *Sarah couched her reprimand in tactful words.*

court (kôrt), *n.* 1. An open space surrounded by walls or buildings. 2. An area marked off for a particular game: *a basketball court.* 3. A king's residence and all his family members and attendants: *the court of Pharaoh.* 4. An assembly held by a king or a judge to administer justice: *The criminal was brought to court.* —*v.* 1. To seek the favor of; try to please: *Absalom courted the Israelites in order to gain support.* 2. To place oneself in a favorable position for something (harmful) to happen; invite: *Riding a bicycle "without hands" is courting an accident.*

cour te sy (kûr′ti sē), *n., pl.* **cour te sies.** 1. Politeness; thoughtfulness; good manners; civility. 2. A favor; an act of consideration: *It is a courtesy to offer one's seat to an older person.*

cred it (kred′it), *n.* 1. Belief in the truth or reality of something; faith; trust: *People should be able to put credit in our words.* 2. A reputation for honesty in money matters; trustworthiness in paying debts: *Persons who have good credit can borrow money easily.* 3. The privilege to buy on the promise to pay later: *The department store extended credit to Mr. Taylor.* 4. Honor; recognition: *credit for one's efforts.* —*v.* 1. To have confidence in; believe; trust: *I can easily credit what you are saying.* 2. To write down as paid; reckon: *The payment was credited to his account.* **—do credit to,** *phrasal verb.* To be an honor to; bring praise to: *David's victory over Goliath did credit to his reputation.*

cur rant (kûr′ənt), *n.* 1. A small raisin used in puddings, cakes, etc. 2. A small, sour berry, usually red, black, or white, used in making jelly and preserves. 3. The bush that produces currants. [from the French phrase "raisins de Corauntz," meaning "raisins of Corinth," the city that exported the raisins]

cur rent (kûr′ənt), *n.* A continuous movement, as of water; flow; stream: *the current of a river, a current of electricity.* —*adj.* Belonging to the present time; now occuring: *current events.* **—cur′rent ly,** *adv.*

cus tom er (kus′tə mər), *n.* A person who buys, especially as a regular shopper.

D

dash (dash), *v.* 1. To strike or throw violently, usually so as to shatter: *Moses dashed the tablets of stone against the rocks.* 2. To hurry; rush: *They dashed away.* 3. To complete hastily. Used with *down* or *off: She dashed off a*

data

depot

letter. —*n.* 1. A hurrying; rushing: *a dash to safety.* 2. A small amount: *a dash of salt.* 3. A punctuation mark (—) that indicates an omission or a sudden, sharp break in thought.

da ta (dā′tə, dat′ə, dä′tə), *n., pl. (but often considered singular).* Facts; information: *The Census Bureau collects data about the people living in the United States. Sing.* **da tum.**

dawn (dôn), *n.* 1. The first appearance of light in the morning; daybreak. 2. A beginning: *the dawn of a new age in history.* —*v.* 1. To begin to grow light in the morning. 2. To begin to grow clear to the understanding: *The truth dawned on him.*

dea con (dē′kən), *n.* An officer in the Christian church who is responsible for the care of needy members.

deal (dēl), *v.,* **dealt, deal ing.** 1. To act toward; treat: *Deal kindly with others.* 2. To have to do; pertain: *This book deals with spelling.* 3. To distribute; mete out: *Food was dealt to the hungry.* 4. To do business; buy and sell. 5. To give; deliver, as a blow: *The soldier dealt Jesus a slap with the hand.* —*n.* 1. An agreement, as to buy or sell: *make a deal.* 2. A portion; amount: *He spent a great deal of his money for transportation. She loved her little brother a great deal.* 3. *Informal.* A bargain: *He got a real deal at the sale.*

debt or (det′ər) *n.* One who owes something to another person.

de ceive (di sēv′), *v.,* **de ceived, de ceiv ing.** 1. To make (someone) believe a falsehood; mislead. 2. To misrepresent the truth; lie. —**de ceiv′er,** *n.*

De cem ber (di sem′bər), *n.* The last month of the year. *Abbr.* **Dec.**

de clare (di klâr′), *v.* 1. To state boldly and positively. 2. To announce formally; proclaim: *The United States declared war on Japan in 1941.* 3. To make known for the purpose of taxation:

had, mā̆de, stär, câre, red, mē, dim, hīde, not, hōme, ôr, oil, tŏŏk, pōōl, loud, sun, tûrn; ch, such; ng, sing; sh, she; th, with; th, the; zh, vision

ə represents *a* in *ago, e* in *open, i* in *pencil, o* in *wagon, u* in *cactus*

declare the goods that were purchased in a foreign country.

de fec tive (di fek′tiv), *adj.* Having a defect; faulty.

def i ni tion (def′ə nish′ən), *n.* An explanation that makes the meaning clear: *Give the definition of* entertain.

de gree (di grē′), *n.* 1. A step or stage, as in a process: *Learning is done by degrees.* 2. Amount; extent: *I have not studied physics to that degree.* 3. A unit of temperature measurement. 4. One of the 360 units into which a circle is divided, used for measuring angles: *There are 90 degrees in a right angle.*

de lay (di lā′), *v.* 1. To put off until later; postpone: *delay one's homework.* 2. To cause (someone) to be late: *A flat tire delayed me.* 3. To linger; loiter: *Do not delay when you are asked to come.* —*n.* The act of delaying; also, the condition of being delayed.

de li cious (di lish′əs), *adj.* Very pleasant and enjoyable, especially to the taste or smell: *a delicious dinner.* —**de li′cious ly,** *adv.* —**de li′cious ness,** *n.*

de liv er y (di liv′ə rē), *n., pl.* **de liv er ies.** 1. A setting free; release: *Israel's delivery from Egypt.* 2. A carrying and giving out; distribution: *mail delivery.* 3. A manner of speaking when giving a lecture, sermon, etc.: *Good delivery helps to make a speech effective.*

de pot (dē′pō, dep′ō), *n.* 1. A railroad or bus station. 2. A warehouse; storehouse. 3. An establishment where military equipment is manufactured, stored, or maintained. [< F *dépôt* < ML *depositum* something deposited]

adj.	adjective	*pl.*	plural
adv.	adverb	*prep.*	preposition
conj.	conjunction	*pron.*	pronoun
interj.	interjection	*sing.*	singular
n.	noun	*v.*	verb

de scrip tion (di skrip′shən), *n.* 1. The act of describing in words. 2. An account that describes: *Write a description of the fire.* 3. Sort; kind; variety: *flowers of every description.*

de sign (di zīn′), *n.* 1. An arrangement of details that is artistic and that serves a certain purpose: *an interesting design on a quilt, the design of the wing.* 2. A plan from which something is to be made; pattern. 3. Intention; plan: *Joseph's brothers had evil designs.* —*v.* To plan in detail: *to design a house.* —**de sign′er,** *n.*

des sert (di zûrt′), *n.* 1. Sweets served after the main course of a meal, as cake, pie, fruit, or pudding. 2. *British.* Fruit or nuts served after sweets at the end of a meal.

des ti na tion (des′tə nā′shən), *n.* The place to which a person or thing is going.

de vel op (di vel′əp), *v.* 1. To grow and mature; result: *Acts develop from thoughts.* 2. To work out in detail: *The author carefully developed his story.* 3. To make (an image on photographic film) visible by the use of chemicals.

de vout (di vout′), *adj.* Sincerely religious; active in worship and prayer. —**de vout′ly,** *adv.* —**de vout′ness,** *n.*

die (dī), *v.,* **died, dy ing.** 1. To stop living; become dead. 2. To cease to operate, burn, sound, etc.: *The engine died. The singing died out.*

dis ap pear (dis′ə pîr′), *v.* 1. To pass from sight; vanish. 2. To pass out of existence; go to nothing.

dis ap point (dis′ə point′), *v.* To fail to meet the expectation of. —**dis ap point′ed** (dis′ə poin′tid), *adj.* Having a desire frustrated; let down because of an unfulfilled hope.

dis ci ple (di sī′pəl), *n.* 1. One who accepts and follows a teacher or a teaching; follower. 2. One of the twelve men whom Jesus called to follow Him; apostle.

dis con tin ue (dis′kən tin′yōō), *v.,* **dis con tin ued, dis con tin u ing.** 1. To stop (an activity or occurrence that has been performed for some time): *discontinue train service, discontinue a job.* 2. To come to an end; cease: *The flow of our creek discontinues in dry weather.*

dis ease (di zēz′), *n.* 1. Sickness; illness in general: *the conquest of disease.* 2. A specific illness, as measles. [from *dis-* (not) and *ease*— not at ease]

dis patch (di spach′), *v.* 1. To send off, as a messenger or message to a particular person or place: *dispatch a telegram.* 2. To do (something) promptly and quickly: *The president dispatched his most important business first.* —*n.* A written message, especially an important or special message: *a dispatch about the earthquake.*

di vi sion (di vizh′ən), *n.* 1. The act of dividing; separation. 2. One of the parts into which something has been divided; portion; section. 3. The operation in arithmetic that is the inverse of multiplication. 4. A difference of opinion; disagreement: *There was a division among the Jews concerning Jesus.*

do mes tic (də mes′tik), *adj.* 1. Tame; not wild: *a domestic animal.* 2. Of the home or family: *domestic duties.* —*n.* A servant in the house, as a cook or maid. —**do mes′ti cal ly,** *adv.*

doubt (dout), *v.* To question the truth or reliability of something; hesitate to believe. —*n.* Hesitation or refusal to believe; uncertainty or unbelief. —**beyond a doubt** or **without a doubt,** *idiom.* Certainly; unquestionably. —**doubt′er,** *n.*

drag (drag), *v.,* **dragged, drag ging.** 1. To draw (something heavy) across the ground. 2. To move too slowly, as time.—*n.* 1. A hindrance; degrading influence: *a drag on his health.* 2. The resistance of air to the forward motion of aircraft.

drive (drīv), *v.,* **drove, driv en.** 1. To push; force; propel. 2. To operate (a vehicle).—*n.* 1. A small road from a highway to a building; driveway. 2. An inward pressure; urge: *a drive to succeed.*

drown (droun), *v.* 1. To die by suffocation in a liquid. 2. To kill by suffocation in a liquid. 3. To make (a sound) hard to hear because of a louder sound: *The noise of the jet drowned out our singing.*

du ty (do͞o′tē, dyo͞o′tē), *n., pl.* **du ties.** 1. What one should do; responsibility: *our duty to help each other.* 2. An assignment; a job: *a cleaning duty.* 3. A tax, usually on an item brought into a country.

E

ear nest[1] (ûr′nist), *adj.* Eager and serious; zealous: *an earnest effort.* **—in earnest,** *idiom.* Determined; serious: *Kenneth was in earnest about memorizing the entire chapter.* **—ear′nest ly,** *adv.* **—ear′nest ness,** *n.*

ear nest[2] (ûr′nist), *n.* 1. Money paid to bind a contract; deposit; security. 2. An assurance of something to come; token; pledge: *"the earnest of our inheritance" (Ephesians 1:14).*

ech o (ek′ō), *n., pl.* **ech oes.** A repeated sound caused by the reflection of an original sound. —*v.* 1. To reflect a sound or be heard as a reflected sound: *This hall echoes. My voice echoed.* 2. To repeat what someone else says: *The little boy echoed his big brother's words.* **—ech′o er,** *n.* [< ME < OF < L *echo* < Gk. *ēchē* sound]

ed u ca tion (ej′ə kā′shən), *n.* 1. Systematic training in various skills, habits, and characteristics through instruction and study. 2. Knowledge

had, māde, stär, câre, red, mē, dim, hīde, not, hōme, ôr, oil, to͞ok, po͞ol, loud, sun, tûrn; ch, such; ng, sing; sh, she; th, with; <u>th</u>, the; zh, vision

ə represents *a* in *ago, e* in *open, i* in *pencil, o* in *wagon, u* in *cactus*

and skills gained through study; that which one has learned: *His education was lacking because he had not applied himself to his lessons.*

ef fect (i fekt′), *n.* 1. That which is caused to happen; result: *the effect of the discovery.* 2. Power to produce a result; influence; effectiveness: *Eli's rebuke had little effect on his evil sons.* 3. *pl.* **effects.** Possessions; belongings: *personal effects.* —*v.* To bring about; cause (something) to happen: *The king effected some major changes.* **—in effect,** *idiom.* In essence, although not in actual fact; for all practical purposes: *To run away, in effect, is to admit guilt.* **—take effect,** *phrasal verb.* To become active; become effective or authoritative: *The new law takes effect immediately.*

e lec tri cal (i lek′tri kəl), *adj.* 1. Having to do with electricity. 2. Charged with or operated by electricity: *an electrical appliance.*

e lec tric i ty (i lek tris′i tē), *n.* A form of energy resulting from the motion of electrons and having the ability to produce heat, light, and motion.

else where (els′hwâr′), *adv.* In or to another place; somewhere else.

em bar rass (em bar′əs), *v.* To make self-conscious and ashamed; humiliate.

em broi der y (em broi′də rē), *n., pl.* **em broi der ies.** Artistic needlework; designs sewn in fabric or leather; also, the art of embroidering.

em ploy (em ploi′), *v.* 1. To use, as a means or an instrument: *Jacob employed deceit to obtain the blessing.* 2. To give a job to; hire.

en coun ter (en koun′tər), *n.* 1. A meeting with someone or something, especially when

adj.	adjective	*pl.*	plural
adv.	adverb	*prep.*	preposition
conj.	conjunction	*pron.*	pronoun
interj.	interjection	*sing.*	singular
n.	noun	*v.*	verb

unplanned. 2. A meeting of enemies; battle: *young David's encounter with Goliath. —v.* 1. To meet (unexpectedly). 2. To be faced with; struggle against: *encounter strong opposition.*

en force (en fôrs′), *v.,* **en forced, en forc ing.** To compel the observation of (a rule or law); cause obedience to: *enforce the speed limit.*

en gi neer (en′jə nîr′), *n.* 1. A person who operates or services engines; especially, the operator of a railroad engine. 2. A person who designs engines, roads, bridges, and so forth: *a civil engineer. —v.* To plan or manage skillfully: *The chairman engineered the project from start to finish.*

E phe sians (i fē′zhənz), *n.* The book in the New Testament consisting of Paul's letter to the church at Ephesus. *Abbr.* **Eph.**

e quip ment (i kwip′mənt), *n.* Tools and supplies with which work is done: *an electrician's equipment.*

er ror (er′ər), *n.* Something incorrect; a mistake: *a spelling error.* [< ME *errour* , < L *errare* to err]

es pe cial ly (e spesh′ə lē), *adv.* To a special extent; more than others; particularly.

es ti mate (es′tə mit), *n.* An approximate idea, especially about the answer to an arithmetic problem; a rough calculation. *—v.* (es′tə māt′), **es ti mat ed, es ti mat ing.** To form an approximate opinion about (a size, amount, etc.); calculate roughly.

et cet er a (et set′ər ə). And so forth; and the rest. *Abbr.* **etc.** [from the Latin words for "and other things"]

e ter nal (i tûr′nəl), *adj.* 1. Without end; everlasting; also, without beginning or end: *eternal life, the eternal God.* 2. Fixed; unchanging: *the eternal Word of God.*

e ter ni ty (i tûr′ni tē), *n., pl.* **e ter ni ties.** A duration without beginning or end; long, immeasurable duration as opposed to time.

ev er last ing (ev′ər las′ting), *adj.* Lasting forever; endless; eternal.

ex act ly (ig zakt′lē), *adv.* 1. In an exact manner; accurately; precisely: *Obey the directions exactly.* 2. Altogether; just: *It was exactly what I wanted.*

ex am (eg zam′), *n.* An examination.

ex am i na tion (ig zam′ə nā′shən), *n.* 1. The act of examining; inspection: *examination of the proof.* 2. A test of one's knowledge and skills.

ex am ple (ig zam′pəl), *n.* 1. A sample; representative specimen: *an example of his kindness.* 2. A person or thing worthy of imitation: *"Be thou an example."* 3. An arithmetic problem: *an example in addition.*

ex cess (ik ses′, ek′ses′), *n.* 1. A portion that is too much: *We sold the excess.* 2. That which is more than necessary: *excess in eating. —adj.* Extra; surplus: *excess weight.*

ex cite ment (ik sīt′mənt′), *n.* 1. The condition of having one's feelings stirred up; agitation. 2. A person or thing that stirs up feelings: *The new baby was an excitement to the whole family.*

ex claim (iks klām′), *v.* To speak suddenly and strongly; cry out.

ex er cise (ek′sər sīz′), *n.* 1. Use; practice: *the exercise of one's abilities, the exercise of care.* 2. That which improves one's strength or ability: *physical exercise, a reading exercise. —v.,* **ex er cised, ex er cis ing.** 1. To make use of; practice: *exercise kindness.* 2. To perform

expedition

fit

exercise or give exercise to: *exercise every day, exercise the mind.*

ex pe di tion (ek′spə dish′ən), *n.* 1. A trip for a special purpose, such as exploration; also, the persons, vehicles, etc., that go on such a trip: *an expedition to the South Pole.* 2. Speed and efficiency: *Elaine tidied the kitchen with expedition.*

ex pen sive (ik spen′siv), *adj.* Costing much money or loss; high priced: *The war, though quickly won, was expensive in terms of human lives.*

ex pe ri ence (ik spîr′ē əns), *n.* 1. Something that happens to a person, often unplanned: *a pleasant experience.* 2. Knowledge and skill gained by direct contact: *experience in farming.* —*v.,* **ex pe ri enced, ex pe ri enc ing.** To have happen to one; go through; endure or enjoy: *experience trials, experience great happiness.*

ex press (ik spres′), *v.* 1. To put into words; state: *express an idea.* 2. To indicate by action or look: *We can express joy by smiling.* 3. To squeeze out (a liquid): *The juice was expressed from the oranges.* —*n.* A fast means of sending something: *Send this package by express.* —*adj.* Fast; swift, as a means of transportation: *an express train.*

ex pres sion (ik spresh′ən), *n.* 1. The putting of thoughts into words; communication. 2. A particular word or phrase used in communication: *The expression "going to stay" has two meanings.* 3. The look on one's face: *a sad expression.* 4. A bringing out of the beauty, meaning, and feeling of a song, a story, etc.: *Read with expression.*

F

fac to ry (fak′tə rē), *n., pl.* **fac tor ies.** An establishment where things are manufactured.

fail ure (fāl′yər), *n.* 1. The fact or state of failing; also, a person or thing that fails: *The invention*

had, māde, stär, câre, red, mē, dim, hīde, not, hōme, ôr, oil, tŏŏk, pōōl, loud, sun, tûrn; ch, such; ng, sing; sh, she; th, with; <u>th</u>, the; zh, vision

ə represents *a* in *ago, e* in *open, i* in *pencil, o* in *wagon, u* in *cactus*

was a failure. 2. A failing to produce a harvest: *crop failure.* 3. Inability to pay debts; bankruptcy: *business failure.*

fash ion (fash′ən), *n.* 1. A way of making, doing, acting, etc.; manner: *The little boy was going about in a bewildered fashion.* 2. The kind of dress, manners, or speech that is the most popular (at a given time); style: *The fashion for the women in Rome was to braid strands of gold into their hair.* —*v.* To make; shape, mold: *fashion a knife out of a sharp piece of metal.*

fau cet (fô′sit), *n.* A device for controlling the flow of a liquid, as from a pipe; tap; spigot.

Feb ru ar y (feb′rōō er′ē), *n.* The second month. *Abbr.* **Feb.**

fierce (fîrs), *adj.* 1. Wild; savage; ferocious: *a fierce lion.* 2. Violent; raging; intense: *fierce hatred.*

fig ure (fig′yər), *n.* 1. A symbol that stands for a number; a digit: *the figure 7.* 2. A visible form, especially of a person; a shape: *a three-sided figure, a figure walking in the distance.* —*v.* 1. To use figures in calculation; compute. 2. To be noticeable; stand out: *Moses figures in Israel's deliverance from Egypt.*

fi nal (fī′nəl), *adj.* 1. At the end; last. 2. Conclusive; decisive: *the final authority.*

fir ma ment (fûr′mə mənt), *n.* The heavens; sky.

fit[1] (fit), *adj.,* **fit ter, fit test.** 1. Suitable: *fit to eat.* 2. In a good physical condition; healthy and strong. —*v.,* **fit ted, fit ting.** 1. To be suitable or proper for: *The punishment must fit the crime.* 2. To be of the proper size: *This boot fits well.* —*n.* The manner of fitting: *This shoe is*

fit   **generous**

adj.	adjective	*pl.*	plural
adv.	adverb	*prep.*	preposition
conj.	conjunction	*pron.*	pronoun
interj.	interjection	*sing.*	singular
n.	noun	*v.*	verb

a good fit. —**see fit** or **think fit**, *phrasal verb.* To consider best for the conditions: *Do as you see fit.* —**fit′ly**, *adv.* —**fit′ness**, *n.*

fit[2] (fit), *n.* 1. A sudden attack, as of a disease or an emotion: *a fit if epilepsy, a fit of anger.* 2. A short time of doing something that is hard to control; spell: *a fit of coughing.* —**by fits and starts**, *idiom.* Irregularly; not steadily: *work by fits and starts.*

for eign (fôr′in), *adj.* 1. Belonging to another country; not native: *a foreign language.* 2. Unfamiliar; strange: *Such an idea is foreign to me.*

for tu nate (fôr′chə nit), *adj.* 1. Happening by fortune; coming by favorable chance: *a fortunate turn of events.* 2. Favored with good fortune; blessed: *a fortunate son.* —**for′tu nate ly**, *adv.*

for ward (fôr′wərd), *adv.* Toward what is in front; onward; ahead: *March forward.* —*adj.* Bold; presumptuous: *Do not be so forward as to invite yourself.* —*v.* To send on, as mail: *The post office forwarded our mail after we moved.*

foul (foul), *adj.* 1. Very dirty; filthy; nasty. 2. Wicked; vile: *a foul deed.* 3. Unfavorable; adverse: *foul weather.* 4. Out of bounds: *a foul ball.* —*v.* To make dirty; pollute. —*n.* In a game, something done against the rules.

foun tain (foun′tən), *n.* 1. A stream of liquid forced into the air and falling in drops or in a spray. 2. A place where a jet of water is forced upward for drinking. 3. Source: *Jesus is the fountain of eternal life.*

fowl (foul), *n., pl.* **fowls** or **fowl.** 1. A bird, especially a large domestic bird, such as a chicken, that is raised for food. 2. The flesh of fowl.

fu ner al (fyōō′nər əl), *n.* A service held in connection with the burial of a dead body. —*adj.* Suitable for a funeral: *a funeral hymn.*

fu ri ous (fyōōr′ē əs), *adj.* 1. Full of fury; controlled by wild, fierce anger. 2. Fierce; raging: *a furious wind.* —**fur′i ous ly**, *adv.*

fur nace (fûr′nis), *n.* A structure containing an enclosed chamber in which a hot fire is made to heat a building, to melt metal, etc.

fur ther (fûr′thər), *adj.,* A comparative of **far.** Additional; more: *further explanation.* —*adv.* A comparative of **far.** To a greater degree; more: *He went further into detail.* —*v.* To help forward; advance; promote: *further the cause of religious freedom.* —*Usage note.* Use **farther** for measurable distances. Use **further** for nonphysical dimensions.

G

Ga la tians (gə lā′shənz), *n.* The book in the New Testament consisting of Paul's letter to the believers in Galatia. *Abbr.* **Gal.**

ga rage (gə räzh′, gə räj′), *n.* A building in which motor vehicles are parked or serviced.

gar bage (gär′bij), *n.* 1. Unwanted or unusable matter discarded from a kitchen, as peelings, eggshells, and spoiled food. 2. Trash; rubbish.

gen er a tion (jen′ə rā′shən), *n.* 1. A group of people born during the same period of time. 2. A step in a natural lineage: *Grandfather, father, and grandson are three generations.* 3. The production of something: *the generation of electricity.*

gen er ous (jen′ər əs), *adj.* 1. Willing to share freely; not greedy; liberal. 2. Gracious and noble: *The generous merchant bought the slave* *to free him.* 3. Abundant; large; plentiful: *a generous serving.* —**gen′er ous ly,** *adv.*

gen tle man (gen′təl mən), *n., pl.* **gen tle men.** 1. A man who is courteous and considerate. 2. Any man—a courteous term used in speaking about a man when in his presence: *This gentleman would like to speak with you.*

Geth sem a ne (geth sem′ə nē), *n.* An olive grove at the foot of the Mount of Olives in which Jesus prayed just before He was arrested.

glo ri fy (glôr′ə fī′), *v.,* **glo ri fied, glo ri fy ing.** 1. To give glory to; praise; worship: *glorify God.* 2. To make more beautiful: *At night the sky is glorified by millions of stars.*

gnaw ing (nô′ing). Form of **gnaw.** *v.* Chewing at and wearing away. —*n.* A constant dull feeling of distress or emptiness, as of hunger: *the gnawing in his stomach.*

god li ness (god′lē nis), *n.* The state of being godly; piety; holiness.

Gos pel (gos′pəl), *n.* 1. The Good News about salvation through Jesus Christ. 2. One of the accounts of Jesus' life and teachings written by Matthew, Mark, Luke, or John. 3. **gospel.** Anything which a person believes to be authoritative, especially when it is a substitute for the Gospel: *a gospel of being saved by works.*

gos sip (gos′ip), *n.* 1. Idle talk about other people and their affairs, often not true and sometimes malicious. 2. A person known to engage freely in gossip. —*v.* To take part in gossip; talk idly.

gov ern ment (guv′ərn mənt), *n.* 1. The ruling of a specific group of people, as a country or a state; jurisdiction. 2. Those who rule, as a king or president and his officials.

gov er nor (guv′ər nər), *n.* 1. The ruler of a state, province, city, etc. 2. A device that controls the speed of a machine.

had, māde, stär, câre, red, mē, dim, hīde, not, hōme, ôr, oil, tŏŏk, pōōl, loud, sun, tûrn; ch, such; ng, sing; sh, she; th, with; th, the; zh, vision

ə represents *a* in *ago, e* in *open, i* in *pencil, o* in *wagon, u* in *cactus*

gram mar (gram′ər), *n.* 1. The principles that govern the correct usage of a language. 2. Correctness in observing the principles of a language: *We study English to improve our grammar.*

grate ful (grāt′fəl), *adj.* 1. Appreciative; thankful. 2. Pleasurable and welcome: *the grateful sight of an oasis.* —**grate′ful ly,** *adv.*

grease (grēs), *n.* A thick, oily substance. —*v.* (*also* grēz), **greased, greas ing.** To apply grease or oil to: *grease a cake pan.*

greet ing (grē′ting), *n.* A friendly word, as to someone whom one has not seen for some time; a salutation.

grief (grēf), *n.* Deep sorrow; great sadness; also, a person who causes sorrow: *The wayward son was a grief to his parents.*

grieve (grēv), *v.,* **grieved, griev ing.** 1. To feel grief; mourn. 2. To cause grief to; sadden: *"Grieve not the holy Spirit of God."*

groan (grōn), *v.* To make a low sound because of pain, grief, or disappointment; moan. —*n.* The sound made in groaning; a moan.

gro cer y (grō′sə rē), *n.* 1. A store that sells food and household supplies. 2. *pl.* **gro cer ies.** Food and household supplies sold at a grocery.

guard (gärd), *v.* 1. To care for in order to keep safe; watch over. 2. To maintain control over; restrain: *Guard your temper.* —*n.* 1. A person or group who guards, especially one or more soldiers. 2. A careful watch: *The soldiers kept a guard on their prisoners.* —**off guard,** *idiom.* Unprepared; not watchful: *I was caught off guard by the question.*

adj.	adjective	*pl.*	plural
adv.	adverb	*prep.*	preposition
conj.	conjunction	*pron.*	pronoun
interj.	interjection	*sing.*	singular
n.	noun	*v.*	verb

H

hap pi ness (hap′ē nis), *n.* A state of being happy; joyfulness; gladness.

hap py (hap′ē), *adj.,* **hap pi er, hap pi est.** 1. Joyful and glad. 2. Satisfied; contented: *Be happy with what you have.* —**hap′pi ly,** *adv.*

head ache (hed′āk′), *n.* A pain in the head.

hedge (hej), *n.* A fence of bushes growing close together. —*v.,* **hedged, hedg ing.** 1. To surround with a hedge or with restrictions that hinder freedom: *to feel hedged in.* 2. To avoid giving a direct answer; evade a questions: *John hedged when his mother asked where he had been.*

height (hīt), *n.* 1. The distance from the bottom to the top of something; tallness. 2. A high place or position: *a mountain height.* 3. A very high degree: *the height of fame.*

heir (âr), *n.* A person who inherits or will inherit something.

hem[1] (hem), *n.* A finished edge on cloth or a garment, made by folding over the cloth and sewing it down. —*v.,* **hemmed, hem ming.** 1. To make a hem. 2. To surround and shut in; enclose: *hemmed in by mountains.*

hem[2] (hem), *n.* The sound made in clearing the throat, often used to cover embarrassment or to attract attention. —*v.,* **hemmed, hem ming.** To make the hem sound.

here to fore (hîr′tə fôr′), *adv.* Before this time; until now; previously.

he ro (hîr′ō), *n., pl.* **he roes.** A person who displays outstanding courage in time of danger.

hon est ly (on′ist lē), *adv.* In an honest manner; truthfully; fairly: *Deal honestly with everyone.*

hon es ty (on′is tē), *n.* The quality of being honest; uprightness; integrity: *Honesty compelled her to return the extra change.*

hon or a ble (on′ər ə bəl), *adj.* 1. Worthy of honor; noble: *an honorable deed.* 2. Having a sense of what is right and proper; noble; upright: *Joseph and Daniel were honorable men.* Also *British* **hon our a ble.** —**hon′or a bly,** *adv.*

Ho se a (hō zē′ə, hō zā′ə), *n.* One of the minor prophets; also, the Old Testament book that bears his name.

how's (houz). The contraction for **how is** or **how has.**

hu man i ty (hyo͞o man′i tē), *n., pl.* **hu man i ties.** 1. The human race; mankind. 2. The quality of being human; human nature. 3. *pl.* The study of classical Greek and Latin literature.

hum ble (hum′bəl), *adj.* 1. Low in station or rank; not important or grand; modest: *a humble cottage.* 2. Not proud; meek; lowly. —*v.,* **hum bled, hum bling.** To make humble; reduce the pride of; abase. —**hum′bly,** *adv.* —**hum′ble ness,** *n.*

hun ger (hung′gər), *n.* 1. A desire or feeling caused by the lack of food. 2. Any strong desire: *a hunger for companionship.* —*v.* To experience hunger.

hy giene (hī′jēn′), *n.* The science of health; the rules that promote good health.

I

ig no rant (ig′nər ənt), *adj.* 1. Having little or no education; untaught. 2. Lacking knowledge about a particular thing; uninformed; unaware: *I was ignorant of your plans.* —**ig′no rant ly,** *adv.*

im me di ate ly (i mē′dē it lē), *adv.* 1. At once; without delay. 2. Directly beside, behind, etc., with nothing between: *Sandra sat immediately behind Viola.*

in clude (in klōōd′), *v.,* **in clud ed, in clud ing.** 1. To have as one of its parts; contain: *The New Testament includes a number of Paul's epistles.* 2. To consider along with other items in a reckoning, as of a price. *The cost of labor is included in the price.*

in crease (in′krēs′), *n.* An amount added; a gain: *an increase of ten pounds.* —*v.* (in krēs′), **in creased, in creas ing.** 1. To make greater in amount, size, etc.; enlarge. 2. To become greater; grow; gain.

in de pend ence (in′di pen′dəns), *n.* 1. Freedom from control by others; liberty. 2. The state of not being dependent on others for one's needs; ability to support oneself.

in dus tri al (in dus′trē əl), *adj.* Of industry; relating to factories where things are made by machines, as distinguished from manual labor and farming: *an industrial worker.* —**in dus′tri al ly,** *adv.*

in fant (in′fənt), *n.* A very young child; baby. —*adj.* 1. For a very young child: *infant formula.* 2. Just beginning to develop; not long established: *an infant project.*

in flu ence (in′flōō əns), *n.* The power to cause something to happen without using force; also, a person or thing that has this power: *Older children have an influence on younger children; they are a good or a bad influence.* —*v.,* **in flu enced, in flu enc ing.** To have an effect upon, especially the mind; persuade; effect: *Peter tried to influence Jesus not to die on the cross.*

in her it (in her′it), *v.* 1. To receive something after someone dies; receive as an heir. 2. To receive (natural characteristics) from one's parents: *I inherited black hair from my father.*

had, māde, stär, câre, red, mē, dim, hīde, not, hōme, ôr, oil, tŏŏk, pōōl, loud, sun, tûrn; ch, such; ng, sing; sh, she; th, with; t̲h̲, the; zh, vision

ə represents *a* in *ago, e* in *open, i* in *pencil, o* in *wagon, u* in *cactus*

in iq ui ty (i nik′wi tē), *n., pl.* **in iq ui ties.** A great sin; wicked deed; injustice. [from the Latin prefix *in-* (not) and the word *aequus* (equal)—inequity, unfairness]

in ju ry (in′jə rē), *n., pl.* **in ju ries.** 1. A physical or mental hurt; harm; damage: *an injury to one's arm, an injury to one's reputation.* 2. Injustice; unfairness: *Jesus never did an injury to anyone.*

in sect (in′sekt′), *n.* A small animal with three body parts and six legs, as an ant, a fly, a bee, or a grasshopper.

in struc tion (in struk′shən), *n.* 1. The act of instructing; teaching; also, the material that is taught. 2. *pl.* Direction; orders: *The policeman received instructions to return to headquarters immediately.*

in struc tor (in struk′tər), *n.* One who instructs; a teacher.

in sur ance (in shŏŏr′əns), *n.* Protection against loss, provided when many people pay money (premiums) into a fund and it is used to pay their losses due to fire, theft, accident, etc.

in ter na tion al (in′tər nash′ə nəl), *adj.* 1. Relating to or dealing with various nations: *an international agreement, an international airport.* 2. Between two nations: *an international boundary line.* —**in′ter na′tion al ly,** *adv.*

in tro duce (in′trə dōōs′, in′trə dyōōs′), *v.,* **in tro duced, in tro duc ing.** 1. To make (a person) acquainted with (another person). 2. To bring into use or notice; launch: *introduce a new idea.* 3. To put in; insert: *introduce a breathing tube.* 4. To begin; start; open: *how to introduce an essay.*

adj.	adjective	*pl.*	plural
adv.	adverb	*prep.*	preposition
conj.	conjunction	*pron.*	pronoun
interj.	interjection	*sing.*	singular
n.	noun	*v.*	verb

in vi ta tion (in'vi tā'shən), *n.* A request extended for someone to come to a certain place or do a certain thing: an inviting.

in voice (in'vois), *n.* A list of items purchased, including the price of each item, discounts, or additional costs, etc.

ir ri gate (îr'i gāt'), *v.,* **ir ri gat ed, ir ri gat ing.** 1. To supply water to (dry land) for the purpose of raising crops. 2. To apply a stream of water to for cleansing; wash out: *The nurse irrigated the cut before the doctor put in stitches.*

J

Jan u ar y (jan'yoo er'ē), *n.* The first month. *Abbr.* **Jan.**

jeal ous (jel'əs), *adj.* 1. Spiteful through the fear of losing one's position to (a rival): *Saul was jealous of David.* 2. Demanding total love and obedience; not tolerating the worship of another person or thing: *The Lord is a jealous God.* —**jeal'ous ly,** *adv.*

Je ho vah (ji hō'və), *n.* The sacred Old Testament name for God, represented by LORD in most Bibles. [from the Hebrew letters for YHWH, related to *hayah* (to be)—"I AM" (Exodus 3:14)]

Je ru sa lem (jə roo'sə ləm), *n.* The ancient capital of Judah and Judea and the modern capital of Israel, located 14 miles (23 km) west of the Dead Sea and 2,550 feet (777 m) above sea level.

jew el (joo'əl), *n.* 1. A precious stone; gem. 2. A person or thing of rare excellence or value: *A true friend is a jewel.* —*v.* To adorn with jewels or things that look like jewels: *The night sky is jeweled with innumerable stars.*

jour ney (jûr'nē), *n., pl.* **jour neys.** A traveling from one place to another; trip. —*v.,* **jour neyed, jour ney ing.** To take a trip; travel.

ju ry (joor'ē), *n., pl.* **ju ries.** A group of persons (usually twelve) who are responsible to decide in court whether an accused person is guilty or innocent.

K

ker o sene (ker'ə sēn', kar'ə sēn') *n.* A thin oil distilled from petroleum and used in lamps, stoves, and engines; also called coal oil. Also **kerosine.** [< Gk. *kēros* wax + *-ene*]

king dom (king'dəm), *n.* 1. The land and people ruled by a king or queen; nation; realm. 2. A division of the things that exist in nature: *the mineral kingdom, the plant kingdom.*

kneel (nēl), *v.,* **knelt** or **kneeled, kneel ing.** To rest upon the bent knees, as for prayer.

knife (nīf), *n., pl.* **knives** (nīvz). An instrument with a sharp edge, used for cutting: *a paring knife, a mower knife.*

knock (nok), *v.* 1. To hit sharply with something hard, especially the knuckles. 2. To make the sound of knocking, as an engine. 3. To hit and cause to fall: *I did not mean to knock you down.* —*n.* A sound made by knocking.

knowl edge (nol'ij), *n.* 1. That which is known; known facts; information. 2. A knowing; familiarity with: *knowledge of good and evil.*

L

la bor (lā'bər), *n.* 1. Efforts; work; toil. 2. Working people as a group: *the needs of labor.* —*v.* To do work, especially hard work; toil. Also *British* **labour.** —**la'bor er,** *n.*

la dy (lā'dē), *n., pl.* **ladies.** 1. A woman who is courteous and considerate. 2. Any woman—a courteous term used especially in speaking about a woman when in her presence: *Who is the lady sitting beside you?* 3. **Lady.** A title used by women of high rank in England: *Lady Astor.*

laun dry (lôn′drē), *n., pl.* **laun dries.** 1. A room or building where clothes are washed. 2. Clothes to be washed or that have been washed. 3. The work of washing clothes: *Laundry was hard work before washers were invented.*

law yer (lô′yər), *n.* A person who has studied law and is authorized to give legal advice to people and represent them in court.

league[1] (lēg), *n.* A union of persons, groups of people, or nations for a specific purpose; an alliance. —*v.,* **leagued, leagu ing.** To form a league; ally. [< ME *liege* < MF *ligue* < OItal. *lega* < *ligare* to bind]

league[2] (lēg), *n.* An old measure of distance usually equal to about 3 miles (4.8 km).

leath er (leth′ər), *n.* An animal skin having the hair removed and having been prepared for use by tanning. —*adj.* Made of leather: *a leather belt.*

length (lengkth, length), *n.* How long something is, either in space or time; the distance from one end to the other or from the beginning to the end.

light ning (līt′ning), *n.* A sudden flash of light in the atmosphere caused by the discharge of electricity between electrified parts of a cloud or between a cloud and the earth.

lin ger (ling′gər), *v.* To stay on; tarry as though unwilling to leave: *They lingered in the city of Sodom.*

lone li ness (lōn′lē nis), *n.* 1. Sadness caused by a lack of companionship or sympathy. 2. The state of being without many people; desolateness: *the loneliness of the wilderness.*

had, māde, stär, câre, red, mē, dim, hīde, not, hōme, ôr, oil, tŏŏk, pōōl, loud, sun, tûrn; ch, such; ng, sing; sh, she; th, with; th, the; zh, vision

ə represents *a* in *ago, e* in *open, i* in *pencil, o* in *wagon, u* in *cactus*

los ing (lōō′zing), *v.* Present form of **lose.** —*n.* The act of giving up a possession through carelessness, by accident, or by natural process: *the losing of a tooth.* —*adj.* Not winning; with little chance for victory or success: *a losing battle.*

loy al (loi′əl), *adj.* Devoted and faithful, as to a responsibility, a person, or a government. —**loy′al ly,** *adv.*

M

ma chin er y (mə shē′nə rē), *n., pl.* **ma chin er ies.** Machines or machine parts as a group: *farm machinery, moving machinery.*

man u fac ture (man′yə fak′chər), *v.,* **man u fac tured, man u fac tur ing.** 1. To make (things) from raw materials, usually with machines and in large numbers. 2. To process (partially finished materials) into finished products: *manufacture steel wire into nails.* 3. To make up; invent; fabricate (something false): *manufacture a theory about how life began.* —*n.* The making or processing of things, usually in large numbers. —**man′u fac′tur er,** *n.*

ma te ri al (mə tîr′ē əl), *n.* 1. That of which something is made; matter; substance. 2. Cloth; fabric. —*adj.* 1. Natural; physical: *material possessions.* 2. Important; major: *A material factor in success is diligence and perseverance.*

ma ture (mə tŏŏr′, mə tyŏŏr′, mə chŏŏr′), *adj.* 1. Fully developed; completely grown; ripe. 2. Fully worked out, with the details well organized: *a mature plan.* —*v.,* **ma tured, ma tur ing.** To come or bring to full development: *Some children mature faster than others. The experiences of life help to mature us.*

adj.	adjective	*pl.*	plural
adv.	adverb	*prep.*	preposition
conj.	conjunction	*pron.*	pronoun
interj.	interjection	*sing.*	singular
n.	noun	*v.*	verb

mean while (mēn′hwīl′), *adv.* At the same time: *Alice washed the dishes; meanwhile, Amy swept the floors. —n.* The time between; meantime: *Since there was an hour to wait for the next plane, Mr. Sanders read in the meanwhile.*

meas ure (mezh′ər), *v.,* **meas ured, meas ur ing.** 1. To find the size, weight, length, etc., of (something). 2. To set apart or mark off by measuring: *The clerk measured off three yards of material for Mother.* 3. To be of a given size: *Typing paper measures 8½ x 11 inches. —n.* 1. A standard unit of measure, as a foot, a pound, or an hour. 2. A limit; bound: *joy without measure.* 3. Action: *a strong measure to enforce the law.* 4. A portion of music between two measure bars. **—measure up,** *phrasal verb.* To meet or fulfill, as an expectation.

me di um (mē′dē əm), *adj.* Of a middle size, position, or quality; neither very much nor very little: *medium heat, a medium height. —n., pl.* **me di ums** or **me di a.** That through which something is done; agency; means: *Money is the medium with which we buy and sell.* [< L < neuter of *medius* middle]

mer chant (mûr′chənt), *n.* A person who buys and sells goods for a profit, including a storekeeper. *—adj.* Having to do with merchandise; trading: *a merchant route.*

mer cy (mûr′sē), *n., pl.* **mer cies.** 1. More kindness than what is deserved or expected; compassion: *mercy on an offender.* 2. Something to appreciate; a blessing: *We should thank God for all the mercies He bestows upon us.* **—at the mercy of,** *idiom.* Completely in the power of; unable to avoid punishment from: *Saul was at the mercy of David, but David spared his life.*

Mes si ah (mi sī′ə), *n.* The Deliverer promised by God throughout the Old Testament, who would bruise the head of the serpent (Genesis 3:15); the "Anointed One" (Christ).

met al (met′əl), *n.* A substance that has a shiny surface, can be melted, can be drawn or hammered into various shapes, and is a good conductor of electricity. Iron, silver, and aluminum are metals, and alloys such as brass and steel are also metals. *—adj.* Made of metal: *a metal blade.*

meth od (meth′əd), *n.* 1. A way of doing something, especially by an organized plan: *a method of solving an arithmetic problem.* 2. Orderliness; organization: *Without a method we will not accomplish much.*

mil li gram (mil′i gram), *n.* One-thousandth of a gram. *Abbr.* **mg** (no period).

mil li me ter (mil′ə mē′ter), *n.* One-thousandth of a meter. *Abbr.* **mm** (no period).

mil lion (mil′yən), *n.* One thousand times one thousand; 1,000,000.

min er (mī′nər), *n.* A person who works in a mine.

mir a cle (mîr′ə kəl), *n.* 1. A supernatural happening or deed: *the miracles of Jesus.* 2. Something so wonderful or unexpected that it seems supernatural: *It was a miracle that no one was hurt.*

mir ror (mîr′ər), *n.* A glass in which a reflection can be seen; a looking glass. *—v.* 1. To reflect as a mirror does: *The still water mirrored the beautiful sunset.* 2. To express in accurate detail; show very clearly: *Mary's sad face mirrored her deep sorrow.*

mis sion ar y (mish′ə ner′ē), *n., pl.* **mis sion ar ies.** A person who spreads the Gospel: *All*

Christians should be missionaries. —adj. Of or about missionaries: *a missionary story.*

mis spell (mis spel′), *v.,* **mis spelled** or **mis spelt, mis spell ing.** To spell wrong: *It is a sign of carelessness to misspell many words.*

mod er ate (mod′ər it), *adj.* 1. Within proper bounds; not extreme; temperate: *a moderate speed.* 2. Of a medium or average size, quality, and so forth; sufficient but not extraordinary: *a moderate salary. —v.* (mod′ə rāt′), **mod er at ed, mod er at ing.** 1. To make or become less extreme or violent; restrain or abate: *The soldiers' presence moderated the fury of the mob. The storm moderated.* 2. To act as a chairperson; preside. **—mod′er ate ly,** *adv.*

mois ture (mois′chər), *n.* A slight wetness; water or other liquid scattered as tiny droplets in the air or across the surface of something.

mor tal (môr′təl), *adj.* 1. Subject to death; sure to die sometime: *mortal man.* 2. Causing or likely to cause death; deadly; fatal: *a mortal wound.* 3. Very serious; causing death to the soul: *a mortal sin. —n.* A being that is subject to death, especially a person: *We mortals must prepare for life after death.* **—mor′tal ly,** *adv.*

moss (môs, mos), *n.* A mass of very small green plants that grow close together in tufts or like a carpet on rocks, decaying logs, tree trunks, etc.

mu se um (myo͞o zē′əm), *n.* A building or room where items of certain interests are displayed, as of scientific, historical, artistic, and cultural interests.

mu si cal (myo͞o′zi kəl), *adj.* 1. Having to do with music: *musical symbols.* 2. Pleasing to hear; melodious: *a musical voice.* 3. Fond of or well taught in music: *a musical family.*

had, māde, stär, câre, red, mē, dim, hīde, not, hōme, ôr, oil, to͝ok, po͞ol, loud, sun, tûrn; ch, such; ng, sing; sh, she; th, with; <u>th</u>, the; zh, vision

ə represents *a* in *ago, e* in *open, i* in *pencil, o* in *wagon, u* in *cactus*

N

Na hum (nā′həm), *n.* One of the minor prophets; also, the Old Testament book that bears his name.

na tive (nā′tiv), *n.* 1. A person who has lived in a given area all his life: *a native of America.* 2. An animal or a plant that comes from a certain place: *The kangaroo is a native of Australia. —adj.* 1. Belonging to a person because of the nation he is from: *one's native language.* 2. Natural, not learned; inborn: *a native ability to write poetry.*

nat u ral (nach′ər əl), *adj.* 1. In accordance with nature; not altered by refining, training, or other factors: *natural resources, a natural response to an insult.* 2. Not learned; inborn; native: *a natural ability.* 3. True to life; realistic: *Her drawing looked really natural. —n.* A musical symbol that cancels the effect of a sharp or flat; also, a pitch not affected by a sharp or flat. **—nat′u ral ly,** *adv.* **—nat′u ral ness,** *n.*

Naz a reth (naz′ər əth), *n.* The town in southern Galilee where Jesus grew up.

nec es sar y (nes′i ser′ē), *adj.* 1. Needed to accomplish a particular result; required; essential: *Water is necessary to maintain life.* 2. That cannot be logically disproven; undeniable: *a necessary conclusion. —n., pl.* **nec es sar ies.** Something impossible to do without; an essential; a necessity: *the necessaries of life.* **—nec′es sar′i ly,** *adv.*

nei ther (nē′thər, nī′thər), *conj.* 1. Not either. Used with *nor* to indicate that two possibilities or alternatives are negative: *Neither she nor*

nephew   oyster

adj.	adjective	*pl.*	plural
adv.	adverb	*prep.*	preposition
conj.	conjunction	*pron.*	pronoun
interj.	interjection	*sing.*	singular
n.	noun	*v.*	verb

I will be able to attend. 2. Nor yet: *Pharaoh did not know the Lord; neither would he let Israel go.* —*adj.* Not either of two: *Neither boy was present.* —*pron.* Not either one (of two antecedents): *Both (children) like to read, but neither enjoys writing.*

neph ew (nef′yo͞o), *n.* The son of one's brother, sister, brother-in-law, or sister-in-law. [< ME *nevew* < L *nepos* grandson, nephew]

nick el (nik′əl), *n.* 1. A silvery-white metal. 2. A coin of the United States and Canada made from nickel and copper; a five-cent piece.

now a days (nou′ə dāz′), *adv.* In these days; at the present time: *Nowadays people travel 100 miles without thinking much of it.*

O

ob ser va tion (ob′zər vā′shən), *n.* 1. The act or practice of seeing and noticing: *Our observation is often much poorer than our sight.* 2. A close examination, as of data for scientific purposes; also, a record of such an examination: *the scientist's observations.* 3. The fact of being observed: *The thief escaped observation.* 4. A comment; remark: *the observation, "It could have been worse."*

oc cur (ə kûr′), *v.,* **oc curred, oc cur ring.** 1. To happen; take place; come about. 2. To be found; exist: *Three sets of double letters occur in the word* bookkeeper. 3. To enter one's mind; suggest itself: *It just occurred to him.*

of fer (ô′fər, of′ər), *v.* 1. To present for acceptance or rejection. 2. To present for consideration, as an idea; suggest; propose: *offer advice.* 3. To make an attempt at; try: *offer no resistance.*

—*n.* The act of offering: also, that which is offered: *an offer to buy a house.*

on ion (un′yən), *n.* The bulb of a plant in the lily family, having a sharp, strong odor and flavor.

op po site (op′ə zit), *adj.* Completely different in direction, meaning, or character; contrary: *East is opposite of west. Happiness and sadness are opposite feelings.* —*n.* A person or thing that is opposite: *A giant is the opposite of a midget.* —*prep.* On the other side from; across from: *the house opposite our house.* **—op′po site ly,** *adv.* **—op′po site ness,** *n.*

or chard (ôr′chərd), *n.* A grove of trees grown for their fruit.

or dain (ôr dān′), *v.* 1. To order; decree; establish: *The new law ordains more severe penalties for speeding.* 2. To appoint as a minister in a Christian church.

ore (ôr), *n.* Natural matter, as rocks, that contains a valuable metal or other substance: *iron ore, sulfur ore.*

o ver alls (ō′vər ôlz′), *n., pl.* Loose trousers, often with suspenders and a part that covers the chest, that are worn over other clothes to keep them clean.

o ver look (ō′vər lo͝ok′), *v.* 1. To fail to observe; miss: *Here are three problems that you overlooked.* 2. To disregard; excuse, as an offense: *The teacher overlooked our tardiness the first time, but warned us not to let it happen again.* 3. To provide a view from above: *The cabin overlooked the entire valley.* —*n.* (ō′vər lo͝ok′). An elevated place, as on a mountain, that affords a view of the scene below.

oys ter (oi′stər), *n.* A mollusk with a shell in two halves and joined along one edge, especially the common kind that is used for food or the related kind that produces pearls.

pajama

phone

P

pa ja ma (pə jä′mə, pə jam′ə), *n.* A loose-fitting garment in which to sleep, consisting of trousers and a shirt. Often plural. Also *British* **pyjama.**

par a ble (par′ə bəl), *n.* A short story that teaches a spiritual truth by the use of natural things.

par a graph (par′ə graf′), *n.* A group of sentences that develops one thought and that has the first line indented, usually a division of a longer composition. —*v.* To divide into paragraphs.

par don (pär′dən), *v.* 1. To forgive: *The Lord will pardon a repentant sinner.* 2. To cancel the penalty due to (an offender): *Washington pardoned the traitor.* —*n.* 1. The act of pardoning. 2. A document that declares a pardoning.

pass o ver (pas′ō′vər), *n.* 1. The lamb killed and eaten at the Jews' Passover feast. 2. **Passover.** The Jewish feast held annually in the spring to celebrate Israel's deliverance from Egypt, also including the weeklong Feast of Unleavened Bread observed immediately after the Passover night.

pa tience (pā′shəns), *n.* Calmness in enduring something unpleasant, as pain, trouble, or delay: *the patience of Job.*

pat tern (pat′ərn), *n.* 1. An arrangement of details according to a plan; a design. 2. A model or guide used to make something: *a shirt pattern.* 3. Any arrangement that occurs regularly: *a thought pattern.* —*v.* To follow (an example); copy: *pattern after the life of Christ.*

pave ment (pāv′mənt), *n.* A hard surface, as of stone or concrete, on which to walk or drive.

peck[1] (pek), *v.* 1. To hit with the beak or with something pointed. 2. To make by pecking: *The bird pecked a hole in the tree.* —*n.* A stroke made with the beak or with something pointed.

had, māde, stär, câre, red, mē, dim, hīde, not, hōme, ôr, oil, tŏŏk, pōōl, loud, sun, tûrn; ch, such; ng, sing; sh, she; th, with; <u>th</u>, the; zh, vision

ə represents *a* in *ago, e* in *open, i* in *pencil, o* in *wagon, u* in *cactus*

peck[2] (pek), *n.* A dry measure equal to one-fourth of a bushel or eight quarts. *Abbr.* **pk.**

pen man ship (pen′mən ship′), *n.* Handwriting, especially when it is of good quality.

pen ny (pen′ē), *n., pl.* **pen nies.** 1. A copper coin of the United States or Canada that is worth one cent. 2. Also *British* **pence.** A coin worth one-hundredth of a pound, or, prior to 1971, one-twelfth of a shilling.

per cent age (pər sen′tij), *n.* 1. Rate per hundred; part of each hundred: *the percentage that is commonly sold.* 2. Part; proportion related to a whole, but often in a more general sense than an exact part of each hundred: *Only a small percentage of the people could read and write in Bible times.*

per mis sion (pər mish′ən), *n.* Consent; authorization: *Father gave us permission to walk home.*

per son al i ty (pûr′sə nal′i tē), *n., pl.* **per son al i ties.** 1. The group of characteristics that make each person an individual, different from all other persons. 2. *pl.* Remarks of a personal nature about another person, usually to belittle him: *We should avoid personalities in our conversations.*

Phi le mon (fi lē′mən), *n.* The book in the New Testament consisting of Paul's letter to Philemon. *Abbr.* **Philem.**

Phi lip pi ans (fi lip′ē ənz), *n.* The book in the New Testament consisting of Paul's letter to the church at Philippi. *Abbr.* **Phil.**

phone (fōn), *Informal.* —*n.* A telephone. —*v.,* **phoned, phon ing.** To call with a telephone.

adj.	adjective	*pl.*	plural
adv.	adverb	*prep.*	preposition
conj.	conjunction	*pron.*	pronoun
interj.	interjection	*sing.*	singular
n.	noun	*v.*	verb

phys i cal (fiz′i kəl), *adj.* 1. Of the body, as distinguished from the mind or spirit; natural: *a physical illness.* 2. Of natural, tangible matter and the laws that govern it: *the physical world, a physical impossibility.*

pick le (pik′əl), *n.* A vegetable (especially the cucumber) preserved in salt water, vinegar, and other spices.

pier (pîr), *n.* 1. A structure extending out over water, used as a walkway or a landing place for boats; dock; wharf. 2. A solid support made of stone or concrete, usually with a bridge resting upon it; a pillar. 3. The solid portion of a wall between windows and doors.

pi geon (pij′ən), *n.* A bird with short legs, a small head, and a plump body; a dove.

plain (plān), *adj.* 1. Clear; simple to understand. 2. Without ornamentation or luxury: *a plain house.* 3. Solid colored; not figured: *plain cloth.* —*n.* A broad stretch of level, treeless land; a prairie.

poi son (poi′zən), *n.* 1. A substance that harms or kills a living organism. 2. Anything that is harmful to one's mind, morals, etc.: *the poison of jealousy.* —*v.* To harm or kill with poison: *poison one's mind, poison rats and mice.*

post of fice (pōst′ ô′fis), *n.* A government office that handles mail and sells stamps.

prac tice (prak′tis), *n.* 1. An action done over and over for skill, or done often as a custom: *the practice of writing neatly.* 2. Skill gained through practicing: *When I tried to skate, I discovered that I was out of practice.* —*v.,* **prac ticed, prac tic ing.** 1. To perform (an action) over and over to improve one's skill: *Practice*

making this letter. 2. To do often as a custom: *Practice kindness in dealing with others.* Also *British* **practise.**

pre fer (pri fûr′), *v.,* **pre ferred, pre fer ring.** 1. To value more highly; esteem above: *"in honour preferring one another."* 2. To choose (something) as being more desirable than (something else); like better: *Janet prefers cooking to sewing.* 3. To offer (in court); present: *Several charges were preferred against the accused man.*

pre pare (pri pâr′), *v.,* **pre pared, pre par ing.** 1. To make ready or get ready: *Mother prepared the lunches. The children prepared for school.* 2. To make (a finished product) by a certain method; process: *prepare aluminum from bauxite.* —**pre par′er,** *n.*

pret ty (prit′ē), *adj.,* **pret ti er, pret ti est.** Pleasing in appearance; lovely. —**pret′ti ly,** *adv.* —**pret′ti ness,** *n.*

price (prīs), *n.* 1. The amount asked or paid for an item that is for sale; the cost to the buyer. 2. The cost of anything: *a high price for one's carelessness.* —*v.,* **priced, pric ing.** 1. To set the price of: *During the gold rush, eggs in California were priced at $1 apiece.* 2. To ask about the price of: *price a used car.*

prin ci pal (prin′sə pəl), *adj.* Most important; main; chief: *"Wisdom is the principal thing."* —*n.* 1. A person who is at the head, especially in a school. 2. The money on which interest is paid. —**prin′ci pal ly,** *adv.*

prin ci ple (prin′sə pəl), *n.* 1. A truth, rule, or belief; a fundamental: *Love is the principle of Christian conduct.* 2. A scientific rule that explains how things act: *the principle of gravitation.* 3. High moral standards; integrity; uprightness: *a man of principle.*

pro cure (prō cyo͝or′), *v.,* **pro cured, pro cur ing.** To get; obtain, especially by difficult means.

pro duce (prə dōōs′, prə dyōōs′), *v.*, **pro duced, pro duc ing.** 1. To make; manufacture; yield. 2. To cause (a result); bring about: *Good thoughts produce good deeds.* —*n.* (prod′ōōs, prō′dōōs). That which is produced, especially by a garden: *selling produce at the market.* —**pro duc′er**, *n.*

pro nounce (prə nouns′), *v.*, **pro nounced, pro nounc ing.** 1. To say, with special attention given to the sounds: *Pronounce this word.* 2. To state formally and positively: *Judgment was pronounced.*

pro pel ler (prə pel′ər), *n.* A shaft with blades mounted on it at an angle, used to propel ships or planes.

proph e cy (prof′i sē), *n., pl.* **proph e cies.** The foretelling of future events; prediction; also, the thing foretold.

proph e sy (prof′i sī), *v.*, **proph e sied, proph e sy ing.** 1. To make a prophecy; foretell; predict. 2. To speak under the inspiration of God to instruct or encourage: *"Ye may all prophesy one by one" (1 Corinthians 14:31).*

prove (prōōv), *v.*, **proved, proved** or **prov en, prov ing.** 1. To show the truth or accuracy of. 2. To try out; test: *prove a new method.* 3. To turn out; be found to be: *The trip proved interesting.*

Psalms (sämz), *n.* The Old Testament book of hymns, most of which were written by David.

pub lic (pub′lik), *adj.* Having to do with all the people; used by all the people, owned by all the people, etc.: *public property, a public library.* —*n.* All the people: *His deed became known to the public.* —**pub′lic ly,** *adv.*

pub li ca tion (pub′li kā′shən), *n.* 1. The printing of books, newspapers, magazines, etc. 2. Something that is published, as a book or magazine.

had, māde, stär, câre, red, mē, dim, hīde, not, hōme, ôr, oil, tōōk, pōōl, loud, sun, tûrn; ch, such; ng, sing; sh, she; th, with; <u>th</u>, the; zh, vision

ə represents *a* in *ago, e* in *open, i* in *pencil, o* in *wagon, u* in *cactus*

pub lish (pub′lish), *v.* 1. To print and offer to the public, as a book, newspaper, or magazine. 2. To make known publicly; spread (information) abroad: *Do not publish everything you are told.*

puz zle (puz′əl), *n.* 1. A problem that is hard to solve. 2. A problem requiring patience and good reasoning ability, for which the solution is to be found as a form of recreation: *a jigsaw puzzle, a crossword puzzle.* —*v.*, **puz zled, puz zling.** 1. To baffle; perplex: *How he got up there puzzles me.* 2. To study (something difficult) so as to understand it: *puzzle over the strange writing.*

Q

qual i fied (kwol′ə fīd), *adj.* 1. Fitted (as for a responsibility) because of meeting certain standards; competent: *a qualified physician.* 2. Limited in some way; modified: *give only qualified approval.*

qual i ty (kwol′i tē), *n., pl.* **qual i ties.** 1. That which makes something what it is; a characteristic: *An important quality of clay is pliability.* 2. Kind; sort; type: *the quality of a sound.* 3. Degree of excellence: *good quality, poor quality.* 4. Merit; excellence: *Strive for quality in your work.*

quar rel (kwôr′əl), *n.* An unfriendly disagreement; a dispute. —*v.*, **quar reled, quar rel ing.** To take part in a dispute, usually by fighting with words.

quo ta tion (kwō tā′shən), *n.* The act of repeating the exact words of another speaker or writer; also, the words repeated: *a quotation from the Bible.*

radar   represent

adj.	adjective	*pl.*	plural
adv.	adverb	*prep.*	preposition
conj.	conjunction	*pron.*	pronoun
interj.	interjection	*sing.*	singular
n.	noun	*v.*	verb

R

ra dar (rā′där), *n.* An instrument that locates and tracks objects by beaming radio waves toward them and receiving their reflections. [from ra(dio) d(etecting) a(nd) r(anging)]

read i ly (red′ə lē), *adv.* In a ready manner; willingly, quickly and easily: *The students could answer the questions readily because they had studied the lesson well.*

re cent ly (rē′sənt lē), *adv.* In the recent past; not long ago.

rec i pe (res′ə pē′), *n.* 1. A list of ingredients, along with instructions for combining them, cooking them, etc., by which to prepare something to eat. 2. Any set of directions for doing something or achieving a certain result; a formula: *What is your recipe for growing such large potatoes?*

Re deem er (ri dē′mər), *n.* 1. Jesus Christ, who paid the price to redeem mankind from sin. 2. **redeemer.** A person who redeems another, as by purchasing his freedom from slavery.

re duce (ri do͞os′, ri dyo͞os′), *v.*, **re duced, re duc ing.** 1. To make less in number, size, weight, etc.; diminish. 2. To bring to lower condition: *The Egyptians reduced the Israelites to slavery. Fire reduced the building to ashes.* 3. To simplify (a mathematical expression): *reduce a fraction.*

ref er ence (ref′ər əns), *n.* 1. The act of referring; the calling of attention to a particular thing; mention: *a reference to the mildness of that winter. The Bible makes no reference to a death angel.* 2. A sentence or passage referred to, especially in the Bible. 3. A person who

can recommend someone, especially as to his working ability; also the recommendation of such a person: *Can you name a previous employer as a reference? —adj.* Used to obtain information: *A dictionary is an important reference book.*

re gard ing (ri gär′ding), *prep.* Concerning; about: *the news regarding the accident.*

reg u lar ly (reg′yə lər lē), *adv.* 1. Usually, customarily: *The stores are regularly open from dawn to dusk.* 2. Again and again; repeatedly. 3. With even spacing; uniformly: *The sick man seemed to be breathing regularly again.*

rein deer (rān′dîr′), *n., pl.* **rein deer** or **rein deers.** A large deer with branching antlers whose home is in northern regions. It is raised domestically as a pack animal and for its milk, meat, and hide. [< ME *reindere* < ON *hreinn* reindeer + ME *der* animal]

re lief (ri lēf′), *n.* 1. The act of relieving, as pain or difficulty; lessoning or removing. 2. That which relieves; help; aid: *The churches sent relief to their needy brethren.* 3. In sculpture, the projection of images from a surface: *a picture carved in relief.*

re lig ious (ri lij′əs), *adj.* 1. Having to do with religion: *a religious picture.* 2. Devoted to religion; devout: *a religious person.* 3. Strict; thorough; careful: *religious attention to the necessary details.* **—re lig′ious ly,** *adv.*

re ply (ri plī′), *v.*, **re plied, re ply ing.** To answer, either with words or with actions; respond: *He replied by turning on the light. —n., pl.* **re plies.** An answer; a response: *Please send your reply immediately.*

rep re sent (rep′ri zent′), *v.* 1. To stand for; symbolize: *The serpent on the pole represented Christ on the cross.* 2. To act for as agent: *An ambassador represents his country.* 3. To describe as having certain qualities; set forth:

The vacuum cleaner was not what the sales-man had represented it to be.

re quire (ri kwīr′), *v.*, **re quired, re quir ing.**
1. To need: *More workers are required.* 2. To demand; insist upon: *Our teacher requires neat handwriting.*

re search (ri sûrch′, rē′sûrch′), *n.* A thorough search for the facts about something, as by reading, experimenting, or asking the opinions of many people; investigation. *—v.* To conduct research; investigate. **—re search′er,** *n.*

re serve (ri zûrv′), *v.*, **re served, re serv ing.** To hold back; set aside for a certain use: *Ananias reserved some of the money but pretended to give it all. —n.* 1. Something set aside, especially public land: *a game reserve.* 2. A store, supply: *a reserve of extra energy.* 3. Self-control; temperance in speech and action: *A person who is too forward does not have much reserve.*

re spect a ble (ri spek′tə bəl), *adj.* 1. Worthy of respect: *a respectable citizen.* 2. Fairly good but not extra-ordinary; acceptable: *respectable grades.* **—re spect′a bly,** *adv.*

Rev e la tion (rev′ə lā′shən), *n.* The last book of the New Testament. *Abbr.* **Rev.**

rev er ence (rev′ər əns), *n.* 1. A feeling of deep respect; a mixture of fear and adoration. 2. An act of deep respect, as a bow: *Mordecai refused to do reverence to Haman. —v.,* **rev er enced, rev er enc ing.** To respect deeply; fear: *reverence the God of heaven.*

re verse (ri vûrs′), *n.* 1. The contrary; the opposite thing: *Coming is the reverse of going.* 2. A mechanism or setting that causes backward action. *—adj.* Opposite; contrary in position, order, direction, etc.: *the reverse side of a coin. —v.,* **re versed, re vers ing.** To change to the opposite, as a motion, a method, or a command: *reverse the flow, reverse a policy, reverse a previous order.*

had, māde, stär, câre, red, mē, dim, hīde, not, hōme, ôr, oil, to͝ok, po͞ol, loud, sun, tûrn; ch, such; ng, sing; sh, she; th, with; <u>th</u>, the; zh, vision

ə represents *a* in *ago, e* in *open, i* in *pencil, o* in *wagon, u* in *cactus*

ru ral (ro͝or′əl), *adj.* Having to do with the country as distinguished from the city; not urban: *rural living.*

S

sales man (sālz′mən), *n., pl.* **sales men.** A man hired to sell something.

sat is fac to ry (sat′is fak′tə rē), *adj.* Satisfying; adequate; acceptable: *The injured man was making satisfactory progress.* **—sat′is fac′to ri ly,** *adv.*

sat is fy (sat′is fī′), *v.,* **sat is fied, sat is fy ing.**
1. To fulfill, as a need, a desire, or an obligation: *satisfy one's thirst, satisfy a requirement.*
2. To remove doubt from; convince: *Father was satisfied that the man was telling the truth.*

scen er y (sē′nə rē), *n., pl.* **scen er ies.** The appearance of a landscape, especially when it has natural features that are beautiful.

schol ar ship (skol′ər ship′), *n.* 1. The achievements of a scholar; the learning of one who is diligent and able in study. 2. The character of a scholar: *Good scholarship must not cease after a person leaves school.* 3. Money given to a qualified student to help him continue his education.

scis sors (siz′ərs), *n., sing.* or *pl.* An instrument with two blades so positioned that they can be brought together to cut something, as paper or cloth.

Scrip ture (skrip′chər), *n.* The Bible or a passage from the Bible. [from the Latin word *scriptura,* related to *scriptus* (written)]

search (sûrch), *n.* 1. The act of looking for; a diligent seeking: *the search for the lost child.*

adj.	adjective	*pl.*	plural
adv.	adverb	*prep.*	preposition
conj.	conjunction	*pron.*	pronoun
interj.	interjection	*sing.*	singular
n.	noun	*v.*	verb

2. Careful examination or probing for a special reason: *a search of the burglar for hidden weapons.* —*v.* To conduct a search; seek for or examine: *search for a book, search a house.* —**search′er,** *n.*

se cret (sē′krit), *adj.* Not known to others: *a secret message.* —*n.* 1. That which is hidden or unknown: *the secrets of the ocean.* 2. A hidden reason; key: *the secret of success.* —**se′cret ly,** *adv.*

se cure (si kyŏŏr′), *adj.* 1. Safe: *The child felt secure in his mother's arms.* 2. Certain; assured: *There is a secure reward for faithfulness.* —*v.,* **se cured, se cur ing.** 1. To attach or close firmly; fasten: *secure a hook to the wall, secure a door.* 2. To get; obtain: *secure the necessary materials.* —**se cure′ly,** *adv.*

seek (sēk), *v.,* **sought, seek ing.** 1. To look for; try to find by searching. 2. To try to obtain or achieve: *seek help, seek peace.*

Sep tem ber (sep tem′bər), *n.* The ninth month. *Abbr.* **Sept.**

se ries (sîr′ēz), *n., pl.* **ser ies.** 1. A number of like things in a row; a succession, either in space or in time: *a series of windows, a series of events.* 2. A certain order: *an alphabetical series.*

se ri ous (sîr′ē əs), *adj.* 1. Not lighthearted; sober; thoughtful. 2. Grave; important; weighty: *a serious responsibility.* 3. Involving much harm or loss: *a serious accident.* —**se′ri ous ly,** *adv.* —**se′ri ous ness,** *n.*

ser vant (sûr′vənt), *n.* 1. One who serves, especially as a slave; a domestic. 2. One who serves in a responsible position: *"Moses was a servant of the LORD."*

se vere (sə vîr′), *adj.* 1. Stern; harsh: *a severe punishment.* 2. Very painful, violent, or stressful: *a severe headache, a severe storm, a severe temptation.* 3. Demanding; exacting: *New drugs must meet severe standards.* —**se vere′ly,** *adv.*

shel ter (shel′tər), *n.* 1. A covering or protection against the weather, danger, etc. 2. A refuge; protection: *shelter from persecution.* —*v.* To shield; protect.

shield (shēld), *n.* 1. A broad piece of defensive armor carried on the arm in ancient times. 2. Something that protects: *A broad hat is a good shield against the hot sun.* —*v.* To protect; guard: *shield a child from harm.*

shine (shīn), *v.,* **shone** or **shined, shin ing.** 1. To give forth light; glow. 2. To do very well; excel: *shine in one's schoolwork.* 3. To make shiny; polish: *shine the furniture.* —*n.* A brightness; glowing: *the shine of a fire.*

shone (shōn), *v.* Past form of **shine.**

sin cere (sin sîr′), *adj.* Not deceitful; honest; genuine: *sincere gratitude.* —**sin cere′ly,** *adv.*

sis ter (sis′tər), *n.* A daughter of one's father and mother.

sit u a tion (sich′ŏŏ ā′shən), *n.* 1. Condition as affected by circumstances; case: *one's situation in life.* 2. The place where something is located; position; location: *Because of its situation, the house was frequently flooded.*

so ci e ty (sə sī′i tē), *n., pl.* **so ci e ties.** 1. All people as a group: *the problems of society.* 2. All people of a particular group, as defined by time or place: *the society of Jesus' day, the American society.* 3. Companionship; association because of friendship; also, one's friends.

solve (solv), *v.,* **solved, solv ing.** To find the answer to (a problem).

Song of Sol o mon (sông, song əv sol′ə mən), *n.* The Old Testament book after Ecclesiastes, consisting of a song written by King Solomon. *Abbr.* **Song of Sol.**

sought (sôt), *v.* Past form of **seek.**

source (sôrs), *n.* 1. That from which something is obtained or an action comes forth: *One source of information is a dictionary. A thought is the source of a deed.* 2. The beginning of a brook or river, often a spring.

sta tion ar y (stā′shə ner′ē), *adj.* 1. In a fixed station; not moving; standing still: *a stationary vehicle.* 2. Not easily movable; not portable: *The sawmill was driven by a stationary diesel engine.* 3. Not changing; stable: *The price has been stationary for over a year.*

sta tion er y (stā′shə ner′ē), *n.* Writing materials, including paper, cards, envelopes, and sometimes pens and pencils.

steal (stēl), *v.,* **stole, sto len, steal ing.** 1. To take what belongs to someone else, without his consent and usually without his knowledge. 2. To win (love, loyalty, etc.) that rightly belongs to someone else: *Absalom stole the hearts of the people.* 3. To move secretly and quietly: *steal away for prayer.*

stock (stok), *n.* 1. Things kept in store for later use or to be sold; a supply: *a stock of food for the winter, a stock of merchandise.* 2. Farm animals; livestock. 3. The main stem of a plant, as the trunk of a tree. 4. *pl.* A framework with holes for the feet and sometimes the hands, used long ago as a means of punishment. —*v.* To store for later use or to be sold; supply or keep in supply: *stock food away, stock shelves with merchandise.* —*adj.* Commonly used, purchased, and so forth; standard: *shirts in stock sizes.* —**take stock.** To take inventory; evaluate one's situation.

stole¹ (stōl), *v.* Past form of **steal**.

stole² (stōl), *n.* A long scarf often made of fur, worn around the shoulders by women.

had, māde, stär, câre, red, mē, dim, hīde, not, hōme, ôr, oil, to͝ok, po͞ol, loud, sun, tûrn; ch, such; ng, sing; sh, she; th, with; <u>th</u>, the; zh, vision

ə represents *a* in *ago, e* in *open, i* in *pencil, o* in *wagon, u* in *cactus*

strength (strengkth, strength), *n.* 1. The quality of being strong; power; vigor; force: *the strength of the wind.* 2. Degree of intensity or concentration, as a color, a flavor, etc.: *When colors fade, they lose their strength.*

stretch (strech), *v.* 1. To extend by drawing: *stretch a rubber band.* 2. To extend one or more limbs, especially in reaching for something. 3. To continue throughout a given space or time; be continuous; spread or extend: *The wheat fields stretched for miles in every direction.* 4. To exaggerate: *stretch a story.* —*n.* An area; length; extent: *a stretch of sand.*

stroke (strōk), *n.* 1. A striking; knock. 2. One of a series of rhythmic pulses, sounds, etc.: *The clock sounded three strokes.* 3. A sudden attack that generally results in paralysis: *Grandmother suffered a stroke.* —*v.,* **stroked, strok ing.** To pass the hand over, usually to show affection; caress.

stud y (stud′ē), *v.,* **stud ied, stud y ing.** 1. To try to learn by reading, observing, and thinking. 2. To put forth diligent effort; try hard: *"Study to shew thyself approved unto God."* —*n., pl.* **stud ies.** 1. An effort to learn by reading, observing, and thinking. 2. A school subject, as reading, arithmetic, or history. 3. A room in which to study.

suc cess ful (sək ses′fəl), *adj.* Having sucess; resulting as desired; fruitful: *a successful invention.* —**suc cess′ful ly,** *adv.*

sug gest (səg jest′), *v.* 1. To set forth for consideration; propose: *What solution do you suggest?* 2. To cause one to think of (something related); bring to mind: *Snow and ice suggest winter.*

adj.	adjective	*pl.*	plural
adv.	adverb	*prep.*	preposition
conj.	conjunction	*pron.*	pronoun
interj.	interjection	*sing.*	singular
n.	noun	*v.*	verb

3. To indicate indirectly; hint: *The children's clothing suggested that the family was poor.*

su preme (sŏŏ prēm′), *adj.* 1. Highest; above all in authority: *a supreme court.* 2. Highest in degree, quality or importance: *The supreme test of love is to give one's life for another person.* **—su preme′ly,** *adv.*

sur face (sûr′fəs), *n.* 1. The outer face of something, usually the upper side: *the surface of the road.* 2. The mere ourward appearance: *On the surface it appeared as if the problem was solved.* —*v.,* **sur faced, sur fac ing.** 1. To put a surface on; make smooth and even: *surface a road.* 2. To come to the surface of water: *The whale surfaced and took several breaths.* 3. To become evident as if by surfacing; appear: *A new problem has surfaced.*

swear (swâr), *v.,* **swore, sworn, swear ing.** 1. To make an oath; lift the right hand in appeal to God to confirm the truthfulness of one's statements: *Jesus said, "Swear not at all" (Matthew 5:34).* 2. To use profane language; curse.

syl la ble (sil′ə bəl), *n.* 1. A word or part of a word uttered as a unit, having one vowel sound and often one or more consonant sounds. 2. A division of a printed word that may be separated from the rest of the word at the end of a line (unless it consists of only one letter at the beginning or end of a word).

syn a gogue (sin′ə gog′, sin′ə gôg′), *n.* A building used by the Jews for religious meetings. [from the Greek prefix *syn-* (together) and the word *agein* (bring)]

T

tab er na cle (tab′ər nak′əl), *n.* 1. In the Bible, a temporary dwelling; tent; particularly, the movable sanctuary used by the Israelites on their journey to Canaan. 2. The human body, regarded as a temporary dwelling place of the soul (2 Peter 1:14).

tai lor (tā′lər), *n.* A person who makes outer clothing to order. —*v.* 1. To work as a tailor. 2. To make (something) suitable for a specific purpose: *The story was tailored for young readers.*

tax (taks), *n.* Money paid by people and businesses to the government and used to hire public employees, to maintain roads, to defend the nation, etc. —*v.* 1. To require (someone) to pay a tax. 3. To place a heavy demand upon; burden: *The heavy load taxed his strength.*

tel e graph (tel′i graf′), *n.* A device or system used to transmit coded messages by wire or radio. —*v.* To send a message by telegraph. [< Gk. *tēle* far off + Gk. *graphē* writing]

tel e phone (tel′ə fōn′), *n.* A device or system used to transmit speech or sound by wire or radio. —*v.,* **tel e phoned, tel e phon ing.** To use a telephone to communicate with (someone).

ter ri to ry (ter′i tôr′ē), *n.* 1. A region; land, especially when it belongs to a particular person or nation: *Mexican territory.* 2. A tract of land owned and governed by a nation and not incorporated as a state or province: *the Northwest Territories.*

tes ta ment (tes′tə mənt), *n.* 1. Instructions that state what is to be done with a person's property after he dies; a will. 2. **Testament.** One of the two main divisions of the Bible; the Old or New Testament (usually the New Testament).

theirs (t͟hârz), *pron.* Something belonging to them: *That car is theirs.*

there fore (thâr′fôr′), *adv.* For that reason: *"I believed, and therefore have I spoken."*

there's (thârz). Contraction for **there has** or **there is.**

they're (thâr). Contraction for **they are.**

tick le (tik′əl), *v.,* **tick led, tick ling.** 1. To touch (someone) in such a way that it causes him to laugh or twitch. 2. To tingle or itch: *My arm tickles.* 3. To please; delight: *The little girl was tickled with her new shoes.* —*n.* A tingling or itchy feeling: *A tickle in his throat made him cough.*

tithe (tīth), *n.* A tenth (of one's wages, harvest, etc.); the fraction established in the Old Testament as the portion belonging to God (Malachi 3:8–12). —*v.,* **tithed, tith ing.** To give as a tithe.

tongue (tung), *n.* 1. The muscular organ in the mouth, used for tasting and (in man) for speaking. 2. Something that resembles the tongue: *a wagon tongue.* 3. A way of talking; speech: *a gracious tongue.* 4. A language: *an unknown tongue.* —**hold one's tongue.** To refrain from speaking, keep still.

tow el (tou′əl), *n.* A piece of cloth or paper used to dry something.

traf fic (traf′ik), *n.* 1. People and vehicles moving along a way of travel: *a large flow of traffic.* 2. Buying and selling; trade; market (often immoral and illegal): *slave traffic in the 1800s.* —*v.,* **traf ficked, traf fick ing.** To buy and sell; deal (often illegally): *The criminals trafficked in stolen goods.* —**traf′fick er,** *n.*

trans fer (trans fûr′, trans′fər), *v.,* **trans ferred, trans fer ring.** 1. To cause (something) to pass from one person or thing to another. 2. To pass from one vehicle or route to another in travel: *transfer from bus to train.* 3. To convey a drawing on special paper to some other surface. —*n.* (trans′fər). 1. The act of transferring. 2. A ticket that allows a passenger to transfer. 3. A

had, māde, stär, câre, red, mē, dim, hīde, not, hōme, ôr, oil, to͝ok, po͞ol, loud, sun, tûrn; ch, such; ng, sing; sh, she; th, with; th, the; zh, vision

ə represents *a* in *ago, e* in *open, i* in *pencil, o* in *wagon, u* in *cactus*

drawing or design that can be or has been conveyed to another surface.

type writ er (tīp′rī′tər), *n.* A machine for writing that produces printed characters.

U

un be liev er (un′bi lē′vər), *n.* A person who does not believe, especially one who does not have religious beliefs.

u ni ver sal (yo͞o′nə vûr′səl), *adj.* 1. Having to do with all, especially with all people: *the universal need for salvation.* 2. Existing or happening everywhere: *Walking is a universal activity.* —**u′ni ver′sal ly,** *adv.*

un pleas ant (un plez′ənt), *adj.* Not pleasant; not enjoyable. —**un pleas′ant ly,** *adv.* —**un pleas′ant ness,** *n.*

u su al ly (yo͞o′zho͞o ə lē), *adv.* Commonly; most generally; customarily: *There are usually five school days in a week.*

V

val u a ble (val′yo͞o ə bəl, val′yə bəl), *adj.* Having much value; precious in terms of money or some other standard: *valuable tools, valuable advice.* —*n.* Something that has value, as an article of gold or silver: *Valuables are commonly stored at banks in safe-deposit boxes.*

van i ty (van′i tē), *n., pl.* **van i ties.** 1. The quality of being vain; pride and conceit: *Haman suffered for his vanity.* 2. The lack of true and lasting worth: *the vanity of riches.* 3. A table or counter with drawers and an upright mirror; a dressing table.

adj.	adjective	*pl.*	plural
adv.	adverb	*prep.*	preposition
conj.	conjunction	*pron.*	pronoun
interj.	interjection	*sing.*	singular
n.	noun	*v.*	verb

var y (vâr′ē), *v.*, **var ied, var y ing.** 1. To change (something); make (something) different: *vary the loudness of singing.* 2. To change; be different: *The number of daylight hours varies throughout the year.*

veil (vāl), *n.* 1. A piece of material worn or hung up to hide something: *the veil on Moses' face, the veil in the temple.* 2. Anything that hides like a veil: *a veil of fog.* —*v.* To cover or hide with or as with a veil: *Clouds veiled the sun. The report was veiled in figurative language.* Also *Archaic* **vail.**

vice-pres i dent (vīs′ prez′i dənt), *n.* The person next in rank to the president. He takes the president's place when necessary, and he becomes the new president if the regular president dies, becomes disabled, resigns, or is expelled from office.

vol ume (vol′yо̄o̅m, vol′yəm), *n.* 1. A book, especially a heavy book or one that belongs to a set. 2. The space occupied by something: *Volume has thee dimensions; length, width, and height.* 3. A quantity; an amount: *a large volume of sales.* 4. The quantity of sound; loudness.

voy age (voi′ij), *n.* 1. A journey by water, usually of some distance. 2. A journey through the air or through space: *a voyage in a jet plane, the voyage of a space ship.* —*v.*, **voy aged, voy ag ing.** To go on a voyage.

W

watch ful (woch′fəl), *adj.* Watching carefully; alert; vigilant. —**watch′ful ly,** *adv.* —**watch′ful ness,** *n.*

weap on (wep′ən), *n.* 1. An instrument with which to fight, as a sword, a gun, or a missile. The claws and teeth of animals are also weapons. 2. Any means of attack or defense: *Paul's pen was a powerful weapon against apostasy.*

weigh (wā), *v.* 1. To find the weight of. 2. To have a certain weight: *This box weighs ten pounds.* 3. To lie heavily upon (the mind); be of great concern: *The problems weighed upon the teacher.* 4. To consider carefully: *Weigh all the facts before you decide.* —**weigh′er,** *n.*

weight (wāt), *n.* 1. The tendency of something to move toward the center of the earth; heaviness. 2. An object used to create pressure because of its weight: *A weight kept the papers from blowing away.* 3. A burden; heavy load: *a weight of guilt.* 4. Worth; value: *the weight of a respected man's counsel.* —*v.* To place weight upon; burden. —**carry weight.** To be meaningful and worthwhile: *Our words should carry weight.*

weren't (wûrnt). Contraction for **were not.**

what ev er (hwot ev′ər), *pron.* 1. Anything that: *Do whatever is necessary.* 2. No matter what: *Whatever happened, Joseph was determined to be faithful.* —*adj.* 1. Any (item) that; whichever (thing): *He seems to succeed at whatever work he does.* 2. At all; of any kind: *No vehicles whatever were around.*

what's (hwots). Contraction for **what has** or **what is.**

whence (hwens), *adv.* From what place or source; from where: *He asked whence I came. Whence is all this noise?* —*conj.* To the place from which; where: *The men returned whence they had come.*

where's (hwârz). Contraction for **where has** or **where is.**

wheth er (hwet͟h′ər), *conj.* A word used to show one of two or more choices or possibilities, usually with *or: Paul was determined to remain faithful whether it meant life or death. I could not tell whether the temperature was rising, falling, or staying the same.*

whirl (hwûrl), *v.* To revolve rapidly. 2. To move swiftly: *He came whirling into the room.* 3. To have a feeling of spinning: *Sue's head was whirling because of how swiftly things had changed.* —*n.* A confused state: *My mind was in a whirl.*

who'd (hŏod). Contraction for **who had** or **who would.**

who'll (hŏol). Contraction for **who shall** or **who will.**

width (width), *n.* 1. How wide something is; breadth. 2. A piece having a certain width, as of fabric: *It took four widths to make the quilt.*

wind mill (wind′mil′), *n.* A machine driven by the force of the wind blowing against a wheel with vanes or sails. Most windmills are used to pump water.

wolf (wŏolf), *n., pl.* **wolves.** A wild animal in the dog family. —*v.* To eat greedily; gulp down: *A person who wolfs his food is displaying poor manners.*

wor ry (wûr′ē), *v.,* **wor ried, wor ry ing.** 1. To be anxious and uneasy: *Do not worry about the future.* 2. To make anxious and uneasy: *Many problems worried the president.* 3. To bother; annoy: *worried her with all the details.* 4. To hurt or kill by biting and shaking: *The dog was worrying the kitten.* —*n., pl.* **wor ries.** 1. Anxiety and uneasiness. 2. A care; concern.

wor ship (wûr′ship), *v.* To give honor and reverence to, especially in a religious service; venerate: *Worship the Lord.* —*n.* Honor and reverence, usually expressed by actions such as praying and singing.

worst (wûrst), *adj.* Superlative of **bad, ill.** Least good; most ill, evil, harmful, etc. —*adv.* Superlative of **badly, ill.** Least well; in the manner of degree most ill, evil, harmful, etc. —*n.* Something that is worst: *We have not yet seen the worst.*

had, māde, stär, câre, red, mē, dim, hīde, not, hōme, ôr, oil, tŏok, pŏol, loud, sun, tûrn; ch, such; ng, sing; sh, she; th, with; th, the; zh, vision

ə represents *a* in *ago, e* in *open, i* in *pencil, o* in *wagon, u* in *cactus*

wor thy (wûr′thē), *adj.* 1. Having worth: *a worthy cause.* 2. Meriting; deserving: *worthy of praise.* —*n., pl.* **wor thies.** A highly honorable person; a person to be admired: *the worthies listed in Hebrews 11.* —**wor′thi ly,** *adv.* —**wor′thi ness,** *n.*

wrap (rap), *v.,* **wrapped** or **wrapt, wrap ping.** 1. To enclose by winding in paper, cloth, foil, etc. 2. To veil; envelop: *wrapped in secrecy.* —*n.* 1. A garment wound or folded about oneself, as a shawl. 2. *pl.* Outer garments, as coats, caps, and scarves: *Hang up your wraps.* [< ME *wrappen*]

wreck (rek), *n.* 1. The destruction of an automobile, a ship, or some other vehicle, usually by collision. 2. The ruined remains of a vehicle: *The wreck was towed away.* 3. Any destruction: *the wreck of one's health.* —*v.* To destroy; ruin: *wreck a person's reputation with slander.*

wres tle (res′əl), *v.,* **wres tled, wres tling.** 1. To try to force (a person) to the floor. 2. To struggle; contend: *"We wrestle not against flesh and blood."* —*n.* 1. A wrestling match. 2. Any hard struggle: *a wrestle with a bad habit.* —**wres′tler,** *n.*

Y

your self (yŏor self′, yər self′), *pron., pl.* **your selves.** 1. The intensive form of **you,** used for emphasis: *You yourself said that.* 2. The reflexive form of **you,** used to show that the doer of the action is also the receiver: *You can see yourself in a mirror.* 3. In your normal condition; your usual self: *Be yourself; do not try to impress people.*